MARINE CORPS TANK BATTLES IN VIETNAM

Marine Corps Tank Battles in Vietnam

By
OSCAR E. GILBERT

CASEMATE
Philadelphia & Oxford

Published in the United States of America and Great Britain in 2007 by
CASEMATE PUBLISHERS
1950 Lawrence Road, Havertown, PA 19083, USA
and
The Old Music Hall, 106–108 Cowley Road, Oxford OX4 1JE, UK

Reprinted in paperback 2017

Paperback edition: ISBN 978-1-61200-532-4

Cataloging-in-publication data is available from the Library of Congress and the British Library.

Printed and bound in the United States of America

For a complete list of Casemate titles, please contact:

CASEMATE PUBLISHERS (US)
Telephone (610) 853-9131
Fax (610) 853-9146
Email: casemate@casematepublishers.com
www.casematepublishers.com

CASEMATE PUBLISHERS (UK)
Telephone (01865) 241249
Email: casemate-uk@casematepublishers.co.uk
www.casematepublishers.co.uk

CONTENTS

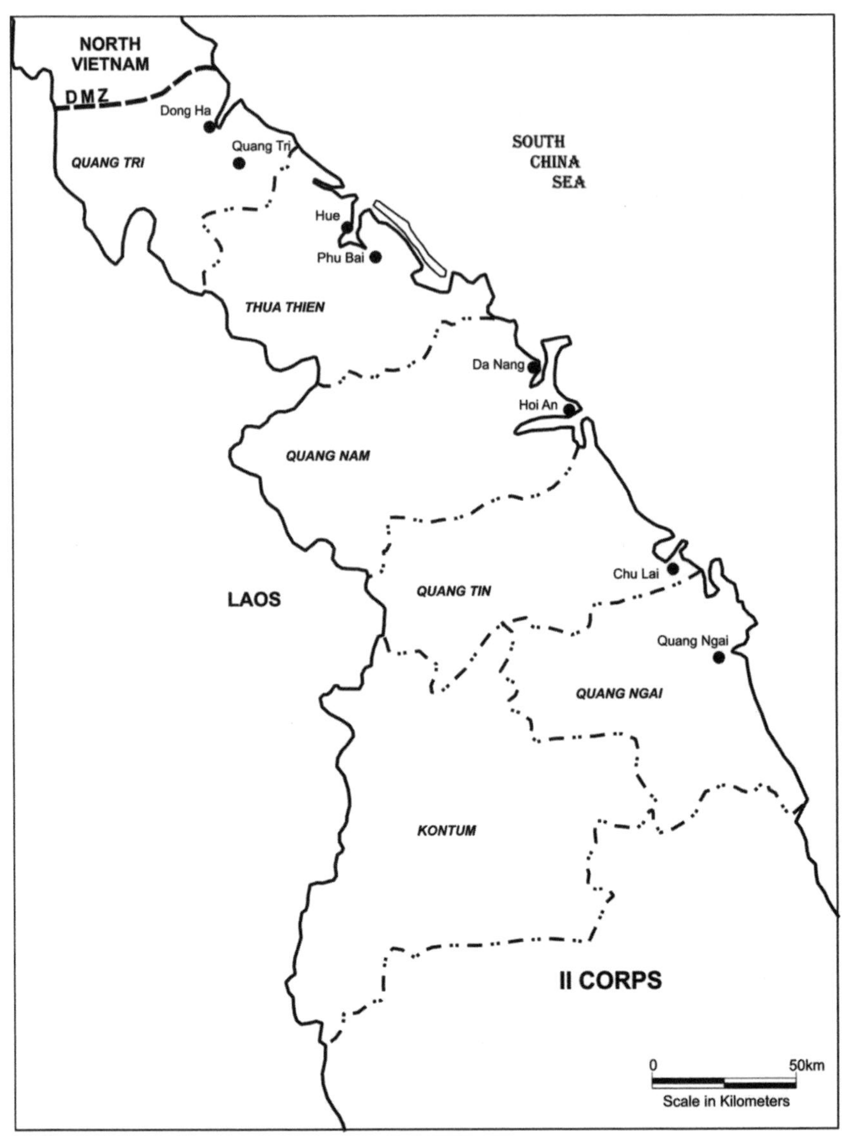

The vast bulk of Marine Corps operations in South Vietnam took place in I Corps, the northernmost sector of the country bordering the DMZ.

PREFACE: A Complex and Undocumented War

All wars are both alike and unique. Each one is alike in that it contains that bizarre mix of horror, brutality, and waste on a massive scale that somehow brings out both the best and the worst in everyone it touches. Each war is unique in the why, where, and how it is fought, and in the way that it touches its victims. The veterans of one war may identify and sympathize with those of another, but the experience of a man who waded through the bloody tide at Tarawa alongside comrades with whom he had trained for months was vastly different from that of the man who flew to Southeast Asia on a civilian airliner to fight alongside a group of relative strangers.

Vietnam carried war to a whole other level of complexity and ambiguity—militarily, politically and morally. There was an almost conventional war against the forces of the North Vietnamese Army, fought with artillery and maneuvering units of uniformed infantry amid a landscape almost devoid of civilians. At the other extreme was a far more personal war for the "hearts and minds" of a largely peasant population, where small units from both sides fought each other while intermixed with the civilians in their ancestral villages and homes.

For the individual, the war gave rise to dreadful moral ambiguities. Was a child a spy, a saboteur, or merely friendly and hungry? Was the guy who sold you a hot beer the same one who lobbed mortar rounds at you last night? Why could you pat a farmer on the back and give him a new hoe, but kill him without compunction if he wandered across an arbitrary line on a map and into a free-fire zone?

It was a war in which you could depend only upon your enemy. He would be professional, brave, tenacious, resourceful, and merciless. You could not depend upon your ally. In one day and place he might be loyal and courageous. In another time and place he might be feckless, corrupt, inept, cowardly, or even murderous if it suited his purpose of the day.

Depending upon where you were in the complex landscape it was a war fought amid shifting sand dunes, the stinking mud of rice paddies, steaming jungle, steep and stony mountains where the cold night chilled you to the bone, or all of the above.

The only clear division between how the war was experienced was geographic, with a conventional war against the NVA north of the Hai Van Pass, and a guerrilla war against the VC south of the pass. Even that distinction eventually fell away.

The nature and prosecution of military operations was far different from those of previous wars. An operation in Vietnam could be defined in any one of several ways. To the military amateur the concept of an operation is usually assumed to be some group of units undertaking a military endeavor directed toward some goal, fighting in a specific area during some defined period of time. Many operations like STARLITE and DEWEY CANYON were just such operations.

In Vietnam an operation might also be defined as any military activity within a specific geographic area. It was not unusual for a unit to be engaged in a named operation, but when it crossed some defined boundary—often a grid line on a map—it was suddenly engaged in a different operation. Some were both, as in October 1966 when Operation PRAIRIE transitioned from an offensive field operation to an "operating area."

Still other operations were thematic, defined by a specific type of activity such as COUNTY FAIR (combined civic actions and searches for local VC agents) or DECKHOUSE (amphibious raids). The Marine Corps conducted 195 such named operations, of all types, over the course of the war.

Unlike in previous wars, the Corps imitated the Army practice of creating ad hoc temporary brigades for specific operations, made up of whatever units were available. This practice allowed greater tactical flexibility, but created other problems when a battalion, company, or even a platoon was suddenly placed under an unfamiliar command structure.

Most confusing, some units in the tank battalions were simply redesignated. A platoon might be told to drive north and report to a new unit. Overnight a platoon might find itself part of a different battalion, in a different division. Small wonder that most Marines do not know to this day the names of the operations in which they participated.

Underpinning everything was the question of why America was fighting the war. It is true that there was a flawed contemporary vision of monolithic communism marching toward world domination—flawed because we could not see the nationalistic cracks in the global communist movement. The North Vietnamese under Ho Chi Minh had a clear vision of what they wanted to achieve: the forceful reunification of Vietnam. We seemed to have no overarching political counter-plan, at least not one with a clear strategy for victory. We lacked even a definition of victory. Our only definition of success was to keep the enemy from winning, and it was a recipe for failure.

The Vietnam War was unlike almost all of America's wars in that thirty-five years after it ended the story of how, or even why, we fought it baffles historians. However, the war was very much like other wars on a more primal level. At the time the men, and a few women, who fought in Vietnam had one crystal clear vision of why they were there. It was because fate had cast them all together, eye deep in hell. They needed each other as they never would again in this world.

To add to its other ambiguities, the Vietnam War is quite poorly documented at the operational level. The common perception of the military is that they are obsessive compilers of documentation and paperwork. That much is true, and there is a form and a process for everything. Often, though, the executors of the process are nineteen-year-old clerks who don't want to be there, supervised by harried staff officers with too much to do. This alliance records everything, and then at various intervals they burn the records.

Typically the starting point for any researcher into Marine Corps operations in any conflict is the usually excellent series of official histories compiled by the Marine Corps Historical Branch. Compared to other wars, the official histories for Vietnam are strangely limited in their mention of the role of supporting arms, other than the Air Wing, which kept separate records. This is an artifact of how forces were structured, how the war was fought, and in particular it is an artifact of the unit level at which records were kept.

For both the Army and the Marine Corps in Vietnam the basic record keeping entity was the battalion. For the Marine Corps tank battalions the most useful basic records are the monthly Command Chronologies, with their intelligence summaries and numerous other sections. If you are interested in details of headquarters location, personnel and disciplinary actions, total ammunition expended, and replacement and repair of equipment, then this is the primary source.

The most useful component, the Sequential Listing of Significant Events, is a monthly "roll-up" of actions and events of which the tank battalion staff was aware. Unfortunately it is a rather dry accounting of such events as:

> 04 MAR 69 A MEDCAP was conducted at Quang Tri treating 54 adults and 66 children.
>
> and
>
> 11 MAR 69 H53 at grid 111548 engaged 2 NVA. While returning fire on enemy snipers, the .50 cal MG exploded, causing superficial wounds on right thigh of the Retriever Commander.[1]

The limitation of such records is that they were compiled from events of which the battalion was immediately aware, or that were reported at long intervals—sometimes monthly—by subordinate but functionally isolated companies or platoons. The tank battalion's companies, platoons, or even two- or three-tank sections were invariably parceled out in direct support of Marine Corps infantry units, the US Army, or even allied units like the Army of the Republic of Vietnam or the Republic of Korea Marine Corps. As a result most of the actual combat operations of the battalion's sub-units were never reported in any significant detail. The individual responsible for reporting the action, an exhausted NCO or lieutenant, was simultaneously coping with numerous other tasks such as re-supply, daily maintenance, and staying alive while he tried to remember and document for the monthly report what had happened weeks earlier.

The tank battalion was responsible for the administrative and logistical support of its widely separated platoons, but not their day-to-day tactical employment. Many of the actions of small units such as isolated platoons or even two-tank sections were simply never reported. The efforts of even the most energetic and conscientious tank battalion commander and his staff (particularly the S-3, who was responsible for recording the journal) could not offset the united effects of distance, limited communications, and incessant fighting.

Tanker and retired Lt. Colonel Ray Stewart believes that the battalion staff officer who knew most about the activities of the individual units was the S-4, logistics, but of course his purview did not include the specifics of combat actions. Once the tanks were placed in support of an infantry unit, the grunts were responsible for operational, administrative, and logistical control.

The real accountings of combat actions in which the tanks were intimately involved lie in the battalion journals of the infantry units they supported, but two factors limit the utility of even those records. The first, and most pervasive, factor is that the infantry units seldom recorded the activities or involvement of supporting arms. Timing, effects, and ordnance expended in air and artillery attacks, the most widely used and effective supporting arms, are mentioned only in the case of spectacular events. The activities, or even the presence, of tanks often goes entirely unmentioned.

Ray Stewart has pored over the records of the big field operations in detail, and discovered surprisingly little recorded information about the use of tanks. "Even though they would show in the task organization ... it won't tell you how the tanks were used. They (the infantry) were running a battalion-size operation. That's only one platoon of tanks. They'd break that platoon up into a couple of sections and that would then be parceled out to the companies. The companies would use those tanks as blocking forces or to run water up to the guys up on the line. However they were used, they weren't reported on. They won't tell you how the hell they were used. You can tell who they were attached to, but the (tank) company commanders didn't go back and tell the battalion commanders a lot of incidents."

Perhaps this is because of the eternal love-hate relationship between tanks and infantry. The infantry always regarded tanks as bullet magnets, and they were. Even the thinly armored Ontos tank destroyers avoided them. One Ontos crewmen said that in a typical reaction force column: "The tank came last because they were RPG and B-40 "magnets" and that was not a good way to start a reaction op."[2]

The NVA and VC regarded tanks as symbols of American power, and went to extraordinary efforts to destroy them. They were hard to protect, and it was dangerous just to be around them. On the other hand they hauled your food, water, and ammunition, provided transport on a hot day, and evacuated your dead and wounded under the most extreme conditions. And there was nothing quite as useful as your very own direct-fire cannon to address your most serious tactical issues.

The second problem that limits research is the sheer volume of material in the infantry battalion records. Infantry units were involved in incessant fighting *everywhere*, for years on end. Tens of thousands of pages in daily journals must be pored over line by line to identify the location and nature of tank unit actions in support of the infantry on the few occasions when they happen to be mentioned. This daunting task confronts every researcher who undertakes a detailed study of the day-to-day fighting in Vietnam. Jim Coan's excellent *Con Thien: The Hill of Angels* describes in detail the nature and course of the fighting that took place within a small, arbitrary circle drawn around that bitterly contested dirt fortress. The basic research took years of grinding effort.

For all of these reasons I have relied far less upon official records than in the previous two books in this series on Marine Corps tanks. This book does not pretend to be an exhaustive history of tank actions in the Vietnam War; that subject is simply too enormous in scope. However in the final analysis the true history of the Vietnam War, for the tank crewmen and for everyone who was there, lies not in the official records but in the memories of those who fought the thousands of tiny actions that made up the mosaic. Here the experiences of a handful must stand for the experiences of the thousands who served in tank units during the course of America's most complex war.

With oral histories the argument is often made that recollections recorded years after the fact are inherently suspect. Over the course of a decade, I have found that the memories recorded long afterward often seem to be the most honest and reliable.

Debriefing interviews recorded soon after events suffer from several shortcomings. Men interviewed soon after an action are still often emotionally numbed. They fall back upon their training, and provide a coldly dispassionate "just the bare facts" description of events, devoid of an in-depth intellectual analysis and emotional context that only time can provide. Young men in our society were (and mostly still are) conditioned to be "macho," with all the braggadocio and self-deception that the expectation entails. They tend to provide the tough-Marine interview they think the interviewer expects of them. That is why the best battlefield memoirs like Gene Sledge's superb *With the Old Breed at Peleliu and Okinawa* are written decades after the fact.

For Vietnam, the greatest complication is the loss of any sense of time. For combat troops Vietnam was a mentally paralyzing series of the same battles fought over the same ground against the same enemy units. Unlike other wars, the individual lacked the simple temporal or spatial context of "this event occurred on Peleliu, that event occurred on Okinawa." The memory of a particular event, no matter how graphic or traumatic, can easily become dislocated in time, so that the individual may not precisely remember even the year in which it occurred. I have encountered this phenomenon more with Vietnam veterans than with others. As much as possible I have tried to accurately fix events in time, but some of the experiences recorded here are without doubt out of their precise sequence in time. If it confuses the reader, rest assured that it is equally frustrating to both the veterans and to me.

The Vietnam Tankers Historical Foundation is currently engaged in an enormous project to document the involvement of the tank units and the individual experiences of the men in them. Their first goal is to identify and place various units in their map positions on the sprawling battlefield throughout the course of the war. Their second, and in my opinion far more important, goal is to record the experiences of the men in the tank units before they are forever lost to time.

It is an uphill struggle against tremendous odds. But then, that's what Marines are best at.

ACKNOWLEDGMENTS

Official documentation of the war in Vietnam at the small unit level is inconsistent and indeed often absent altogether. For this reason it is particularly important to acknowledge the contributions of the representative men interviewed; their names re listed separately in the section on interview sources. Several of the same individuals provided personal photographs, and they are acknowledged in the photo captions.

Don Gagnon (Master Gunnery Sergeant, USMC, Retired) provided invaluable help in suggesting contacts, and his name recognition in tank veteran circles opened many doors. This is the fourth book for which Don has provided his invaluable assistance.

Ray Stewart (Lt. Colonel USMC, Retired) suggested veterans for interviews and provided insights into tank usage and doctrines. Most valuable, however, was his help in sorting through records and databases in order to construct a demographic "cross-section" of men who served at various times in the long Vietnam War. As noted in the references, I have drawn heavily upon his summaries of tank actions prepared for The Sponson Box magazine.

Lloyd "Pappy" Reynolds acts as the webmaster for both his own site devoted to the 3rd Tank Battalion along the DMZ, and the USMC Vietnam Tankers Association. He was instrumental in locating some individuals, and was very free with his time and assistance. Ray and Pappy are the moving forces behind the Vietnam Map project which seeks to fix the locations of various tank units through time. A massive work very much in progress, it is suggested as an adjunct source of information to those wishing more detail on tank actions in Vietnam.

Joe Sleger (Colonel, USMC, Retired) provided copies of period documents, and introductions to other individuals.

Dieter Stenger, formerly of the USMC Museum Branch, and the staff members of the Marine Corps Historical Center and the National Archives provided invaluable assistance in locating the majority of the photographs.

Guy Wolfenbarger did not have the opportunity to contribute to this work because of family circumstances, but previous conversations with him are incorporated in small and unacknowledged ways.

Ken Estes (Lt. Colonel, USMC, Retired) and Alvin Hubert were invaluable as sounding boards, and providing the occasional conversation that makes work worthwhile.

My daughter Jillian and my son Bill helped with initial editing and ran all the errands that contribute to the small bits that somehow accumulate into large contributions. Bill also undertook the final edit while I receovered from a medical problem.

I would also like to acknowledge the publisher and staff of Casemate for encouragement to compile this book, their editorial tasks, but most of all for their patience while I struggled with a complex, confusing, and sometimes painful task.

Finally, I have to acknowledge my wife Cathy. No one else had to listen to my daily complaints, or tolerate me awakening at 0500 hours with an idea of how to resolve a nagging problem.

ED GILBERT
Katy, Texas
January 2008

PROLOGUE

Above all, this book is not concerned with Poetry,
The subject of it is War, and the pity of War.
The Poetry is in the pity.
All a poet can do is warn.

Wilfred Owen, preface to *Poems*

At 0330 hours any Marine at the Gio Linh Combat Base could see and hear for himself what was going on at the new base ten kilometers to the southwest, but there was nothing you could do to help. The distant rumble that rose and fell in waves and the flickering lights meant that men from both sides were dying at the place the Vietnamese called The Hill Of Angels.

No matter what you might think of the politics that motivated the average "Mister Nguyen" of the North Vietnamese Army, you could seldom fault his courage or combat skills. Fifteen minutes earlier it had been a quiet night like many others, but hundreds of NVA infantry and sappers had slipped quietly up to the base of the hill, skillfully evading roving patrols and small listening posts that ringed the hill but also absorbed most of its manpower.

A torrent of artillery fire drowned out the blasts of satchel charges hurled by elite sappers advancing through their own artillery fire, and many positions fell before the Marines could react. Gunnery Sergeant Barnett Person's three tanks were a major part of the force defending the north slope of the hill, but minutes into the attack two were already useless hulks. Their crewmen were dead or wounded, or if they were a bit luckier, fighting for their lives in the maelstrom outside. For now, Person and his tank would have to fight it out where he sat. An infantry officer had sited Person's tank just forward of his Command Post, where he could more easily control the tank's firepower. But that decision meant that Person could not back his tank out of the shallow pit where it sat. The decision had sacrificed the mobility that was an important part of the tank's shock power in combat, and more important, gave it some small chance to evade the RPG rockets that arced through the night like footballs trailing showers of sparks.

All around the tank the situation was already desperate. Tongues of orange fire from NVA flamethrowers flashed amid the whiter light of flares and explosions as the enemy moved down the thinly held trench lines. Teenaged Marines and NVA infantry fought with grenades, guns, bayonets, and knives in the dark bowels of bunkers.

In the confusion no one detected the NVA sappers who clambered onto the engine deck behind the turret of Person's tank, and jammed a satchel charge under the gypsy rack, the pipe and steel mesh bin that held personal gear and anything else when the tank was on the move. The blast bounced the heavy tank on its suspension, and threw up all the dirt that accumulates inside the crew space, but the tank and its crew still lived. The gunner traversed the turret, but it ground to a stop, jammed by the twisted gypsy rack. An attempt to traverse the other way led to the same result; the tank would have to see this fight out with only limited turret traverse.

In the flickering light Person caught sight of the sapper team, which had retreated to a position in front of the tank and crouched on the ground, apparently preparing more satchel charges. Despite what Hollywood writers and historians tell us, combat seldom produces inspiring quotes. Person reacted with a standard fire command instilled by long habit: "Gunner! Canister! Enemy on ground!"

The second word gave the loader a critical fraction of a second head start to grab a heavy, square-nosed M338 shell, flip it over, jam it into the moving breech of the ninety-millimeter gun, snatch his hand out of the way as the breech block snapped shut, and shout "Up" at the top of his lungs. Almost instantly the gunner shouted "On the way!" and pressed his electrical trigger.

Thousands of small steel balls spewed out of the tank gun at supersonic velocities and shredded the six enemies beyond all recognition as human beings. But there was no time to think of that as Person searched for another threat to his survival. It was three hours until dawn, and countless enemies roamed the ground on all sides. May 8, 1967 would be a very long night at Con Thien.

* * *

With the possible exception of the brief and relatively cost-free war against Iraq in 1991, none of our wars have ever been one of the "popular" wars of our national mythology. Tory loyalists made up a significant portion of the population in the War of Independence. Internal economic divisions drove the New England states to the brink of secession in the War of 1812. In our historical blindness, we forget the war-weariness that gripped the nation in the final year of "The Good War" of 1941–1945, when both money and young lives to sacrifice were in increasingly short supply.

The veterans of Vietnam were not only victims of the misconceptions of the true place of war in our society, but of a unique confluence of social changes in American society. The Vietnam War was in many regards the most socially divisive in our national history, in some ways more so than the Civil War. Southerners used to call that conflict The War Between the States, which is perhaps a more descriptive term; it was on the whole a conflict between regions. The Vietnam War came to divide generation from generation, parent from child, and spouse from spouse in American society. Why?

When the war began, Americans were fearful of a monolithic Communism bent on conquering the world. Vietnam was depicted as the critical first in an inevitable series of small conflicts. The popular model was the "domino theory." If we allowed Vietnam to fall, then Thailand would fall, then the Philippines, until at last, as the propaganda saying went, we would fight the Communists on the beaches of California. Only during the course of the conflict did we come to realize the schisms within the Communist world. Indeed the dominoes would not fall, because Communism held little appeal for the people of Thailand or the Philippines. The successes of the Communists in Vietnam were in fact the result of their cynical manipulation of powerful Vietnamese nationalism. Americans came to suspect that they had been sold a war under false pretenses. The traditional unpopularity of war to Americans was aggravated by the revelation.

America was also experiencing several independent internal upheavals. By its very nature, American society has long been accepting of social mavericks. Our national heroes are the mountain man Jim Bridger, the outlaw Jesse James, and Johnny Appleseed, not lawyers, accountants, and shopkeepers. The counter-cultural "hippie" movement was both a massive example of this national tendency and a reaction to the atypical (and often legally enforced) conformity that had marked American society in the 1950s and early 1960s. It was a revolt of privileged youth against the comfortable conformity of a generation that had survived the Depression, won a global war, and thought things were just fine, thanks.

Unfortunately the counter-culture brought with it destructive elements. Use of illegal drugs was widespread, and included not only old foes like heroin, but LSD (which ironically grew out of government experiments), the first "designer drug." Marijuana gained new acceptance as an expression of the counter-culture. (Most young Marines undoubtedly approved of the concurrent sexual revolution).

On the whole the "hippie" movement was non-violent, but there was of course a complete spectrum of unsavory human behavior. Radical factions like the Weathermen turned to extreme violence in an effort to blindly overthrow the government, with no real vision of its replacement. The non-violent Civil Rights movement similarly spun off various radical wings, extending to outright criminal groups like the Symbionese Liberation Army.

As the Vietnam War dragged on and became increasingly unpopular, the more radical elements took their fury out on the returning troops. Communist sympathizers were of course glad to exploit the frustration and incite trouble, and many in the anti-war movement aped Communist propaganda without clearly considering the consequences. For their part, "conservative" elements in both society and government over-reacted with paranoia, exemplified by Richard Nixon and J. Edgar Hoover, and sometimes with deadly violence against its own citizens, as at Kent State University. Of course all this was dragged into the normally coherent military by the draft, and troops going to and from Vietnam had to cope with a brutally fractured society that sometimes vented its resentments on the returning veterans. More typically, society just ignored them out of either embarrassment or apathy.

Vietnam veterans were also victims of a sort of benign national lie. An entire generation had been raised on images of glorious parades and wild celebrations that greeted returning victors. In reality most returning veterans of past conflicts had never met with such receptions. The much-photographed celebrations that marked VE and VJ Days were spontaneous, and mainly benefited young trainees who had not yet gone overseas. There were a few "show" parades in places like New York, but by the time most veterans returned, months or even years later, society was back on a peacetime footing. The war was over. Returning veterans were supposed to hitch up their britches, don their gray flannel suits, and succeed in the post-war boom if they could.

By the end of World War II the government had come a long way toward providing care for the physically maimed, but in the 1950s there was no such thing as Post-Traumatic Stress Disorder. If you were among those mentally or emotionally damaged by war beyond coping, you were a drunk, an addict, or crazy. It was a problem for you and your family to deal with. Post-Traumatic Stress Disorder was still not a recognized problem at the end of the Vietnam War.

Over a period of years the men—and women—who served in the Vietnam War slipped back into a society that at best ignored them and at worst scorned them, unable to tell their stories of achievements in a lost and controversial war.

In the end veterans simply turned to each other, trying to look out for one another after the war as they had done in it. For all too many other Americans, acceptance of what had happened to them would be a long time in coming. True understanding could never, ever come for those who were not there. Acceptance would have to do.

CHAPTER 1

TWO THOUSAND YEARS OF WAR

"We have a secret weapon.... It is called Nationalism."
Ho Chi Minh

We badly underestimated our enemy.

With the arrogance of citizens of a young and vigorous nation, Americans tend to pay little attention to the long and often complex histories of other lands. What we ignored about Vietnam was that it was assembled from many disparate kingdoms over two thousand years of unrelenting and savage warfare, and possessed a long and proud history of resistance to occupiers from both neighboring and distant lands. Like so many peoples, the Vietnamese squabbled amongst themselves – to deadly effect—but their most ruthless struggles were against the many foreign troops that had marched over the unhappy land for centuries before America was even dreamt of.

The exact ethnic origins of the Vietnamese are lost in history, but they are a people who moved south out of China's Yangtze Basin to displace the indigenous tribesmen whom the French and later the Americans would one day call *montagnards*.[1] Although careful to distinguish themselves from the Chinese, the Vietnamese built a culture along Confucian Chinese lines, complete with a Mandarin intellectual class. With an economy based on wet rice agriculture, the Vietnamese largely left the mountains to the hill tribes.

In 208 BC the renegade Chinese warlord Trieu Da established his kingdom in Canton. From there he governed a small empire that included northern Vietnam and southern China. In 111 BC, forces of the Chinese Emperor Wu Ti overran the kingdom; it was the beginning of a thousand years under the Chinese yoke. Chinese colonists and indigenous Vietnamese staged numerous revolts, with varying degrees of success. Several prominent revolutionary leaders were women, and women held higher status in Vietnamese culture than would have been conceivable in China, or in Europe for that matter. One revolt, led by two sisters, successfully evicted the Chinese, who returned two years later to crush the short-lived independent state.

In the south the Hindu kingdoms of Funan and Champa ruled over what is now the Mekong Delta and most of southern and southeastern Vietnam, respectively. Funan fell to the Khmer (Cambodian) Empire in the 6th century AD. In the 10th century AD a series of bloody revolts against the tottering Tang Dynasty of China culminated in a spectacular naval victory by Ngo Quyen in 938 AD, and the establishment of an independent Vietnamese state. From 1009 until 1225 AD the Ly Dynasty ruled from a base near modern Hanoi. Sandwiched among the Chinese and Khmer Empires and the Kingdom of Champa, the Vietnamese were in a near constant state of war. Between 1057 and 1061 the Chinese again battered unsuccessfully at the Vietnamese borders. Under the Tran Dynasty in the thirty-year span between 1257 and 1287, General Tran Hung Dao decisively repulsed three major invasions by the Mongol armies of Kublai Khan.

In 1400 a renegade general, Ho Quy Li, usurped the throne and in the ensuing struggle to retain his position invited the hated Chinese back into Vietnam. The Chinese Ming Dynasty imposed a brutal occupation marked by serfdom and an attempt to destroy the Vietnamese culture. From 1418 until 1426 Vietnamese rebels fought a series of savage battles against the Chinese, culminating in a decisive Chinese defeat near modern Hanoi at the hands of Le Loi, one of the towering figures of Vietnamese history. Le Loi instituted many reforms, and his heir, Le Thanh Tong, led Vietnam to its era of greatest power.

Under the lengthy Le Dynasty the real powers were rival clans, the Trinh and the Mac (eventually destroyed by the Trinh) in the north and the Nguyen in the south. For nearly a hundred years in the 14th and 15th centuries the Nguyen waged a prolonged and brutal war against Champa. In 1471 the Vietnamese captured the Champa capital and slaughtered its inhabitants.

THE COLONIAL ERA

In 1516 Portuguese traders appeared, followed by the Spanish and the French. Through trade and the introduction of modern technologies and

Christianity, eventually to be followed by colonial rule, the French exerted a lasting impact on the region.

Between 1700 and 1760 the Nguyen at last wrested control of the Mekong Delta from the Khmer Empire, and the modern Vietnamese nation took shape.

During the long struggle between the Trinh and Nguyen, the two Tay Son brothers revolted against the moribund Le Dynasty and seized Hanoi in 1786. They were immediately confronted by another Chinese invasion, which they repulsed in 1788.

Soon Vietnam began to feel the influence of rivalries on the other side of the globe. The French, driven out of their richest colonies in the Americas, became the dominant European economic and social influence in Indochina. Oddly enough, the French government had little interest in the Southeast Asian backwater. Instead, the Roman Catholic Bishop in the small city of Saigon, Pigneau de Behaine, raised a force of European mercenaries who helped the usurper Nguyen Anh seize control of the Delta and Saigon in 1788 while the Tay Sons were distracted by events in the north. With French assistance Anh captured the major economic center, Hanoi, in 1802 and from his new imperial capital at Hue became Emperor Gia Long, ruling over all of Vietnam.

Gia Long's heirs were rightly suspicious of French influence and the rising influence of the Roman Catholic faith. This suspicion was manifested through the persecution of Christian converts. The French bombarded the port of Danang in 1847 in retaliation, but otherwise the situation continued at a low boil.

The accession of Napoleon III, with his global imperialistic ambitions, affected both Southeast Asia and far away Mexico. In 1857 the revitalized French demanded trade concessions in Vietnam. When rebuffed they used the pretext of protecting native Catholics against persecution (which they had tolerated since about 1820) to invade. Danang fell to the French in September 1858, and Saigon the following February. Despite extensive Spanish aid, the French—crippled by the failure of the Christian Vietnamese to support their "liberators"—soon became bogged down, defeated by terrain unsuited to European armies, the climate, and tropical diseases. After a protracted campaign, in April 1863 the Vietnamese ruler Tu Duc ceded control of the major seaports of Saigon and Haiphong to the French.

Unfortunately for Tu Duc he soon enough repeated the mistake of Ho Quy Li, soliciting French aid in suppressing an 1867 revolt among his own citizens. The cost was the dismemberment of Vietnam. The French gained outright control of southern Vietnam, which they renamed Cochin China. Stung by their defeat in the Franco-Prussian War and taking advantage of Tu Duc's death with no heir, the French once more moved against Vietnam. In August 1883 they bombarded the Imperial City at Hue, and threatened the big commercial center at Hanoi. The terrified and vacillating court advisors succumbed to French threats. The sack of Hue and treaty of 25 August 1885 completed the dismemberment of Vietnam and established the Protectorates of Tonkin (northern Vietnam) and Annan (central Vietnam). In 1887 the French created the illusion of legitimacy with the Indochinese Union, made up of the three bits of Vietnam, the Cambodian Protectorate (which they had conquered in 1863), and eventually Laos (ceded by Thailand in 1893). Though the Vietnamese retained their Emperor, he was ruler in name only.

While they never formalized the barbarities of some other European colonial administrations, the French still proved cruel masters. The motivation was for quick financial profit from a land poor in any of the mineral or agricultural resources coveted by the European powers. The French exploited the country by proxy, ruling through a tiny minority of trusted indigenous Roman Catholic administrators and landlords. The landlords in turn used their positions and manipulated the repressive system of laws, burdensome taxes, and trade monopolies on virtually every product to seize ever-increasing tracts of agricultural land and to exploit the peasants as sharecroppers and indentured workers. Soon the French, and a few thousand fabulously wealthy Vietnamese collaborators, controlled the entire wealth of the nation. It was a situation ripe for small resistance movements, which were brutally suppressed by the French.

THE COMMUNIST RESISTANCE

In 1926 an obscure and self-educated man of Mandarin origins living in China formed the Revolutionary League of the Youth of Vietnam, or Thanh Nien. Born in the north of Vietnam as Nguyen Sinh Cung, as a boy he witnessed the bloody aftermath of several revolts against French rule. He ran away to the south, shipped out as a merchant seaman (calling himself Van Ba) and visited numerous ports before fetching up in New York City as a laborer. Moving on to London as a pastry chef named Nguyen Tat Thanh, he eventually joined the large Vietnamese expatriate community in Paris, under the new name Nguyen Ai Quoc.

Six years in Paris converted him from an idealistic nationalist to a socialist, and he moved on to Moscow (as Linh), where he briefly associated with the likes of Trotsky and Stalin as they struggled for the dead Lenin's crown. Moving on to China and adopting the name Thanh Nien, he fled the massacre when Chiang Kai-shek turned on his Communist allies. He moved from Moscow to France to Siam (Thailand) to Hong Kong, where he helped found the Vietnamese Communist party. He spent another dozen years wandering the globe under uncounted assumed names.

Following the fall of France to the Nazis in 1940, Japan seized the opportunity to informally incorporate Vietnam into their sham Greater East Asia Co-prosperity Sphere. Faced with a considerable demand for troops, the Japanese allowed Vichy France to rule by proxy, along with the collaborationist figurehead Emperor Bao Dai.

In 1941 the itinerant revolutionary slipped across the border from China, returning to his beloved homeland after thirty years. In a cave he met with confidants such as Pham Van Dong and history professor Vo Nguyen Giap to form the Viet Nam Doc Lap Dong Minh (Vietnam Independence League), or Viet Minh. The wanderer was ambitious and a shrewd judge of character. His years on the run had hardened him into a ruthless and pragmatic man who could skillfully utilize the talents of others for his own ends, or destroy his opponents with equal ease. Assuming yet another name and persona, Ho Chi Minh ("Bringer of Light"), the revolutionary had at last found his mission in life.

By 1942 the Viet Minh armed forces under Vo Nguyen Giap were, with the aid of the Chinese (both Nationalist and Communist factions), British, and Americans, conducting an armed resistance to the Japanese occupation. In March 1945 the Japanese launched a takeover worthy of a Shakespeare play, inviting French military officers to dine with them. They seized the officers, and killed or captured the leaderless troops. These events prompted increased aid to the resistance through the Deer Mission, run by the American Office of Strategic Services (OSS), predecessor of the Central Intelligence Agency (CIA).

As the Japanese Empire collapsed, on 2 September 1945 Ho Chi Minh took the opportunity to proclaim the Democratic Republic of Vietnam (DRV) in the north. The puppet Emperor Bao Dai abdicated to become a senior advisor, and both the northern factions and the

Communist-dominated Provisional Executive Committee of South Vietnam (PECSVN) sought Allied recognition through moderation. Instead the great powers, meeting at Potsdam, Germany, divvied up the nation. North of the 16th Parallel the Nationalist Chinese occupiers more or less ignored Ho's machinations, and his presumptive government operated openly. In the south the British were far more repressive. Fearful of the effects of Asian nationalism on their own tottering Empire in India, Major General Douglas Gracey used his 20th Indian Division, liberated French prisoners, and Japanese Army units under British leadership to ruthlessly suppress the PECSVN and impose harsh conditions on the populace.

On 23 September a peculiar alliance of Vichy and Gaullist French forces stormed the Viet Minh party headquarters. As the French and Vietnamese jockeyed for position, Ho admitted non-Communists to his DRV government, and in November dissolved the Indochinese Communist Party. In March 1946 the Chinese and French reached an agreement for Chinese withdrawal. With both sides still weak, Ho agreed to let 25,000 French and French-led native troops garrison the country. The French in turn agreed to recognize the DRV as an independent state within the French Union, and withdraw their forces by 1952. Other nationalist forces denounced the agreement, prompting the French and Viet Minh to combine forces to destroy them.

Now confident in their power, the French immediately reneged on the deal. In June 1946 they declared Cochin China autonomous, and "granted" the powers promised to the DRV to the French-controlled Indochina Federation. By mid-October the French felt confident enough to reassert control in the north, seizing Haiphong. A revolt on 19–20 November collapsed but at considerable cost to the French, and on 23 November the French bombarded the city's native quarter, killing over 6,000 civilians. Giap and his military forces slipped away into the interior to pursue a guerrilla strategy. Bao Dai briefly fled the country until the French reinstalled him as a puppet.

Bao Dai and the French were also engaged in other uneasy alliances in the south. The Cao Dai were a local religious sect who practiced a mixed Asian and Christian theology, but more importantly had what amounted to a 30,000-man private army. The schismatic Hao Hao Buddhist sect in the Delta commanded another 15,000-man army. The most influential was the Binh Xuyen organized crime cartel that controlled all the vices of the ethnic Chinese Cholon District of Saigon; their

2,500 "soldiers," augmented by bribed police and hired muscle effectively kept the Viet Minh out of Saigon proper.

The French continued to dally, waiting for American aid, making no effort to pacify the countryside—the source of the Viet Minh's strength - through meaningful reform, and hamstrung by their constitutional ban on using French conscripts outside Europe. The Viet Minh grew in power after the fall of China to Mao Tse Tung's Communists.

THE WAR AGAINST FRANCE

In September and October 1950 the Viet Minh captured two large border forts along the rugged ridges that form the border with China, and decimated the French relief columns. Strategically more important than the 6,000 French casualties and loss of materiel was that the actions secured an overland supply route from China. Overconfidence now led Giap to face the French in conventional battles for control of the populous Red River valley west of Hanoi, and between January and June 1951 the French, under their new commander, General Jean de Lattre, inflicted three major defeats on the Viet Minh. The road bound French were unable to pursue and exploit their victories, so Viet Minh power remained relatively intact.

In October 1951 the French repulsed an attempt to seize another border fort, Ngiah Lo, and in November a French airborne assault secured the big Viet Minh staging area at Hoa Binh. Though a tactical victory, the French were unable to open a land route and the force was left stranded in the countryside. Following the death of de Lattre from cancer, General Raoul Salan oversaw a costly breakout from Hoa Binh.

Both sides licked their wounds through most of 1952, until in mid-October Giap at last captured Ngiah Lo, securing yet more of his logistical lifeline. In late October 30,000 French and Vietnamese troops drove west into the Red River valley from Hanoi, but the offensive floundered to a halt amid relentless ambushes and its own logistical shortcomings.

In May 1953 General Henri Navarre replaced Salan, but by now the French effort was failing from the unreliability of the native troops that made up most of their force. Despite American aid, the ruinous financial costs and the ever-increasing demands for troops made the war increasingly unpopular in France.

In late 1953 a French airborne attack secured the isolated village of

Dien Bien Phu, in a valley near the Laotian border. The place itself had no strategic value, but Navarre saw it as a remote place for a "land-air base." In his vision, he could supply the position by air while the Viet Minh would exhaust themselves in both the struggle to move troops into the region and futile assaults, giving the French increased bargaining power in peace negotiations in Geneva. Navarre underestimated his own logistical limitations, and particularly his requirements for artillery. But most of all he underestimated Giap. Through immense effort the Viet Minh dragged American artillery and munitions, captured in Korea and China, to the remote valley.

In March 1954 the Viet Minh commenced unrelenting bombardments and costly infantry assaults, nibbling away at the French fortress. The Americans continued to supply the French, but General Matthew Ridgway advised against direct intervention in the form of long-range B-29 strikes, much less the nuclear intervention desired by some. On 7 May 1954 Dien Bien Phu fell, eleven thousand French and Vietnamese troops entered a brutal captivity, and the French lost all bargaining position in the Geneva negotiations.

An International Control Commission (ICC) made up of delegates from Canada, Poland, and India was to oversee the partition of Vietnam, with the proviso that two years later open elections would decide issues of reunification and the form of a new government. Immediately Colonel Edward G. Lansdale (US Air Force and CIA) of the Saigon Military Mission began to persuade about 900,000 refugees —mostly Catholics—to flee the North, gutting the country of many of its educated citizens. This exodus would have serious consequences, as the wealthy refugee elite came to dominate the politics and economy of the otherwise Buddhist south. At the same time about 100,000 southerners went north, weakening the Communist infrastructure in the south.

By 9 October the last of the French troops had left Hanoi. Joe Sleger had fought with Able Company, 1st Tank Battalion as part of the Marine Brigade in the Pusan Perimeter, and in the battles for Inchon, Seoul, and the horrific Chosin Campaign in Korea. In February 1952 he was commissioned, in his words, as a "senior second lieutenant."

"I was stationed on board a ship at the time, and the contingent of ships that I was with went into the Bay of Tonkin. Eight Marine officers were put ashore in Haiphong, and we had eight enlisted men with us who could speak French. We made contact with the French bureau of operations for the Tonkin area. We assisted them with evacuating their own forces, their colonial forces, and the Foreign Legion troops from the port of Haiphong."

PARTITION AND CORRUPTION

The revolutionaries now faced the daunting task of actually running a country, complicated by the loss of so many skilled workers and administrators in the southward exodus. Botched land reform led to rebellion in late 1956, and thousands of peasants were killed or relocated. This bought the even more disorganized government in the south a brief respite.

Emperor Bao Dai, the nominal ruler in the south, found himself on the horns of a dilemma. He needed a capable premiere, but one who posed no political threat. His choice was a poor one. Ngo Dinh Diem was an honest and capable administrator who had served briefly in the cabinet in the 1930s, but refused to collaborate with the Japanese. He went into voluntary exile, in part in the US, where he made influential contacts. He at first refused to work with either Ho or Bao Dai as a puppet, though both wooed him. Bao Dai eventually granted Diem full control over both the civil and military arms of the new government in the south. Diem controlled the South Vietnam National Army (SVNA), an organization crafted by and in some ways still loyal to the French.

The industrious Lansdale soon persuaded Diem to consolidate power by eliminating the private armies, covertly providing arms and money for the struggle. Diem instead chose a more traditional technique, buying off the Cao Dai and Hao Hao with cabinet posts and millions of dollars in American aid money. The more affluent Binh Xuyen refused to be bought off, and in February 1955 Diem unleashed the SVNA, driving the Binh Xuyen into the Rung Sat. For the next two decades the Binh Xuyen survived in these swamps near Saigon, and the Rung Sat Special Zone remained a thorn in the side of the South Vietnamese and later the Americans. Diem skillfully convinced the Cao Dai to stand aside as he eliminated the Hao Hao; then he turned on the Cao Dai. The survivors of both organizations became welcomed members of the rump Viet Minh organization that remained in the south.

Even as the struggle against the sects was going on, Diem convened an illegal national assembly that called for the dismissal of Bao Dai. In an October 1955 referendum in which 133% of the population voted,

Bao Dai was overthrown. Diem then turned his considerable energies to eliminating the last vestiges of French influence.

Neither Ho nor Diem had any intention of abiding by the election provisions of the peace accords, and simply failed to conduct the elections scheduled for July.

Taking a leaf from Ho's book, Diem formed the Can Lao Kan Vi party to ensure that a shadow government loyal to his family retained control of all aspects of the administration. "Land reform" required the peasants to purchase their land from the government. Heavy taxation and usurious loans assured that most of the land ended up in the hands of Diem's loyalists.

Unfortunately Diem failed to follow another of "Uncle Ho's" calculated practices that had helped to calm unrest in the north. Ho emulated Mohandas Gandhi by donning peasant garb and adopting a simple lifestyle. Diem, who lacked Ho's charisma, instead aped the French colonialists in dress and lifestyle, further distancing himself from his subjects. A November 1960 coup that demanded less family domination prompted Diem to negotiate reform, but while negotiating Diem surrounded the plotters, captured them, and dismissed the promised reforms.

With the finalization of his control over the north, Ho was now free to turn his attentions to the "liberation" of the south. In 1960 Ho announced the formation of the new National Front, eventually to become better known by the name bestowed by the South Vietnamese and Americans: the Viet Cong (VC).

Again the great power politics of the West began to play out in Indochina. The departure of the French set into motion a long and complex three-sided civil war in Laos, controversial at the time but today little remembered in America. Neither the US nor the Soviet Union wanted to fight over insignificant Laos, and by mid-1961 peace talks were under way in Geneva. At the last minute the main US ally in the country derailed the talks by massing troops along the northern border, and the North Vietnamese attacked. The end result was a Laos neutral in name only, with a continuing shadow war fought by the Communist Pathet Lao and the US-backed Meo tribesmen.

Facing relentless political attacks by the Republicans for the Bay of Pigs fiasco in Cuba, and the "loss" of Laos (which no one much wanted to fight for anyway), President Kennedy decided to draw a line in the sand in Vietnam.

By 1961 the situation in South Vietnam was grim. Still stubbornly resisting any sort of reform despite Washington's pressure, Diem feared coups more than the Communists. Most units of the Army of the Republic of Vietnam (ARVN) were not under a central command. Field commands were instead under the local political province chiefs, men chosen for their personal loyalty to Diem. As a result, the regime controlled less than half of its own country. In late 1961 the Communists briefly seized control of Phuoc Vinh, near Saigon itself, staged a show trial and publicly beheaded the province chief. Diem pressed the US for a bilateral defense treaty, and again promised reform.

THE COMING OF THE AMERICANS

In December 1962 the first US combat troops arrived: Air Force "advisors" who actually flew combat missions, Army Special Forces, and military and civil advisors. More than the Communists, Diem feared the rise of a populist military officer and the threat of a coup, and he punished ARVN officers who achieved victories. Major operations were deliberately botched. By early 1963 things were spiraling out of control. Senior American military officers and Embassy officials were determined to put the best possible face on the news, even at the cost of passing on news they knew to be false. Exasperated junior officers were leaking contradictory information to the American press.

In May 1963 the government in Hue allowed special flags to be flown in celebration of the archbishop's (Diem's brother's) birthday. Then in early June they denied a Buddhist request to fly traditional flags in celebration of Buddha's birthday. The ensuing demonstrations cost nine lives, and spread as far as Saigon. Diem again botched the negotiations designed to halt the violence, allowing Madame Ngo Dinh Nhu (a Catholic and Diem's sister-in-law) to taunt the Buddhists, denouncing them as Communist sympathizers. Buddhist monks, or *bonze*, began a traditional protest campaign, immolating themselves with gasoline in public places, and students joined in public demonstrations.

As the Buddhist protests mounted, Diem paid lip service to American demands for reform, but allowed Madame Nhu to continue to publicly taunt the Buddhists. Then he began to harass and censor the American press, who smuggled reports out by way of sympathetic American officers. On 21 August Diem's brother, Ngo Dinh Nhu, staged a massive raid on the Buddhist temples by special police and ARVN

Special Forces disguised as ARVN soldiers. This led to another round of protests by students, but more importantly, it enraged any senior ARVN officers who still held on to a shred of professionalism or patriotism.

The protests escalated throughout September, and the ARVN generals put out feelers to determine how the Americans would respond to a coup. The new American Ambassador, Henry Cabot Lodge, advised Kennedy that Diem would never change, but General Paul Harkins, the commander of the Military Assistance Command, Vietnam (MACV) warned that the generals had no viable replacement for Diem. Lodge advised the ARVN generals that the US considered the change of government an internal matter for the South Vietnamese to resolve. The Americans would not stand in the way of a coup, provided Diem's replacement would serve the welfare of the people and conduct an effective campaign against the Communists. On 1 November 1963, ARVN troops surrounded the Presidential Palace. Diem and Nhu escaped, but were captured the next morning. Placed inside an M113 Armored Personnel Carrier for transport, they were murdered *en route* by "persons unknown."

America itself was soon racked by the assassination of President Kennedy. His successor, Lyndon Johnson, inherited all of Kennedy's advisors and frustrations, and would be the President forever associated with the growing conflict. The US began openly stockpiling military supplies, and sent messages through the ICC that America's patience with the northern attacks was limited. With Johnson also came a new Ambassador (retired Army general Maxwell Taylor, on 2 July) and commander of MACV (General William Westmoreland, on 20 June).

Harkins's apprehensions proved justified. Under General Duong Van Minh ("Big Minh"), the head of a triumvirate that replaced Diem, the government was rife with favoritism and corruption. The VC grew bolder, and military bases and hamlets fell to the enemy. On 30 January 1964, General Nguyen Khanh overthrew Big Minh in a bloodless coup. Khanh attempted social reform, but was hamstrung by the entrenched Diem bureaucracy, conflict with the Buddhists, and the chaos caused by his own purges. The insurgency steadily gained ground.

Joe Sleger again returned to South Vietnam. "I was down in the Delta, when the Marine Corps was sending personnel down there to work with the advisors. It was called 'on the job training.' So I went down there as infantry.

"We worked with the advisors, with the South Vietnamese Marine Corps. We just accompanied them on their operations. During that period I was down there we made six operations, some of which were battalion size. They were just on foot, in the Mekong Delta area."

The battalions of the South Vietnamese Marine Corps, with an airborne brigade, constituted the general reserve force. They were used on particularly hazardous operations, or in particularly difficult terrain.[2]

The Special Landing Forces of the Navy's Seventh Fleet were constantly off the coast of Vietnam. Bob Embesi recalled, "On four of those occasions we did sit off the coast of Vietnam without doing anything. These were at different times right after they would have a coup or an assassination. We would get this news basically through the ship's radio as to what was going on ashore.... Nobody went ashore."

US Navy ships had long been conducting electronic intelligence surveillance (DESOTO operations) in the Gulf of Tonkin. On the night of 2 August 1964, the destroyer *USS Maddox*, on a DESOTO mission, exchanged fire with three North Vietnamese torpedo boats in the Gulf of Tonkin. Two nights later *Maddox* and the *C. Turner Joy* fired on radar contacts in the same area. Though there was considerable doubt among intelligence experts whether the two ships had actually been attacked (they may have fired on the radar returns from their own wakes), Congress hastily passed the Gulf of Tonkin Resolution, signed by Johnson on 11 August. This essentially granted the President war powers without a declaration of war.

Ken Zitz played baseball at Kent State University, and had offers to play in the minor leagues, but faced the draft when he graduated. He interviewed with the Marine Corps college recruiter about a placement in aviation, but could not pass the color vision component of the physical examination. He attended Platoon Leaders Class, and was given a waiver to be a ground officer. He planned to spend three years, with no plans for a career.

At the end of his training, in September 1963, he was given a choice to apply for an MOS, but still could not pass the color vision screening. His second choice was tanks, based on one experience.

The grand finale of officer training at Quantico is the Three Day War. "We were crossing this pretty good size stream, crossing a log about eight feet above the water. There was a little Thai officer in front of me, and a flare went off. Of course he stopped." The troops were told to freeze when a flare went off to avoid motion revealing their position. The stream crossing was in shadow, but "I lost my balance, and fell into the stream. About twenty-five degrees (F).

"Immediately I just turned to ice. It was cold." A training officer led Zitz to a tank positioned on a nearby ridge, and handed him over to the care of the enlisted crewmen. "I had never been in a tank before. It was warm as toast. I took all my clothes off. They gave me some dry clothes and stuff, and I had a coming to Jesus there. I said 'Hey, I might be a tanker. The hell with the infantry.'"

His first duty assignment was 3rd Tank Battalion on Okinawa in 1963. After only two days he was pulled out to play baseball, much to the disgust of the XO. About 1000 one morning in August 1964 another player asked if he had seen the notice on the bulletin board at the gym. The sign said that the baseball season was cancelled. All troops were to report to their parent unit within twenty-four hours.

The very junior officer Ken Zitz was Officer Of The Day when Colonel States Rights Jones reported to assume command of the 3rd Tank Battalion on Okinawa. Many of the senior NCOs looked forward to the arrival of Jones, a veteran of Iwo Jima and very much a leader in the tradition of the "Old Corps." Jones "Walked in, kicked the door closed, and said 'Sit down, Lieutenant.' He reached in his socks, pulled out his Camel cigarettes, and said 'You smoke?'" Jones proceeded to quiz Zitz for half an hour about the state of the battalion as viewed from near the bottom. "He turned that battalion into the wind. It was so-so, and he really got it going."

Tank crewman Kurt Moss had left high school in Virginia to join the Corps at age seventeen in 1963. He was initially assigned to the 2nd Tank Battalion at Camp Lejeune, and was a loader on an M103 heavy tank. In early 1964 some of the new men were given orders to report to 3rd Tank on Okinawa. Moss was assigned to 1st Platoon, A Company. He was later assigned to the 3rd Platoon of Bravo, and sent to the training area at Fuji, Japan, then sent back to his original platoon, still a loader as the junior man, when the unit returned to Okinawa.

Moss said that Jones heard reports about the poor quality of food in the enlisted mess. "He took his rank insignia off, and went through the enlisted men's chow line." He laughed uproariously. "Oh man, they caught the devil about that!"

Jones quickly proceeded to scrounge for officers, NCOs, and experienced enlisted men. Dan Wokaty enlisted in Waco, Texas in 1953, but did not go through boot camp until 1954. He attended Tank School, but the Corps said they had too many tankers, so in June they sent Wokaty to an infantry weapons company in Korea. "There was a Warrant Officer one time who said he didn't know why they even had MOS's in the Marine Corps because nobody worked in that MOS. They always worked in something else."

Wokaty was assigned to firing range duty, but Lt. Colonel Jones wanted him back in tanks. After some wangling, Jones finally pried him loose to help fill out a B Company platoon as a heavy section leader.

Elation over the American actions prompted Khanh to declare himself President, with more sweeping dictatorial powers. He promptly resigned in the face of massive protests, was lured back by the US, and survived a coup attempt. The attempted secession of the hill tribes led to the formation of a High National Council (HNC) of elder technocrats to draft a constitution and form a civil government.

Though Ambassador Taylor's staff was pessimistic, Taylor wanted to provoke North Vietnamese attacks as a means of justifying a bombing campaign against the north. Johnson, however, doubted that Khanh's increasingly shaky regime could survive an all-out Communist attack. On 18 September the destroyers *Morton* and *Persons* fired on North Vietnamese torpedo boats, but rather than risk escalation, Johnson ordered the DESOTO missions suspended. Even an attack on the US airbase at Pleiku, in which five US personnel were killed, 76 wounded, and five B-57 Canberra bombers destroyed, failed to provoke a response. In late November, with the US elections safely past, Johnson succumbed to Taylor's pleas and authorized renewed attacks in Laos and North Vietnam in return for promises of social reform from Khanh.

The offensive proved so insignificant that the North Vietnamese simply ignored it, and of course Khanh ignored his promises. Khanh suppressed more rioting, but he was clearly in trouble with his own backers. A faction of ambitious young officers, the self-named Young Turks, formed the Armed Forces Council to pressure him.[3] In early December they asked Khanh to dismiss all the older generals; when the HNC refused, Khanh used the opportunity to dismiss the Council.

As the exasperated Taylor confronted both Khanh and the Young Turks, the Buddhists rioted in response to increased national conscription, and the VC expanded their terror campaign into Saigon itself. Concerned about the security situation around the bases near the northern cities, the Marines temporarily deployed security forces in the area, keeping a very low profile. The force was a Battalion Landing Team with supporting elements, and belonged to the Seventh Fleet, not MACV.

Ken Zitz was assigned to 3rd Platoon of A Company to accompany a battalion float on the USS *Alamo*, LSD33. He was assigned to shadow the more experienced Lieutenant Ed Mels. "We were steaming off Vietnam for many days and weeks. We didn't know what was happening. We were just getting bits and pieces. This thing in Vietnam was starting up, that we might go in there, we may not go in there. We could see Vietnam, we were off the coast.

"One night about eight or nine o'clock at night, we got the word that they're going to offload into Danang." Nobody knew where Danang was.[4]

"It was a terrible night. The seas were real heavy, and pushing us off(shore). I was in Alpha Three-One, the tank. I don't know where the Platoon Commander (Mels) was. We were backloading onto the Mike boat, a smaller (LCM) boat that just carries one tank, The coxswain was supposed to hold forward power when you do this. You're pushing fifty-four tons of steel against him.

"The coxswain, instead of pushing forward, I guess he had it in neutral or reverse. We start going down the ramp, and I knew we were going to go into the ocean. That's about two hundred feet of water there. We were skidding on that thing and the driver threw it out of reverse, and we just barely got back up into that boat (the LSD). Our hearts were in our throats."

Zitz demanded that the Mike boat be secured to the ship with lines and that the coxswain apply full power to jam the boat against the LSD's ramp. "The Navy Lieutenant was kind of PO'ed. This old crusty mustang, he'd been in the Navy about forty-something years."

The tanks were finally loaded and headed for shore. "We landed at Danang. We got off at a place right below Monkey Mountain; I didn't know it was Monkey Mountain then." Nobody knew what their mission was, or where they were supposed to go.

"This Army Captain came up and met us. I said 'What's going on?' He said 'Well, you see, Lieutenant, this is kind of how it is. There's these guys in the north, and these guys in the south. The guys in north want to take over the country. The south is being backed by the US, and they don't want them to.'

"I said 'You mean it's a civil war?'

"He said 'Lieutenant, you broke the code.'"

The Captain went on to explain a bit more, but Zitz asked, "'Is that good or bad?' He said 'Beats me, brother. I'm just here like you. I'm serving.'"

Since the platoon had no clear assignment and had been cooped up aboard ship for weeks, "Spanish Joe" Martinez broached the idea of going into town to find some beer for the platoon. "It's about ten thirty at night, raining like a cow peeing on a flat rock in West Texas. Spanish Joe and I get in the jeep, Joe's driving, I'm in the right seat, all we've got is our forty-fives. We're going down the road and all of a sudden we pass this patrol. I don't know if it was an NVA patrol, or ARVN, but they were Vietnamese. It could have been VC, I don't know. I said 'Keep going Joe, don't stop.'"

The two found an Air Force compound and located a service club. The Air Force bartender gave them several cases of beer, at no cost.

After a week on the beach, the platoon went back aboard ship and south to the Saigon area. Although no one knew it at the time, this was the first inkling of a problem that would bedevil the Marines in Vietnam for the entire war. The Special Landing Forces like these were technically under Seventh Fleet, and independent of MACV. This made coordination with Marine Corps forces ashore difficult, and irritated Westmoreland mightily.

The amphibious force cruised off the coast and up the Saigon River, but never went ashore. The float battalion then returned to Okinawa.

Following the unofficial Tet Truce of 1–6 February, 1965, the VC stepped up their attacks, killing nine Americans in a 7 February attack on an advisor's compound at Pleiku. The Americans and South Vietnamese retaliated by bombing enemy barracks complexes at Dong Hoi and Vinh on 8 and 9 February (Operation FLAMING DART). On 23 February the VC blew up a hotel housing American advisors, killing twenty-three.

Johnson retaliated by authorizing Operation ROLLING THUNDER, a bombing offensive against the north, to commence on 20 February. Actual execution was delayed until 2 March by yet another coup in Saigon. The coup resulted in the downfall of Khanh and the installation of a civilian, Phan Huy Quat, as premiere, though the military retained actual power.

"AMERICANIZING" THE WAR

Fearful of North Vietnamese retaliatory air attacks against the big logistics and air base at Danang, which was all too close to the Demilitarized Zone, Westmoreland was anxious to beef up defenses at the base.

Between 8 and 16 February the US command deployed the Marine Corps' 1st Light Anti-Aircraft Missile Battalion to defend the base at Danang, although there was not—and never would be—a truly credible air threat from North Vietnam. Deployment of the missile batteries, positioned on high ground west of the base, virtually assured that more US troops would be required to provide security for them. Delta Company, First Battalion, Third Marines (D/1/3)[5] was already in South Vietnam, providing local base security for a Marine helicopter squadron.

Westmoreland began what was to become a pattern of requests for increasingly larger commitments of troops. More experienced in such matters than his Washington superiors, Ambassador Taylor predicted that it would be "very difficult to hold the line" on additional troop commitments requested by Westmoreland, and that the ARVN would displace an increasing share of the fighting onto US troops.

A fundamental decision was whether to use the Army's 173rd Airborne Brigade or the 9th Marine Expeditionary Brigade. An Army brigade could be more readily supported by existing logistical infrastructure aleady in place for the ARVN. The Marines, however, had their own organic logistical support and could provide for themselves from the very beginning without relying upon local support. The ultimate decision was to deploy the Marines.

The Marines were in many ways a significantly different organization than the one that had fought in World War II and Korea. From the inception of the Fleet Marine Force, the fundamental combat unit had been the all-arms, stand-alone division, capable of supporting itself anywhere in the world. Supporting arms such as artillery, tanks, logistics and engineering assets were integral parts of the division organization.

At the end of the Korean War the Marine Corps again found itself competing with the Army for funds and a role in the defense establishment. In an effort to assume the "force in readiness" role, the Army had created its Strategic Army Corps (STRAC), of two airborne and one air-transported infantry divisions. The Marine Corps realized that amphibious forces supported by naval transport had more inherent staying power than airborne forces, but might still be required to deploy by air transport, far from the sea. "Lightness" became the watchword, as part of the Corps' new concept of vertical envelopment, an air mobility doctrine that predated the more familiar air cavalry doctrine by a decade.

In 1956 the FMF Organization and Composition Board (more commonly known as the Hogaboom Board, after its chairman) recommended that the division be pared down and made completely air tranportable. Under the new organization the only mechanized component was to be the Anti-Tank Battalion, equipped with the M50 Ontos tank destroyer originally developed for the Army airborne. The division would retain an integral but reduced Motor Transport function of light and medium trucks. Artillery units would be equipped with the M98 Howtar, a hybrid of the rifled 4.2-inch mortar mounted on a modified M1A1 75mm pack howitzer carriage. All heavier equipment, the beloved amphibian tractors, 105mm and 155mm towed artillery, self-propelled 155mm howitzers, 155mm guns, and 8-inch howitzers, and tanks would all become part of a separate Force Troops organization, corps-level assets that could be attached to the division at need.

Implementation of the Hogaboom Board plan was not achieved by 1965, primarily because of limited funding and technological shortcomings in transport helicopter design. The 105mm and 155mm towed howitzer remained the mainstay of the artillery regiment, and in Vietnam, Howtars or standard 4.2-inch mortars would equip only one additional battery per battalion. Amphibian tractors and tanks were officially not part of the division organization, but the distinction was largely academic. Platoons of tanks still accompanied expeditionary units afloat.

The biggest change was to a size-flexible organization that could deploy a unit appropriate to the task at hand, a Marine Expeditionary Unit (MEU—a small combined-arms brigade built around an infantry battalion), a Marine Expeditionary Brigade (MEB—built around an infantry regiment), or a Marine Expeditionary Force (MEF—a division-scale unit with air assets). The most common was the MEU, with several maintained at sea with the Atlantic, Pacific, and Mediterranean fleets. Each MEU included a platoon of tanks.

The tank battalions and their equipment had changed considerably since 1953. The new M48A3 was two design generations removed from the M26 and M48s of Korea. It still mounted a 90mm main gun, but with a much improved range finding and fire control system with a mechanical computer. New munitions included High Explosive Anti-Tank (HEAT) rounds with shaped-charge warheads capable of drilling through the armor of any known tank. Other rounds included High Explosive (HE), a highly-effective anti-personnel canister round packed with 1,281 steel balls, White Phosphorus Smoke (Smoke WP), the Armor-Piercing Tracer (AP-T) solid shot, Armor-Piercing Capped with Tracer (APC-T), Hypervelocity Armor-Piercing with Tracer (HVAP-T), High Explosive with Tracer (HE-T), High Explosive Plastic with Tracer (HEP-T), and a variety of training rounds. The old .30-caliber machine gun was retained as a coaxial weapon, even though it had been replaced in infantry service by the modern M60.

The crew was reduced to four with the elimination of the assistant driver and his bow machine gun, but the tank commander was provided with an armored cupola with an integral .50-caliber heavy machine gun. The peculiar way of mounting the redesigned machine gun in the cupola was the least popular feature of the tank. The gun was mounted on its side, with a complex feed and ejection mechanism, and was prone to jams. John Wear, who would serve in Vietnam in 1967 and 1968, explained that "You had to fire about four or five rounds, reach your hand underneath and clear the links, and clear the brass. It would fall down on top of the gunner. Then you fired three or four or five more rounds. You had to clear it all the time."

The tank was easy to drive, and the diesel power plant was reliable and reduced the risk of fire. The round-bottomed cast hull was more resistant to mines, always one of the greatest threats to tanks, and the cause of most casualties in both the Pacific and Korean Wars. The design vented a mine blast sideways, often causing repairable damage to the suspension, but saving the lives of the crew.

The one thing that had not changed significantly was the maintenance burden. Ken Pozder, a maintenance NCO and retriever commander in 1st Tank Battalion in 1965, said, "The book says that for every hour of operation, there's four hours of maintenance. That's what it says. You spend a lot of time punching (cleaning) your main gun tube, cleaning your fifty caliber, cleaning your thirty caliber." It took eight men to punch the wire bore brush down the main gun tube, so crews would usually team up for this task.

"The air cleaners took a pretty severe beating. You had to really keep an eye on your air cleaners. The dust and sand. You take three tanks moving in a convoy, and you've got trucks and whatnot in between, it's terrible." The air cleaners were several heavy sheets of felt-like cloth mounted in large rectangular boxes on the track covers. "You unsnapped the lid and pulled the door out, pulled the air cleaner out, and then pulled the air cleaner out of the framework. Then just beat it on the side of the tank, as best you could," like cleaning a carpet. "You could wash them ... but nobody had time to wash them." Cleaning the air cleaners was a weekly task. Other tasks were daily.

Some maintenance requirements were unique to Vietnam. The fuel tanks had to be purged because of the rain and humidity. "You stuck a fuel transfer pump hose down in the bottom of your fuel tank, and pumped off five gallons of fuel onto the ground. Tried to keep all that water out of there. If you didn't, algae would grow, and the algae would get into your fuel filters, and that was it. You quit running until you got it cleaned." The M48A3 had two aluminum fuel cells, one on each side, which cross-fed to a common filter. Both were included in the cleaning ritual.

Adjusting track tension was at least a daily task, because "If you were on an operation, you *did not* want to throw a track. They'd leave you a squad of infantry, if you were lucky" to provide protection while the crew spent hours of backbreaking labor to repair the track.

The M48A3 equipped three gun tank companies, Alpha, Bravo, and Charlie. Each company had three numbered platoons of five tanks each, with two additional tanks in the Headquarters Platoon. The individual platoons could be further subdivided into a heavy (three tank) and light (two tank) section for separate operations. One of the Headquarters Platoon gun tanks was equipped with a dozer blade, though these would not prove to be as tactically significant as in the Pacific or Korea.

The battalion H&S Company included two additional tanks for the CO and XO, but these were more often used as reserve vehicles. Like any military organization, this structure might change with circumstances. Sections or platoons might be transferred between, or attached to, other formations, and in some cases "extra" platoons were organized from additional available vehicles.

The M67A2 was the last of the flame tanks, externally almost identical to the M48A3. The H&S Company included a Flame Section with nine tanks divided in threes. The organization was designed to allow parceling the flame tanks out to support the line platoon gun tanks.

The M103A2, with its 120mm gun and crew of five, was the only American heavy tank to see active service. The M103A2 equipped a fourth (Delta) company in each battalion. Kurt Moss was a loader, gunner, and later a tank commander for the heavy tanks before and after his tour in Vietnam. "It was a hoss of a tank. Everything was heavy. The ammunition was heavy, and it was a brute of a gun. The ammunition was separate loading, the projectile and the casing were separate." There were two loaders, one for the projectile and another for the propellant. "I think it was a fifty-six-pound armor-piercing projectile. When you fired it, you had best be braced back against the turret wall, because it (the lurching of the vehicle) would bruise you up." With no enemy heavy armor threat, the heavy tanks were never sent to Vietnam.

The M51 tank retriever was a hulking monster built on the chassis of the M103A2. It could easily recover and tow the smaller M48A3, and the lift boom was used in heavy repairs to many vehicles. Each line company was allotted one M51, with another in the H&S Company Maintenance Section. The vital role of the retriever is often overlooked, although the retrievers were often included among the first detachments sent into combat areas.

Like many others, Pozder loved the M51. "It would tow an M48A3 tank, fully loaded with ammo, just no problem. You could hook up two of them in fact, and pull it. It had a thousand horsepower engine. That baby, if you could hook onto it, you could pull it."

There were some things that remained the same, particularly the way tankers operated. Jim Carroll said that like many of their World War II counterparts, but unlike his personal experience on Iwo Jima, tank commanders in Vietnam tended to ride exposed in combat. The TCs traded safety for what would today be called better situational awareness, "which of course gave you a greater advantage of visibility, seeing what the hell was going on, and being able to direct your gunner where to shoot. The disadvantage is that if you got a sniper in the area, he could pot you right there in the turret."

Like their predecessors, the tankers of the Vietnam era also tended to adopt personal weapons other than those issued to them. The official small arms of the tank crews were pistols and the much-despised M3A1 "grease gun" submachine gun, a descendant of a World War II design. It was inaccurate and often unreliable, and according to Sergeant John Wear "just sat on the side of the tank." The tankers quickly acquired M14 or M16 rifles, M79 grenade launchers, shotguns, and even the occasional enemy AK-47.[6]

The 9th Marine Expeditionary Brigade,[7] under Brigadier General

Frederick J. Karch (assistant division commander of the 3rd Marine Division, parent formation of the 9th MEB), was embarked aboard the four amphibious assault ships of the Navy's Task Force 76. Karch himself was wary of the assignment and gloomily predicted, "If we go into Danang, we'll disappear into the countryside and never be heard from again."

The Landing Order specified that only 3/9 would land over Red Beach 2, northwest of Danang, while 2/9 remained aboard ship as a floating reserve. The order also stated, "The US Marine force will not, repeat will not, engage in day-to-day actions against the Viet Cong."

H-Hour for the landing was set for 0800 hours on 8 March 1965, but was delayed by high waves that endangered the smaller landing craft. Finally at 0903 the first infantry waded ashore. A crowd of amused Army advisors and young Vietnamese women with flower garlands greeted the chagrined Marines, who came ashore in full battle array. Mike Company remained to secure the beach for landing the Brigade's heavy equipment, while its sister companies moved by truck to their assigned base area.

The next morning Staff Sergeant John Downey's tank led the five M48A3s of 3rd Platoon, Company B, 3rd Tank Battalion across Red Beach 2, to become the first US armored unit in Vietnam.[8] Later in the month the second infantry battalion, 1/3, was airlifted from Okinawa, and the tanks of 1st Platoon, Company A, 3rd Tank Battalion came ashore to complete Westmoreland's request.

Unexpected by either the Marines or Westmoreland, it was the arrival of the tanks that produced a political firestorm. The American public was generally supportive because Johnson had clearly publicized that the deployment was only temporary. General William Westmoreland was appalled by the high-profile landings, the South Vietnamese government had not been advised that the Marine Brigade was coming, and some saw the arrival of heavy equipment like tanks as a clear escalation of the war. Ambassador Taylor stated in no uncertain terms that tanks were "not appropriate for counterinsurgency operations."[9]

The nose of the camel was well and truly under the side of the tent, with the rest of the beast sure to follow.

CHAPTER 2

1965: TAKING MEASURE

"The tanks were certainly the difference between extremely heavy casualties and the number that we actually took. Every place the tanks went they drew a crowd of VC."

Major General Oscar Peatross,
comments on Operation STARLITE, USMC Official History

Both the Vietnamese and the Department of Defense wanted the US landings to be as inconspicuous as possible. The problem was that the 9th Marine Expeditionary Brigade would be capable of sustaining itself, but the assets that provided staying power—the tanks, artillery, ground transport, the forward logistical support units organic to the Brigade, and above all the small fleet of ships that carried it—were very conspicuous. Some officials like Ambassador Taylor had not even considered the issue of the heavy equipment like tanks that were included in the Brigade.

The original landing plan was based on predicted mild weather and low surf conditions. On the morning of 8 March 1965 a cold drizzle, eight-knot winds and ten-foot (3m) waves confronted Task Force 76 and the landing force. The 3rd Battalion, 9th Marines (3/9) quickly went to an alternative plan, which delayed the landings until full daylight. LPD-2, *USS Vancouver,*[1] disgorged landing craft carrying the Brigade's heavy equipment, including five tanks.

One photograph depicted the commander of the 9th MEB, Brigadier General Frederick Karch, bedecked with flowers but wearing a grim expression. Teased by reporters, he explained that he thought it inappropriate to be photographed smiling when civilians back home might soon learn that their loved ones had died in Vietnam. Perhaps he was more prescient than many.

The bulk of another infantry battalion, 1/3, arrived less conspicuously by air later in the day, with the platoon that included Kurt Moss arriving by sea. "We landed at night at Monkey Mountain in Danang."

In keeping with the avowed role of the 9th MEB, the tank platoon's first mission was to guard the airstrip, with a section of tanks at each end of the three-mile long runway.

The tanks were positioned to the side of the runway axis, which was fortunate. Moss: "A bomber took off, I think a B-57 (Canberra), and it seems like they got up maybe a hundred feet in the air, and they just couldn't get any altitude. Went on down across the end of the airstrip and crashed."

There were of course no facilities in place to accommodate the Marines. For tankers like Moss this meant, "We had no tents. We managed to get some cots, and we dug out tank slots with shovels, and slept right behind the tanks using the tarp as a tent. Occasionally we would go over to the Air Force barracks to take a shower, because they had hot running water. They even had good food." The platoon was fed on C-rations, but sometimes they would crank up a tank and drive to where they could obtain hot food, a kind of fifty-ton drive-through. The Marines would also trade for food. "For some reason they [the Air Force personnel] wanted C-rations, so we would trade them C-rations for good food."

For sanitary arrangements, "There was a creek that ran down within a hundred yards or so of the airstrip, and a lot of times we bathed in the creek.

"There were many times we would be out there in the creek and airplanes would be coming by and landing, and we'd be waving at the people as they went by." Any semblance of privacy was of course nonexistent, and they dug a latrine, a four-holer, out in the open.

Since the Corps fully adheres to the old principle that idle hands are the devil's workshop, "They worked us to death, because there were many days when we would take big bundles of sandbags and six-bys, and go down there and load sandbags all day long. Digging zigzag trenches all day, then out on patrol ... all night."

The nearby city offered the only worthwhile diversions, and "About every two weeks we could go on liberty, out in Danang. Now the Air Force had a whorehouse on the base, named the Blue Hawaiian. Off limits to Marines."

Politics and confusion over logistics continued to bedevil the

Marines. The Brigade went ashore with only a fifteen-day supply of food and ammunition. The Department of Defense had denied permission to use mount-out stocks[2] of supplies and ammunition. MACV thought that the Marines would be supported through their own system, since so much of their equipment was not common to the Army or ARVN. Eventually Westmoreland approved temporary support until a Marine logistical support structure could be established.

By 22 March the logistical units were in place, along with two Marine Air Groups. This constituted an MEF-sized force, and Major General William R. "Rip" Collins (commander of the 6th Tank Battalion on Okinawa in 1945) established III MEF on 6 May. Relationships with the ARVN were already strained, and with the civilian populace in revolt an Expeditionary Force was unfortunately similar to the title of the old French Expeditionary Corps. After some indecision Commandant Wallace Greene selected the title III Marine Amphibious Force (III MAF), harking back to World War II terminology, and on 7 May III MEF became III MAF. III MAF would eventually grow to a corps-sized unit but would retain the same title to avoid even the politically-charged term Corps. The Marine Corps force continued to grow at an accelerating pace, and on 5 June Major General Lew Walt assumed command of III MAF and its major component command, 3rd Marine Division.

The nominal mission of the Marines was to provide security for the Danang airfield and base facilities, so the Marines were initially limited to a very small Tactical Area of Responsibility[3](TAOR) in the immediate vicinity of the base. At first only part of one tank company, with two of its three line platoons, was ashore, with the other still aboard ship.

Don Gagnon had fought with the 1st Tank Battalion in the early days of the Korean War, and was the Company Gunnery Sergeant.[4] "The Company Gunnery Sergeant's job in a tank outfit is to re-supply, and see that the outfit has beans, bullets, POLs (petroleum, oils, and lubricants), and if there's a platoon that's out on a blocking position or whatever, he's supposed to go out there and say 'Okay, what do you guys need in rations?' Actually, because we had radio communications they call in and say 'Hey, I need this, this and this'. A lot of times it was compromised because the enemy had radios that they could listen in on."

The role of the tanks was still ill defined, and inside the small perimeter the situation was disorganized. Don Gagnon: "When we set up our CP, we weren't too far from the battalion's S-3[5] and so forth. The helicopters came in ... one right behind the other, and just tore our CP up with their backwash. (Lieutenant) Mels went up to the Three shop and raised hell with them. Says 'You know, you want us in this position, and you bring these helicopters in. We're trying to work, and you blow down all of our tents.' So the Three officer says go down and find another position as close to the CP as you can, (but) out of the way of the helicopters." The company moved into a position on a low hillside, which made it easier to construct protected bunkers to store fuel and ammunition.

"The place he (Mels) chose for a CP was on the fringe of the battalion, the BLT (area), and we just took in that sector. He went to the Three and said okay, we're gonna be from here to here... We'll make up range cards and everything, and that's what we did.

"We would set their tanks out and give them a sector (to defend), put an aiming stake out—an aiming point, just like the artillery—and say okay, you can shoot from there over to that point." The tank crew would then use the gunner's azimuth indicator[6] inside the turret to the limits for aiming in darkness to avoid firing into friendly positions. "The elevation ... you used your (gunner's) quadrant[7] and figure out the elevation, and make your range card accordingly."

Unlike World War II, when it was common to construct an improvised pillbox under the vehicle, in a perimeter defense the tankers fought from inside the tank. "I didn't like to put people on the ground except for the listening post, and before the listening post could do any shooting, he was supposed to come in so he wouldn't be in a crossfire or overhead fire. We had the tank infantry phone, and you could hook up a double-E eight[8] to that system." The listening post went out "Probably fifty yards or so. Two men, one to sleep and one to stay awake."

Inside the area were old French concrete bunkers that stood twelve to fifteen feet off the ground, but "That would be the first thing they would hit, so we didn't use any of those."

On 14 April Westmoreland authorized expansion of the TAOR, but only for defensive patrolling. The Marines chafed under both this restriction and the requirement that they request authorization to engage enemy units actually observed in the open. They began to call their surrounded enclave The Alamo.

In late April Moss's platoon moved out to Hill 327. One of the early missions was to provide indirect fire since the tank guns outranged the 105mm howitzers. "We were firing maybe 19,000 yards" as well as patrolling with the infantry. "At one time we had several outposts up on the side of 327, where we would go at night, just walking up there. You had a radio and stuff like that."

The Marines continued to trade services and favors, some inexplicable. "Some of the guys in the Air Force would even come out and help us hump ammo when we were doing indirect fire. They wanted C-rations, so we let them hump ammo and gave them C-rations. They had a barracks and hot water and everything. Not living out there like a bunch of vagabonds."

At Hill 327 the tanks were located on the left side of the road, just across from the Seabees, Navy Construction Battalion troops. "Thank God for those guys. If it had not been for them I don't know what we would have done. At first we were out there digging out tank slots with picks and shovels and stuff. Once they got there, (we) would gladly do them any favor we could, get them to bring the bulldozer over. Oh my gosh! The greatest bunch of guys there were.

"We had no place to get water or anything. They dug wells, and had water purification points and all kinds of things. I mean, they built roads, and you name it they did it."

The tankers would trade services for construction tasks and good, hot food. "One time one of their vehicles had run over the side of the mountain or something, so we took the tank up there and hooked to it and pulled it back up." The Marines also provided security and other favors.

Less welcome was a nearby battery of self-propelled guns of the 3rd eight-inch Howitzer Battery. These huge guns were the old M55 guns built on the heavy tank chassis with a large enclosed turret. Located between the hill and Danang, "They were maybe two hundred yards (away), so they were firing over top of us. And talking about the concussion and the muzzle blast! Man, it would pick you up. That's a real experience. Not a good experience, being in the front of eight-inch howitzers while they're firing."

Back on Okinawa, Ken Zitz had been assigned to raise his own new platoon to replace Mels's old 3rd Platoon, A Company. He found that Jones was willing to override the normal peacetime practice of assigning billets by seniority. Zitz wanted Sergeant Donald J. Clark for Platoon Sergeant of his A Company platoon, Jones appointed him in preference over several more senior NCOs who wanted a platoon. Zitz's platoon had been formed by men transferred from other units, which had—in time honored military tradition—taken the opportunity to dump many of their less satisfactory men. Zitz recalled that Clark justified his trust by whipping a group of men whom Zitz thought "looked like the Dirty Dozen" and were "the laughing stock of the battalion" on their first firing exercise into a first-class platoon.

One of the late additions to Zitz's platoon was the platoon mechanic, Dan McQueary. Dan enlisted in the Marine Corps from Deer Lodge, Montana in 1954, and served in the infantry and Amtracs. As a Sergeant in 1964 he was assigned to Okinawa, and eventually into Zitz's platoon. Because of his seniority and performance he eventually became a tank commander, unusual for a mechanic. In the middle of May 1965 the platoon was sent to Vietnam, under the operational control of 3/3. On 14 May the platoon landed in Vietnam at Chu Lai.

Zitz described how in the Chu Lai landings, though they were unopposed, "We lost two tanks going in." The Navy LSU, or Landing Ship Utility that carried three tanks, struck a sandbar bout fifty yards offshore. Zitz's tank was the first vehicle off.

"We dropped into about ten feet of water. Water came all the way up to my cupola." McQueary, the platoon mechanic, swam out with a carrier line and the damaged tanks pulled the LSU over the bar. "We had bilge pumps and we got through the surf okay, but when we got on the beach we found out that we had lost our generator. It was salt-damaged, so we were screwed. Another tank, same thing happened. We had two tanks out of action, and we weren't there for five minutes." With no supplies, it took several weeks to secure parts for repairs. "They just sat on the beach there."

Zitz termed the early rules of engagement at Chu Lai as "screwed up." Under the complex rules, "The tanks were not allowed to fire. No 90mm cannon was allowed to fire. It was an order that said 'unless approval was given by MACV.'"

Zitz thinks that an incident that involved him resulted in changes to the rules of engagement. One of the tasks of the platoon was to provide security along the Song Cai Bong river. Zitz took the heavy section with Sergeant Sam Kaleilaeki and a platoon of grunts to a position along the river. Also along was a Vietnamese interpreter riding in the gypsy rack. Zitz gave the interpreter a bullhorn and told him to tell the Vietnamese boatmen that the curfew was 1900 hours, and that boats should come over for inspection.

"About six boats started coming right over" to be inspected. "On the far bank we saw this one, the guy starts the engine up. We saw the puff of smoke. It was a big junk, and he started heading out of the harbor." Zitz moved his tank down to the mouth of the river. "I told Hachi [the interpreter] I said 'Pull that boat in here or we're going to huff and puff and blow him away.' Then the guy dropped his sail and started motoring out of the harbor."

The tank fired a warning shot across the bow. The boat kept going.

"I told Zebal [Ken W. Zebal, the gunner] 'Zebe, put one through the center of mass.' He said 'Roger,' so we fired that HE again.

"I was looking through my scope and I saw it. I called bull's eye. It went right through that junk. That thing was still smoking out. I said 'Gunner, give me a Willy Peter,' white phosphorus. I figured if he's got anything that's explosive, when this thing hits it's going to be the Fourth of July.

"The third round we fired was a Willy Peter. When that thing hit it looked like the last fireworks at the Fourth of July. Crap was flying all over. We had secondary explosions, tertiaries, big explosions, and three guys jumped over the side. They're swimming like rats. Zebe says to me 'Lieutenant, work them over with the fifty.'

"I said 'No, I'm not going to shoot a guy in the water because he's swimming away.' So I didn't do that. I think they were a little bit out of fifty range anyway." It was still a young war.

Zitz was called up to the regimental CP to explain the incident, accompanied by his visibly agitated company commander. Instead of being disciplined, the regimental commander congratulated Zitz. The rules of engagement for the 90mm were relaxed, and the big guns could be used at will.

Dan McQueary also recalled the peculiar security assignment along the river. "At night we would go down along the river and set up defense during the evening time." The unit quickly improvised gunboats, a throwback to a practice first used in the Cape Talasea campaign on New Britain in 1943. "Occasionally on the river they would bring in some LCMs, Navy boats. We'd put tanks on the LCMs." As infantry patrolled along the banks on either side, "We patrolled the river with the tank on it, and we were more or less supporting fire for them, using the tank off the LCM."

Firing the tank's main gun over the side of the LCM was "Kind of interesting. Kind of moved it over to the side a little bit. When we first started out, we went on the LCMs and we noticed that we had some problems with turret rotation and depression of the gun. We shored up the bottom of the LCMs when we boarded, so that lifted us up off the decking of the LCM to give us good traverse of the gun, and elevation and depression of it." The tanks were parked on dunnage, rough-cut timbers used to shore up cargo in the holds of ships. "Usually two (LCMs), they worked in pairs.

"Most of the time we didn't run so much in the daytime with that, we ran at night, up and down the river." In conjunction with the Navy, the improvised gunboats searched the local boat traffic. "Check them out for any type of infiltration or contraband. They (sailors) were doing the boarding. We'd pull up alongside, pull them over and pull them into the boat, and they'd go in. The crews of the tanks would get up with their weapons and provide security for it." The river patrols were intermittent, conducted only when intelligence indicated that there would be enemy traffic along the river.

Just before Zitz's tour ended, Colonel Jones came down and spoke to him. He told Zitz, "'I usually don't make deals, Lieutenant, but if you'll extend for six months you can keep your platoon and stay here.'"

Zitz had just ordered a new convertible back in the States and declined the offer. Jones gave him until the next day to make a final decision. When Zitz stuck to his decision, Jones told him with some foresight that "'You'll be back. This thing ain't going to be over any time soon.' He was right."

Zitz went back to teach at the Basic School at Quantico, as one of the first tactics instructors with actual Vietnam experience. "We got the hero's welcome. We got all this red carpet treatment and we're invited to all kinds of functions." The novelty of Vietnam soon wore off. "Then about six months later everybody forgot about us, because then they start coming back in droves, guys from Vietnam." Zitz got married and extended for a year and was assigned to a forty-seven-week Chinese language school in Monterey California with another tanker, Lieutenant Mike Wunsch.

Kurt Moss remembered that the naïve young Marines thought—like many of their countrymen—that Vietnam would require only a simple show of force to intimidate the locals. At first, in fact, the VC bided their time, assessing their new foe. The only dangers were those inherent in any military operation. "On the 23rd of June our truck driver, (Lance Corporal) Jesse James Jr., was killed in the company area."

James did not know the password system, and when a sentry challenged him he did not respond. After a third challenge, the sentry shot and killed him.[9]

Like any piece of blind, cumbersome, but powerful heavy machinery, a tank is inherently dangerous to be around, even when not in combat. Even small oversights could have serious consequences. One loader shot himself with his own thirty caliber coaxial gun while removing it from the turret for maintenance, and another was seriously injured when his unsecured loader's hatch slammed shut, nearly severing his head.[10]

The first heavy loss of life for A Company was the result of an accident. Kurt Moss: "On the 26th of June we went on a company-sized patrol with Alpha Four-Two (in the lead). Lieutenant Butts was the lead tank. I was on Alpha One-Three, and we were bringing up the rear. On the third river crossing, he sunk his tank. Lieutenant Butts, Corporal Zapanzik, Corporal Swinger, he was the company armorer, Sergeant Eustace, plus an engineer that was riding on the outside drowned." The driver and another tanker managed to swim free and survived.

Somehow the tank had dropped into a pothole in the river bottom, and "I think maybe only about two feet of the tallest antenna that was on the RT-66 radio was above the water. I think it might have been about eighteen, twenty feet of water."

Moss could not be entirely sure what was going on. "We really didn't know what had happened, because at about the same time as they sunk the lead tank, we blew the engine in my tank." On the first river crossing the previous vehicles climbing out of the water had made the bank wet and slick.

"It was scary being out there in the river. George Owens was driving, and Bonell (the tank commander) told him 'Go a little further up the river and then turn left' and we turned directly into the riverbank. Next thing I know I'm looking down and the shroud on the engine is under water. The whole engine is under water.

"George said he saw the water coming and held his breath and kept his foot down. Believe it or not, water was all down in the turret. We started up the bank. The engine was still running. White smoke was coming out of it. Water was coming out of the air cleaners.

"If we had stopped right then and there, it would have saved the engine. Even though there was no water in the oil, we had gotten water in the cylinders, and had bent or kinked several connecting rods." The engine seemed to be running well but on the second crossing, "It put three rods through the block."

The engine blew at about the same time that the lead tank was foundering at the other stream crossing. "The retriever came by a bit later and couldn't get Alpha Four-Two out, so they stopped on the way back to tow us in."

Through the following relatively uneventful weeks the tank platoons were in constant motion. Moss's platoon shuttled between the airstrip and Hill 327. On 30 June the airstrip was attacked, though the tanks, at the extreme ends of the runway, saw no action. In early July the platoon moved out into The Dust Bowl. "That's what we called the area where the 2nd Battalion, 3rd Marines were. All that white sand and whatever."

It was common practice to send one or more experienced people to assess the situation and coordinate with the unit being relieved. Dan Wokaty said, "I went with the advance party to find out all the ins and outs, and what all we had to do. Where we placed our tanks at night for security for the Danang airbase. The rest of the platoon came down, and when they came in we took their positions, and they back loaded back onto the ship, and they went back to Okinawa. We were First Platoon of Bravo Company, Third Tanks, but we became First Platoon of A Company, Third Tanks" with the stroke of an administrative pen, "and we stayed that until the rest of Bravo Company Third Tanks came down."

There were no port facilities that could handle heavy vehicles, so "They offloaded all tanks and Amtracs at Red Beach. They even had a train that I guess went north, then went south. When the Amtracs came off the ship there, for some unbeknown reason they took off and run into the train, and knocked the train completely off the tracks.

"The platoon that I was with, we started out right there on the Danang airbase. But our company headquarters ... was at Freedom Hill" northwest of Danang. The tanks were dug in with the turrets above ground, in turret defilade.

"We just provided security on the Danang airbase with our tanks. They had two tanks on the north end and two on the south end, and usually they'd rotate 'em.... That was to keep sappers from coming in there and blowing up the planes, and doing all kinds of destruction there." The tanks and a company of infantry stood watch at night.

Binoculars and telescopic sights gave the tanks much better night vision capability, and "If they needed something lit up on the ground, why we could light it up 'cause we had searchlights on our tanks." The searchlight could also provide lasting illumination, as opposed to the temporary and flickering light of flares.

General Walt requested the balance of the 3rd Marine Division, and this was authorized as part of a huge force of 44 battalions requested by Westmoreland, who continued to press for troops in ever increasing numbers.

On 7 and 8 July the battalion headquarters for 3rd Tank, along with B Company, arrived to join the other two line companies of the battalion. When the balance of B Company arrived, Wokaty's platoon once again joined them. Kurt Moss's platoon was replaced at Danang by an adjunct platoon from B Company that was simply designated to become part of another battalion.

On 24 July 3rd Tank Battalion was assigned a general support mission. This meant that the tanks would be spread out among the infantry regiments, according to Marine doctrine. At mid-summer Alpha Company would support the 3rd Marines, B Company the 9th Marines, both near Danang. C Company would support the 4th Marines at Chu Lai, with one platoon at Phu Bai with 3/4. In all tactical matters the tank units would operate under the control of the supported command.[11]

Ken Pozder was from a remote area of northern California and "just wanted to get out and see what was going on in the world." With career choices limited to the logging industry or commercial fishing, Pozder chose the Marine Corps in 1956. He began in tracked vehicle maintenance, though like many he never attended a formal school but gained his expertise through on the job training, or OJT in Marine parlance. In 1965 Sergeant Pozder was sent to Vietnam as part of a replacement draft. "You had a couple of days to get your paperwork, and shots that you may have missed, which you got 'em all before you even got there. They threw you on a truck, and out you went. Gave you a rifle." Pozder was assigned to the retriever for Bravo Company, 3rd Tank at Marble Mountain. The retriever was kept busy because "we hit a bunch of mines. It was all sand in that area, and boy they just buried them *everywhere*."

In the early days facilities at the base camps were still fairly primitive. Pozder said that the accommodations at the new Marble Mountain base were strong-back tents, heavy canvas tents stretched over a frame of light timbers. "We had stuff readily available to trade to the Seabees. We could get plywood for a floor, things like that.

"We had good food. There was never any shortage of that. We had our own company mess hall, which was a good deal. What you ate was C-rations, but at least they were presentable. They weren't in a can."

The sanitary facilities were old-fashioned pit latrines dug into the sand, "The good old GI four-holer."

In 1965 ambushes were largely hit-and-run, and the VC would not stick around to fight. "They'd set up a good ambush, usually over a command-detonated mine. Then they'd rake the area with machine guns or whatever they had. RPG's. Then they'd just *sheew*, gone." Such ambushes were sufficiently common that tank escorts became mandatory. "That was a Division deal there that you couldn't go anywhere without two tanks."

Bridges were a problem, particularly for the sixty-ton M51 retriever. "They didn't really have many bridges that we drove tanks across. Usually it was ferries. The engineers have their pontoon ferries, and you just got on a ferry one tank at a time."

As the Marines gradually expanded their operational areas, they became responsible for military operations in an amazingly complex region. Within very short distances—a few miles or kilometers—the terrain could change rapidly from coastal sand dunes to low rolling hills covered by scrub forest, swamps with mazes of waterways navigable by small boats, farmland, or steep jungle-clad mountains impassable to vehicles of any sort. The annual rainfall could be up to 128 inches (325cm). Most of it fell in the monsoon season that peaked in January through March, when low temperatures and the cold *crachin* (French for drizzle) made life in the outdoors cold and miserable. In the dry summer months of June through August the stifling heat, abrasive sand, and blowing dust led to respiratory diseases and increased wear on mechanical devices from rifles to tanks. The population density varied from cities to mountainous valleys never seen by Europeans. The agricultural land outside the cities along the coastal plain was as densely populated as a typical American suburb.

Contrary to popular misconception, Ken Pozder said that the coastal plain and the Marble Mountain area was "beautiful tank country," mostly sandy with few rice paddies, and even those were usually traversable by the tanks. "Once in a while one would get stuck, and battalion came up with this cross-cable system. One or two tanks had these thick cables on them, with eyes on both ends. If one got stuck, you just went out and cross-cabled and pulled them back out."

It was not the mud but the fine sand that gave tankers headaches, clogging air filters and finding its way into moving parts to grind away at the metal. Pozder: "Of course the humidity did a lot too, because the fuel (algae) would grow in the fuel cells and plug up the filters. It was pretty tough in 1965. We had no replacement parts, or very few. New track was almost non-existent. You hit a mine. You'd lose ten or twelve track blocks, and what you ended up doing was replacing them with old stuff that was laying around, or (from) somebody that had hit a mine before and needed a lot more maintenance than what could be accomplished very soon." The maintenance section managed to keep tanks from being deadlined for lack of parts, as "Everybody kind of cobbled things together, and I think we even got some stuff from the Army. You know the Army didn't even have any tanks over there then, but they were building up their supplies. I think we kind of cumshawed stuff from them."

Marine tactical doctrine at all levels emphasizes offensive operations, and commanders continued to agitate for the chance to take the fighting to the VC. On 6 August Westmoreland rescinded orders that limited Marine operations. The first offensive was Operation BLASTOUT I, a foray into a VC stronghold south of the Phong Le Bridge by infantry and LVT transports.[12] The VC evaded significant contact, but ambushed the column as it withdrew along the rivers. In this VC-controlled area the Marines were granted permission to burn a hamlet[13] from which they had taken fire. The event, filmed by a CBS film crew, provided one of the iconic images of the war.

Reinforcements continued to flow in. On 13 August the 7th Marines under Col. Oscar F. Peatross landed at Chu Lai, reinforced by Capt. Allen W. Lamb's B Co., 1st Tank Battalion. Battalion Landing Team 1/7, with the 1st Platoon, B Co., 1st Tanks, arrived on 14 August.[14] Typical of the way the Marines were operating at the time, many of these units would remain only days before being loaded back aboard ship.

Ray Stewart was the Platoon Commander of 3rd Platoon of Captain Allen W. Lamb's Bravo Company, 1st Tank Battalion. Stewart had joined the Marine Corps Reserve in 1955 in high school, and subsequently went on active duty as an enlisted man. After a brief period following that tour, he went back to active duty in the Naval Enlisted

Scientific Education Program. He attended university and was commissioned in 1964.

Stewart's platoon landed with 3/7 at Chu Lai, but without tanks. The battalion then back loaded and returned to the Philippines.

FIRST MAJOR CLASH—OPERATION STARLITE

The first Marine offensive operation would be a classic sweep, designed to seek out and inflict casualties on the enemy, and locate and disrupt his logistical and support functions. The pattern for these operations was established early, and they became symbolic of the war.

In June the Marine Radio Battalion noted an increase in enemy radio traffic emanating from the area of the Van Tuong Peninsula, 24km south of the Chu Lai enclave. On 15 August an enemy deserter reported the presence of the *1st VC Regiment* (*60th* and *80th Battalions*, *52d Company*, and *45th Weapons Battalion*) south of Van Truong Village, in preparation for an attack on the new base at Chu Lai. It was the opportunity Walt had been seeking, and plans were set in motion for an immediate attack on the VC base area. Colonel Oscar Peatross, a World War II Raider and CO of the 7th Marines, would be in command, though his regiment would supply only the operational reserve (3/7).

Operation STARLITE was formulated within forty-eight hours. It had all the features of sweep operations that were to become all too familiar. The tactical plan was complex. Individual units were drawn from multiple commands, with companies from different regiments and even different divisions. This meant that not only were units working with other formations whose leaders might be unfamiliar, but that chains of command were complex and sometimes ambiguous. The supporting tank force, Company B (-) (Rein), was probably the most cobbled-up lot of all. The command element was drawn from Bravo Company(-)/1st Tank (one M48A3 gun tank, three M67 flame tanks, and an M51 retriever). Dan McQueary's 3rd Platoon/Alpha Company/3rd Tank Battalion, and a section from Second Platoon of Charlie Company/3rd Tank supported the main assault elements. The A Company gun tanks were to support BLT3/3, the section from C Company would support BLT 2/4, and the command element would be a general reserve.[15] Since 2/4 would land inland by helicopter the tanks assigned to its support would have to cut across enemy-held country to link up with them.

Ray Stewart was frustrated that "Lieutenant Colonel Botley (3/7) again went in on STARLITE and did not use his tanks. I got ashore because I went as part of his staff." He had a reinforced platoon complete with fuel trucks, communications jeeps, and other gear, but "As it turned out the tanks that were used on STARLITE came down from Chu Lai. Captain Lamb brought down a throw-together task force of tanks from Chu Lai ... Botley leaving his tanks and Ontos aboard the LSD *Point Defiance.*" Stewart believes that Colonel Peatross and his subordinate officers did not have a real grasp of the utility of the tanks.

In contrast, Dan McQueary thought that the infantry officers in 3/3, particularly the CO, Colonel Joseph Muir, were very good with supporting weapons. Unfortunately the quickly improvised operational plan required complex coordination with US Army units, as well as Navy supporting units and air assets. Security in the local ARVN headquarters, riddled with VC agents, had proven so inadequate that the entire operation was concealed from the "allies" until it was underway. The ground was not only unfamiliar, but inadequately reconnoitered. In the maze of hamlets, trails, mixed agricultural land, and scrub forest that all looked alike, it would prove easy for units to get disoriented or misidentify their positions. The only thing that would prevent disaster was the bravery and professionalism of the Marines at the sharp end.

Before going ashore Ray Stewart observed that though the younger men were excited by the prospect of going into combat, many of the older NCOs were more sanguine. "They were not young and enthusiastic. That kind of sums it up."

On 17 August M/3/3, mounted on Amtracs, moved toward the north edge of the operation area, then spread out on foot to secure a blocking line along a stream. At 0615 hours on 18 August the 155mm howitzers of K Battery, 4/12 bombarded three landing zones (LZs RED, WHITE, and BLUE) along the west margin of the area, while Marine jets pounded the LZs and GREEN Beach to the east.

At 0630 Amtracs bearing I/3/3 and K/3/3 landed on GREEN Beach and moved inland, followed an hour later by five M48A3 gun tanks, the three M67s and the VTR from Bravo, and M50A1 Ontos tank destroyers, followed by five more gun tanks. Over the next few days this small armored force would literally be everywhere on the small battlefield. Like many battles in Vietnam, it would prove so confused that it is impossible to track the movements of the tank units across the battlefield. Peatross established his headquarters just inland. At 0645 helicopters deposited G/2/4 in LZ RED, followed at 0730 by E/2/4 (WHITE) and H/2/4 (BLUE).

K/3/3 moved quickly until it encountered heavy resistance along a ridgeline designated Phase Line BANANA,[16] about two kilometers inland, and the reserve L/3/3 was called forward. E/2/4 met heavy resistance almost as soon as it left LZ WHITE, and spent several hours trying to clear a small ridgeline.

The real problem lay at LZ BLUE, where H/2/4 landed literally on top of the *60th VC Battalion*. The surprised VC did not react immediately, but following waves of helicopters were raked by heavy machine gun fire from nearby Hill 43 and the Nam Yen (3) hamlet. The company was totally committed in the effort to drive the VC off Hill 43. The tanks came ashore together, but once ashore "They kind of split us up, once we hit the beach." McQueary's tank section supported India 3/3. The landing was uneventful, but once ashore the company, moving inland from the beach, was redirected to the west and crossed over into 2/4s operational area to attack An Cuong (2). Both platoons of gun tanks supported this southern flank of the Marine attack, but the thickets that separated the fields were natural ambush sites. "Lots of hedgerows and stuff like that. Trenches."

Dan McQueary: "I had a squad of Marines with me, a kid by the name of Sergeant O'Malley, his squad. We were running some clearing operations up in one particular area there. Right away we got in the fan, things started hitting the fan. We took quite a bit of small arms, and then we started taking some anti-tank stuff.

"O'Malley then left us and started out to clear some trench lines. We put supporting fire in on it." An Cuong (2) had turned out to be a fortified VC stronghold. In the fighting a VC disabled McQueary's A34 with a single RPG round. "My tank took a hit at the time."

The infantry was off to the right, and the tanks had closed in on the VC trench lines. "I remember getting on the radio and telling my driver, Milo Plank, I said 'Dammit, Milo, get that hatch closed.' I was looking out and we had the little brown men probably within ten to fifteen feet of the tank at the time, and I figured they were naturally going to assault the tank, and try to drop a grenade or something in the open hatches.

"We were struck right by the gun shield." By some fluke that spared the gunner, "I took most of the shrapnel." McQueary "hung in there as long as I thought I possibly could." The nearby infantry squads were taking heavy casualties. "We stayed there at the area and defended that.

We provided security for some medevacs. They came in and picked up I don't know how many at the time. I was medevaced probably on the third leg of the medevac."

After a confused fight that cost the life of the company commander, India captured the hamlet. According to some accounts, tanks from C Company evacuated the crew of A34, but McQueary believes that the tank continued to operate for a time after he was evacuated.

By mid-afternoon the inevitable confusion of battle, exacerbated by the hasty planning and relative inexperience of some officers, began to pile up. With too few men to secure ground already taken, Marine infantry and tank units moved about like ships in a sea of enemy-occupied hamlets, woods, and fields. The situation was probably worse for the VC commanders with a less integrated communications system and Americans appearing at many separate—and often irrational—places. With neither side willing or able to back away, the confused dogfight swirled through the countryside.

The tanks were dispatched to move cross-country and link up with the units encountering the most trouble, H/2/4 near Hill 43 and I/3/3 near An Cuong (2). One section of C Company tanks assisted in evacuating the A34 crew and moved toward H/2/4's position. The light section of 3d Platoon lost its protecting infantry in the confusion, so it also moved toward H/2/4's position. The remnants of the heavy section, with A33 escorting A35, which was experiencing mechanical problems, returned to the beach. All the functional gun tanks were now operating in support of H/2/4.

After clearing An Cuong (2) India gave it up and moved off toward the BANANA ridge to assist embattled K/3/3, leaving two squads to guard the hulk of a helicopter shot down during the fighting. After securing Hill 43 Hotel 2/4 moved off to link up with I/3/3, which was moving away from them.

Escorted by a mixed platoon of tanks and three Ontos, H/2/4 moved out into the rice fields between Nam Yen (3) and An Cuong (2). Hotel's commander thought that India had also cleared Nam Yen (3), but strong enemy mortar and machine gun fire from Nam Yen (3) and Hill 30 raked the infantry in the open muddy ground. The tanks and Ontos were limited by the deep mud, and Lt. Homer Jenkins, the commander of Hotel, drew them up in a defensive circle to try and protect his men. Supported by fire from the tanks the infantry pushed into Nam Yen (3), but were driven back to the protection of the tanks.

With his position untenable, Jenkins moved the company back toward the LZ. As Hotel fell back, the arrival of medevac helicopters coming down atop the marching company dispersed them, and one platoon became separated. This orphan platoon was pinned down but rescued by the fire of the two squads left behind by I/3/3; the two groups joined up and moved off to seek refuge near An Cuong (2). The tanks and H/2/4's other two platoons were ordered back to LZ BLUE to dig in at 1630 and await reinforcement.

India 3/3 requested flame tank support at about 1100 hours. Back at the operational headquarters near the beach, the senior officers of 3/3 made a mistake that would have been obvious to Marines of an earlier generation. The commander of 3/3, Lt. Colonel Joseph Muir, instructed Major Andrew Comer, his Executive Officer, to dispatch a supply column of five Amtracs escorted by three flame tanks (the only uncommitted tactical unit) to move out toward India's temporary position. Both men thought that India was just forward of the 7th Marines CP, when in reality the company was near An Cuong (2), and on the move in poorly understood ground.

The armored column, without infantry protection, was being sent into the midst of an aroused enemy in a tangle of trails and woodland. It was a classic recipe for disaster. Dan McQueary was later puzzled by this course of action. "I think there were misinstructions given to them, I believe, in where they were supposed to proceed to. And they didn't have communications."

Ray Stewart: "Did these guys know what the hell to do with tanks and armor? No, because if they did they would have known that the Marine Corps has been a tank-infantry coordination (organization). Always tank-infantry. We don't fight tanks separately and we don't fight tanks without our infantry cover, yet that was done on Starlite."

Dan McQueary: "That was the name of the game that we really trained for when we were in Okinawa with Three-Three, was tank-infantry coordination, and the communications with it."

The supply column passed by H/2/4 and promptly got lost in the maze of trails. It was ambushed in enemy ground between An Cuong (2) and Nam Yen (3). Moving along a trail between open paddies and a tree line, the lead vehicles were struck by large explosions. Flame tank B55 was hit and put out of action with two men wounded. The LVTs, attempting to avoid contact, drove into the rice paddy. Three immediately bogged down, and a VC tossed a grenade into a fourth. Under fire from recoilless guns[17] and mortars, the tanks tried to back off the trail to form a defensive circle.

With the flame gun on the rear tank out of action, and numerous casualties, the column was soon fighting for survival as the VC closed in. Without infantry in support the vehicles were vulnerable to close assault. One VC rushed in and threw a satchel charge onto the driver's hatch of tank B53, showering the driver with shards of thick glass from the periscopes. In the confusion a radio operator in one LVT held down the transmit button of his radio, shouting for help but preventing anyone else from talking on the assigned frequency. With weapons rattling all over the countryside observers could not even locate the lost column by sound.

B53 had expended all its .30caliber ammunition, its .50caliber cupola gun was disabled, and the driver wounded. The tank broke contact and headed back toward the headquarters near the beach.

Believing the column was about to be overrun, Colonel Muir called India back toward the CP and instructed Comer to organize a rescue force. Peatross was worried that the column had struck a VC force moving against the operational headquarters.

Tank B53 found its way back to Peatross's headquarters, where the tank commander reported he had not been fired on from An Cuong (2), and felt he could guide a relief force back into the killing zone. At 1300 Comer's relief force—the worn-out I/3/3, some headquarters personnel, and the only uncommitted armor (command tank B51)—moved out. Near Hill 30 the scratch force encountered strong resistance. B51 stopped to engage enemy troops running across its direct front, and was hit by an RPG. The thin-skinned Amtracs, under fire from the front and flanks, left B51 on its own. Unable to identify and engage the enemy, B51 broke contact. When the fire slackened temporarily Comer ordered India to press on through An Cuong (2). They worked their way through the hamlet, but were driven down by heavy fire before they could reach the trapped armored column. The headquarters party remained pinned down in open rice paddies by heavy fire. They gathered in the orphaned platoon from H/2/4, and Comer sent the two squads from I/3/3 toward Hill 30.

Lima 3/7 was brought ashore from the operational reserve to help rescue the supply column.[18] The new unit and the battered India remnants, supported by a cobbled-up armored force consisting of B51, A33, and the big M51 VTR again pressed toward An Cuong (2) against heavy fire. Under pressure from the two infantry companies, and with night coming, the VC broke contact. Rather than push on in the darkness, India, Lima, and the tanks pulled back. The trapped supply column—no longer under pressure—remained in place through the night.

During the night Peatross pulled H/2/4 and Comer's scratch force back, and brought the rest of the operational reserve (India and Mike, 3/7) ashore and put them into the line. The 3/7 was reinforced by Ray Stewart's 3rd Platoon, B Company, 1st Tanks aboard LSD31, the *Point Defiance*. The fighting continued into the darkness and tank A34 was hit again by an RPG, killing McQueary's replacement.[19]

At 0730 on 19 August the Marines pressed forward. By 0900 the fresh companies from 3/7 had entered An Cuong (2) and contacted the survivors of the armored column. Five were dead, most of the rest wounded, and only nine effectives remained after the violent three hour fight.

The tank and recovery crews worked to recover the crippled vehicles scattered around the battlefield. Tank A34 and an Amtrac were too badly damaged, and were destroyed by the engineers.

By 1030 on 19 August the various forces had linked up in a broad front, driving the VC toward the sea and blocking positions to the north and south. The VC fought tenaciously and repeatedly emerged from caves and bunkers to attack the Marines from the rear.

The next day the battered 2/4 and 3/3 were withdrawn, replaced by 1/7 and elements of the 2nd ARVN Division, still smarting under the insult of not being advised of the operation. For five more days the Marines and ARVN soldiers rooted out enemy survivors. The VC had suffered 614 known killed, with nine captured and an unknown number of wounded. The Marines lost 45 killed and 203 wounded. The small tank force of three officers and 44 enlisted men had suffered one dead and 13 wounded, with another killed in the supporting Ontos unit. Clearly the enemy did not find the tanks intimidating.

Dan McQueary was wounded in the legs, back, and arms. He was taken to Chu Lai, then to Danang. After surgery at Danang he was flown to Clark Air Force Base near Manila, and then to Okinawa. After several weeks in the hospital he was sent to the US on convalescent leave. "I figure I was lucky compared to some of them. Oh, well. It goes with raising the right hand."

Another of the wounded was 2nd Lt. Ky Thompson, Ken Zitz's replacement. He lost part of a foot to an RPG.[20]

STARLITE would prove typical of the war. The Marines descended upon a Communist force, inflicted disproportionately heavy casualties, and controlled the battlefield. The VC slipped away and lived to reorganize and fight again another day. Ray Stewart said, "We all came out of Starlite thinking differently about the enemy than when we came in, that's for sure." Stewart said that of course no one could have foreseen 58,000 dead over a period of years. "That could have been just as easily, in our mind, not only the first battle but the last battle. We kicked their ass, and we're never going to see those guys again. The prognosticators of the time said 'Well, you know that VC regiment ceased to exist after Starlite.' Well, yeah, it did, for a couple of weeks. Maybe a couple of months on the outside."

Unfortunately STARLITE was also typical of future tank employment, with tanks sent out in penny-packets, sometimes without infantry support. Both sides deployed small and fairly mobile forces with a low troop density spread over large areas with no continuous lines. Unlike in World War II, it was often impractical or impossible to exert the effort necessary to push tanks into forested or otherwise inaccessible ground before the fighting was over. The problem that confronted US forces was that they needed to control huge tracts of countryside, but they lacked the immense manpower required to occupy land once it was cleared of the enemy. Instead, enemy units moved freely and there were no clear fronts. The answer seemed to be operations that could seek out and destroy enemy forces, trying to neutralize enemy strength and control ground. Similar operations on a smaller battalion scale included STOMP, conducted by 2/7 on 5 through 7 September.

THE WAR WIDENS

The success of STARLITE encouraged III MAF to undertake additional large combined air-amphibious assaults. Operation PIRANHA would include Vietnamese forces in the effort to complete the annihilation of the *1st VC Regiment*. In the predawn hours of 7 September, aircraft bombed and strafed WHITE Beach on the Batangan Peninsula, 12km south of the STARLITE battlefield, and several LZs inland. At 0635 two companies of 1/7 followed LVTE-1s[21] onto the beach, and elements of 3/7 were lifted into LZ OAK. The helicopters then lifted troops from the 2/4 ARVN and the 3rd Battalion of the South Vietnamese Marine Corps into LZs BIRCH and PINE. The initial resistance quickly melted away, and over the next three days the troops swept toward the An Ky Peninsula. Only 1/7 reported any significant contact with the enemy. The infantry found an abandoned hospital and other facilities, but also evidence that the *1st VC Regiment* had decamped about a day earlier. Had they been warned? The VC would return, and the region would remain an enemy stronghold for the rest of the war.[22]

For the most part the VC avoided contact for several months as they sized up the Americans and tried to develop tactics to counter their mobility and firepower. The tanks were not used in any significant way, but primarily to establish blocking positions against which the infantry could attempt to drive the VC.

For other tankers on more routine duties, like Kurt Moss, all through late August "We were on roadblock positions near the river. On the 24th we had got pay records and everything ready preparing to leave, even though we were still going out on patrol and everything that night."

The war was ratcheting up, but "Our tour of duty was up." The group that included Moss should have arrived back in California by 1 September, "but we didn't leave Vietnam until the twenty-ninth of August. I was there my last six months in the Far East."

The Corps was still a relatively small institution, generally peopled by men serving long-term enlistments. It was more like a family, so the departing men were ordered to report to battalion, to be sent off by Colonel States Rights Jones. "He was just up there shaking everybody's hands just like a daddy to his sons. Because we were leaving. We were the first ones in there, and the first to go."

The small group thought they would be leaving by plane, but there were more familial send-offs in store. "So we went down to the Danang airstrip, and General Walt talked with us. No airplanes. So we went down to the Danang River, and went out in an LCU and boarded USS *Lenawee*, APA 195 (an old World War II Attack Transport). That one took us up the coast to Chu Lai, and we got on the USS *Iwo Jima* helicopter carrier, and that one brought us back to Okinawa. We didn't think we would ever get back."

The Marine Corps had numerous commitments other than Vietnam. Moss was sent back to the heavy tank company, Delta Company, of the 2nd Tank Battalion, with the 2nd Marine Division that supported the Atlantic and Mediterranean Fleets, as well as NATO in Europe. By an all too typical administrative oversight, in early August of 1967 he received orders for Vietnam "about a week and a half before I was due to get out. I said 'I'm not gonna extend, I'm not gonna re-enlist, but hey—a week and a half, I'll go.'"

Ray Stewart's platoon from B Company was finally put ashore at Chu Lai. There, "We cleaned sand out of every crevice and crack of our body, and food, because the wind blew across the beach. We were always short of fresh water. We would go for a dip in the South China Sea, and then of course ended up with crotch rot because you couldn't get the salt water off you because we didn't have showers." Eventually conditions improved as the camp took shape.

Stewart explained that the sand was particularly hard on drive sprockets and torsion bars. Drive sprockets were normally reversed at most twice a year, to allow for differential wear. In Vietnam "Those drive sprockets would wear out just so quick. We were swapping drive sprockets every day. There were times they were swapped two or three times until that sprocket was almost worn smooth before we got replacement sprockets."

At night the tankers would be lying in the tent and "You'd hear a big 'Pop!' It would be a torsion bar breaking for no known reason." Other particular problems were the inflatable rings that sealed the turret race ring for fording streams or in beach landings, and the radios. "We'd sit there for hours and hours and hours with abrasive erasers, polishing up the electrodes on the radios."

All this occurred against a policy clash invisible to the American public and the troops in the field. The Marines wanted to apply a "spreading inkblot strategy" to drive the VC out of the populous coastal region, controlling the population instead of territory. Pacification at the village level would deny the enemy recruitment and local resources like food. The fundamental part of this program was aggressive patrolling and establishing good relationships with the villagers.

The tank units, with no clear responsibility except to support the scattered infantry operations, were constantly on the move. In one such relocation Dan Wokaty's platoon crossed the river on barges and joined the rest of the battalion at Marble Mountain. "Once we got over there, we started running patrols with the infantry, because we were supporting Ninth Marines over there. Ninth Marines were having companies that would stay out in, we called it the Impact Area. We supported them out there." The tanks worked as far south as Hoi An.

In planning a sweep the tankers conferred with infantry company commanders. "They'd get us involved in that. They'd tell us what they were gonna do, and they'd ask us where we could provide security. After being out there a couple of times, we knew the layout of the area pretty well, so we knew where we could take our tanks, and where we could assist and help the infantry."

One of the frustrations was that the VC had some unusual local refuges. "There was a leper colony out there too, south of Marble Mountain. I guess the Viet Cong would take position and shoot at us, and then they'd go and hide out in the leper colony. The leper colony was off-limits to us. We never did go in there, shoot the place up or tear it up, or anything."

Suspected VC or sympathizers were taken for interrogation, but it "Seemed like they always came up with the same people. They'd send them back to the rear, and once they got interrogated they'd let them go. The next time we'd sweep the area, they'd be right back in there."

The tanks were probably most useful in extracting the infantry from trouble. "Where infantry was pinned down or something and they needed to get free....We'd pull up there with our tanks, and instead of using the thirty we just cut loose with the ninety millimeter HE, and if it was close enough we'd use HE and WP and sometimes canister if the infantry wasn't in the way. You'd fire that canister or that beehive, that flechette round."

Profligacy with ammunition caused problems with a stingy supply service, just as it had in Korea. "They told us we were gonna have to quit firing so much ammunition down there, 'cause First Platoon of Bravo Company had fired more ammunition than the whole Marine Corps was allotted."

Overriding III MAF's plans, MACV had formulated its own rather vague strategy with no specific goals or dates. The idea was to throw enough troops into the field to "stop losing" by the end of the year. In 1966 US forces would go on the offensive, and at some unspecified future date would bring the enemy to open and decisive battle in the remote interior of the country. Interestingly, this complemented the enemy's strategy. Their primary strategist, General Giap, felt his best chance for ultimate victory was to lure the Americans into the mountainous interior where terrain would help offset the American advantages of mobility and firepower. There, he believed, he could "bleed them mercilessly."

General Walt had already advised MACV that he needed two full Marine divisions to accomplish his diverse missions, and in October the Marine Corps made plans to reactivate the 5th Marine Division.[23] III MAF had already initiated a MIXMASTER operation, with extensive reassignment of personnel. The early units to arrive in Vietnam had come as whole units, which meant that the troops' tour of duty would all end at the same time. The MIXMASTER avoided having to replace entire units, but at the cost of disrupting integrated units.

Ray Stewart said that as the war wore on training was shortened, but unlike Korea the replacements were at least trained tankers. The real problem was unit integrity. "The real downside I suppose was you didn't know who the hell was going to be in that crew the next day. I talk to tankers all the time, and they can't tell me who was in their crew. The first tankers that went over, we trained together, we did everything together.

"You didn't know who the platoon commander was going to be, you didn't know who the supply guy was going to be, you didn't know who was going to be in your crew. Constantly checking date of rank among Lance Corporals to see who was going to drive and who was going to load, who was going to be the TC. It was bedlam."

Sam Binion grew up in Florida, but left home at sixteen and "took off cross country. Ended up in Las Vegas. Worked there a few months, and decided to head back to Florida to go back to school." In January 1962 he stopped off to visit a brother who was stationed with the Air Force in Louisiana. "Sold my car for twenty dollars, and joined the Marine Corps" at seventeen.

In 1965 Binion joined 2nd Platoon, Charlie Company, 3rd Tank as a replacement. "Lew Walt, who was the General there, he met us at Danang and gave us a big speech, telling us that eighty-five percent of the casualties so far had been our own making. It wasn't because of the enemy, it was because of our own stupidity."

The replacements traveled to the Charlie headquarters that night. "That was an experience, because it was night, none us had weapons, and we were scared to death." There was no orientation to the country, just equipment issue. "We were issued our jungle boots. At that time they had the (separate) steel inserts; they weren't made into the boots. The inserts they gave me had blood all over them, so I didn't care for that too much."

For years the VC had instituted an annual "rice tax," openly venturing into the villages to confiscate part of the autumn harvest. In September some of the village chiefs requested Marine protection, and infantry units began patrols as part of GOLDEN FLEECE. On 12 September a village chief told the Marines that VC tax collectors were operating in the hamlets south of Marble Mountain. III MAF immediately dispatched two infantry companies, supported by tanks, Ontos, and LVTs. After a day of heavy fighting, the VC fled. Annual GOLDEN FLEECE programs would become a staple of the Marine mission.

Bob Embesi had returned to Vietnam aboard ship with a platoon from 1st Tank in support of 2/1, stopping en route at Midway and Okinawa.[24] The MEU was designated as a Special Landing Force under Seventh Fleet, and embarked aboard the USS *Point Defiance*.

Gary Gibson, in the same platoon, joined the Corps in 1964 because as a child in Indiana he found a discarded book under a tree. "It was *The Odyssey* and *The Iliad*. Some college student had thrown them away, apparently, in the ditch, and I picked them up when I was eight years old, and read them. I was hooked ever since. I wanted to get me a sword, or a rifle and a bayonet or something, and go charge something. That's all I ever wanted to do when I was growing up." He left high school in the first semester of the tenth grade, and first tried to join the Army, but the recruiter was not in his office. His mother signed the papers allowing him to join the Marines.

Like many others, Gibson "didn't know the Marines had tanks."

Gibson wanted to go to Vietnam. When his company commander instructed him not to sign his name to a posted list of volunteers, "I put my name at the top of the list, and I put my name at the bottom of the list."

In the MEU, built around 2/1, "There were Amtracs, artillery, engineers, air-naval gunfire liaison. There was a small Force Recon group, and of course tanks and motor transport, the whole works. Eighteen hundred men aboard two ships, and we had a helicopter carrier with us too, the USS *Iwo Jima*. We were a self-contained all arms group." After stops in Okinawa and the Philippines, where the jungle training was "one drunken party," the group sailed for Vietnam.

Embesi: "We were making raids trying to find NVA sanctuaries." A typical operation involved helicopter landings inland, coordinated with troops and a section of tanks landing across the beach to drive the enemy inland. The troops would offload over the horizon from the shoreline, and the Amtracs and boats would be towed toward shore, and cut loose for the landing. "If they're watching on the beach, they start heading inland. Get out of your way. Very seldom would they stop and stay there and fight." It was typical for the enemy to leave small forces behind to fire at the landing forces. Of seven landings, four met resistance.

Usually the enemy would slip away after suffering a few casualties. "Later on it was RPGs everywhere, but in the beginning with the Viet Cong it was a different war."

These raids penetrated a few miles from the coast, and the terrain was equally treacherous. Most was firm ground, but on the second raid, DAGGER THRUST II, three tanks were escorting infantry and Amtracs. "We rode inland about three or four miles... and when we went across what looked like a dry river bed, or dry rice paddy, one of the new tractors had stopped out there, and he sunk right down. Never did get it out. We had to blow it in place there. Then when we got inland two or three miles on an objective, as soon as the tanks stopped they sank. I saw what was happening, and the Amtracs that were with us, they were sinking too. So I pulled up on top of a house base, happened to be an old church.... I was the only one that wasn't stuck. They were stuck so bad guys were stepping eight inches off onto the ground from the top of an Amtrac."

The event was memorable for Gibson because when the tank stopped on a sandy area, "The tank commander had me get out of the tank, and he told me ... go out there and find these Amtracs and get them up there because they had one of their tracked vehicles stuck up there."

When Gibson dismounted, "I jumped out of the tank, when I hit the ground ... I could have sworn I felt the ground jiggle a little bit." This was a phenomenon that would bedevil the Marines all along the coastal strip. A cohesive layer of ancient beach and dune sands overlay thick mud saturated with water. Any heavy object—from a man to a tank—that broke through the sand crust quickly sank from sight in the liquid mud below.

"I took off and I went about a hundred yards and I was in heavy cover, wasn't jungle but it was heavy brush and trees.... I didn't know how we got there, I didn't know where anybody was. I thought 'Sonofabitch!'... I took my forty-five out and cocked it."

Gibson found the Amtracs and brought them forward, "But when I came back, our tank had sunk. We had parked over an underground riverbed. Our tank had sunk clear up to the fenders. While the driver was trying to get it out, he threw both tracks underground." The amtrac was buried in the ground up to its upper deck, and "the only thing sticking up was the antennas sticking out of the ground."

The agitated unit commander threatened to destroy the vehicles in place if they could not be extracted by nightfall. "He was getting upset. There was some contact made up ahead, I guess by the helicopters. The rumors controlled what we heard back there, whether there had been some movement up ahead and they were trying to maneuver on us.

"With entrenching tools, them little old two foot-long shovels ... we dug that thing out, and got the tracks back on that thing."

The tankers used Embesi's tank to pull another out of the mire, then successively extricated other vehicles. The Amtracs had to be "pigtailed" (hooked together fore and aft), with all three tanks required to move the first Amtrac. Once a vehicle was in motion, it could churn across the ground fast enough to avoid sinking.[25]

Like many young boys Gibson had "killed millions of little clay troops and such." On one of the raids "I finally got to shoot somebody, which was the end game.

"We were coming up off the beach behind the sand dunes, and there was a big wide bay-like thing, like a river, coming out toward the ocean.

"There was a tree line way out there. They ran up to the tank and hollered they had sniper fire coming from that tree line, and pointed (it) out to my tank commander. So he told me right where to shoot, right at the end of that tree line.

"We ranged out to it, and I took the crosshairs in there, and I dropped a ninety-millimeter round into it. Through my ten-power scope, when that round went off, I saw him come out of the goddamn tree line end over end, and land in the water. He came up swimming."

The grunts later found one dead VC among the trees, but "that one started swimming." Gibson switched over to the thirty-caliber coaxial gun. "I'd fire a burst at him, and he'd just disappear in the geysers. So I thought 'Hmmm, I got him.'

"I'd wait a few seconds, and twenty or thirty feet farther on out, he'd pop back up again, swimming. I'd do it again. I did that four or five times, and each time he's getting farther away. He was already past tracer burnout—he was over five hundred yards away."

Finally, "The tank commander grabbed the override, which takes control away from me. He opened up on him a couple of times. Same thing happened. Then a chopper flew over there, saw us firing, and the door gunner out of that chopper fired a little bit, and they flew on off.

"This guy pops up again" about seven or eight hundred yards away. "I thought 'Goddamnit! There must be a way to get this sonofabitch.' So I just put my aiming circle—a little reticle in there that lights up—put that aiming circle about where I thought he was gonna come up." Gibson held the trigger down, pumping out rounds from the machine gun.

"When his head came up, I thought 'boop-boop-boop-boop-boop,' and walked right across his head, and I got him. He rolled over and his ass cheeks came up in the water, and I popped them full of rounds....I guess I yahooed ... It was better than sex, I tell you what."

The surf and beach conditions encountered on the raids were often more hazardous than the enemy. "That China Sea's a very rough kind of water." In one landing the LCU[26] grounded on the sand, but Embesi warned the commander of A34, the tank ahead of him. "I said 'Don't go off. Let this damn thing float over the sandbar on the next swell or something.' But the bosun up there hollered 'Get off the ship!'

"I told Pop (Kelly) on the radio, don't go. He went anyway. Went about ten feet, and then he dropped in about twenty-five feet of water. When he did that, of course the tank was gone. They popped up. By this time the waves are starting to carry the crew in. They all finally got out of the tank."

When the tank submerged the driver, Lance Corporal Burrell, was trapped when his hatch jammed. The tank commander somehow managed to hook the hatch lever with his foot, freeing the driver.[27]

"Now the U-boat is going around them and we're going in—less weight's on the U-boat, so now it's floated over the sandbar.... We land, and they show up swimming through the surf."

The tank was recovered several days later when Navy divers attached a tow cable, and several other tanks pulled it onto the beach. The tidal surge had ripped the rear armor and engine pack from the tank, as well as most of the internal fittings. On another landing Embesi's own tank was submerged and the crew space flooded, but the driver was able to drive the tank up out of the water, and complete the short operation.[28]

The VC were clearly willing to fight for control of the agricultural lowlands, and on the night of 27–28 October attacked the airbases at Marble Mountain and Chu Lai. On 17 November the revitalized *1st VC*

Regiment took advantage of the monsoon rains and clouds to overrun the local Regional Forces[29] garrison and capture the town of Hiep Duc at the western end of the fertile Que Son Valley, which enters the coastal plain between Danang and Chu Lai. This placed them in position to take two more important towns, Que Son and Viet An, in the center of the valley. The next day Marine helicopters lifted ARVN troops into LZs near the town after air attacks suppressed heavy fire from the NVA *195th AAA Battalion*. The ARVN recaptured the town the next day, but the VC then attacked the town of Thach Tru to the south; clearly they planned to contest ownership of the rice-rich valley. A hastily organized operation, HARVEST MOON/LIEN KIET-18 under a temporary command, Task Force Delta, was planned to disrupt the enemy efforts.[30] The VC planned otherwise.

The battle for control of the strategic valley opened on 8 December, when the ARVN 1/5 and 11th Ranger Battalions moved west out of Thangh Binh toward Hiep Duc, 25km away. The two battalions would guide on Highway 534. The plan was to lift 2/7 into position west of the enemy, and pinch them between the Marines and the advancing ARVN force, with 3/3 as an operational reserve. The 11th Ranger Battalion, advancing north of the highway, walked into a carefully prepared ambush set by the *70th VC Battalion*, losing a third of its force within hours. The battered Rangers withdrew to the northwest, farther from potential aid, and the ARVN force south of the highway was similarly assailed. The ARVN 1/6 was hastily lifted in to help the Rangers.

The next morning at 0645 the VC *60th* and *80th Battalions* fell upon the hapless ARVN force south of the highway, overrunning them and scattering the survivors. The VC again fell upon the ARVN Rangers and 1/6 to the north, but that force held out. At 1000 hours the 2/7 lift was diverted to LZs eight kilometers west of the shattered ARVN force, and the operational reserve, 3/3, was quickly moved by truck and helicopter to an LZ to the southeast. The latter quickly linked up with such ARVN holdouts as they could find, and set out for a hill a kilometer to the northwest. Along the way they were ambushed by strong VC forces, and forced to dig in for the night.

The next day was spent by both sides in preparing to "pile on" once battle was joined, rushing in reinforcements in an effort to inflict maximum casualties on the other side. This too was to become a pattern for the rest of the war.

After conclusion of the DAGGER THRUST raids the SLF built

around 2/1 had been sent to the Philippines for additional training and refitting. They were called back for the new operation. On the morning of 10 December, 2/1 was routed into an LZ southeast of Que Son. The plan was for the three Marine battalions to squeeze the VC between them. Instead the helicopters were hit by powerful antiaircraft fire, and after F/2/1 was landed the other lifts were diverted to LZs to the west. A ferocious ten-hour firefight ensued as the various companies of 2/1 tried to link up, resulting in heavy losses.

Gary Gibson said, "They needed troops and they couldn't use the tanks, it was monsoon time in there. They yanked us off as an infantry platoon. They gave us a bunch of used rifles. Some of them had nicks in them and bloodstains on them. Four magazines apiece, and a bunch of grenades." The 1st Provisional Rifle Company consisted of men from the tank, engineer, and Ontos platoons under Lt. Herb Stiegelman. The assignment was to provide security for a Howtar section.[31]

The provisional platoon was ferried from the USS *Monticello* to the *Iwo Jima* and loaded aboard helicopters. "Which is terrifying. I'd never been on a helicopter. The floor is corrugated, and it's wet, and it's slick. When you're sitting there and you're looking out the door, there's no door, no straps, no handholds. It's not too bad, but when you're at four thousand feet, when he banks to make a turn the floor becomes the wall, and you're looking straight down with nothing between you and the ground. Nothing to hang on to. I remember that. I did not like that.

"We spent seventeen days I think on operation HARVEST MOON up there as infantry."

The morning of 11 December revealed little resistance. The *1st VC Regiment* had slipped away again, probably into the less accessible Phuoc Ha Valley to the south. On 12 December ARC LIGHT strikes were called in for suspected enemy sites, then 2/1 and 3/3 were lifted in to search the valley, but monsoon rains and deep mud slowed movement. The Marines found caches, but no enemy. On 20 December III MAF declared an end to the operation and the troops withdrew.

Throughout this period the tank platoons attached to the BLTs that made up the Special Landing Forces were constantly on the move, extending their operations as far south as the coastline directly south of Saigon. The Navy in particular had held high hopes for amphibious raids conducted by the SLFs, which were controlled by Seventh Fleet and thus independent of MACV. A series of raids, DAGGER THRUST I through V, saw little action, and proved disappointing.

In December A Company, 1st Tank landed at Phu Bai with 2/1.[32] On Christmas Eve, Bob Embesi's platoon from Charlie Company landed at the Navy boat ramp in Hue City, and then traveled Highway One south to Phu Bai. For the first five or so weeks, the company commander allowed liberty—in civilian dress—in Hue, with a regular truck shuttle to the town.[33]

As the year drew to a close the doctrinal squabble between MACV and III MAF was coming to a head, with significant consequences for the Marines. General Walt wanted to emphasize pacification operations, but Westmoreland groused that he did not have enough troops to garrison every village in the country. Westmoreland's plan was that "We'll just go on bleeding them until Hanoi wakes up to the fact that they have bled their country to the point of national disaster for generations." This "strategy" also lent itself to the simple mathematical metrics so beloved of Defense Secretary McNamara. One metric was the body count. Another was "battalion days in the field." Since MACV did not count pacification operations as "days in the field," MACV Operations Officer Brigadier General William E. DuPuy concluded that the Marines were not pulling their weight, and recommended ordering them to undertake field operations against major enemy units in the interior.

Despite all the pre-war training and the experiences of previous wars, there was stil no clear doctrine of how the tanks were to be utilized. Ray Stewart observed, "If you had a company commander, or battalion commander [in the infantry] who really liked tanks, I can tell you that you used a lot of tanks. And if you didn't, if you thought they were nothing but RPG magnets, then you actively avoided them."

One unfortunate pattern that was already emerging was the use of tanks as self-propelled bunkers for local security. Ray Stewart laughed when he recalled that "A couple in my platoon (Rick Smith and Ned Schultz) said, 'Yeah, the goddamn Lieutenant put us up on a roadblock when we got there, and six months later came back and said it was time to go home. Didn't see that sumbitch for six months."

On 7 December 1965 Westmoreland issued orders to III MAF for a January operation along the I Corps/II Corps boundary. For the Marines it would initiate a whole new war.

CHAPTER 3

1966: THE NVA MOVES SOUTH

"We'll just go on bleeding them until Hanoi wakes up to the fact that they have bled their country to the point of national disaster for generations."

General William Childs Westmoreland

As the New Year began, Brigadier General DuPuy put increased pressure on the commanders of III MAF to increase the body count. Despite all prior experience, many Marine officers seemed to have unlearned the lessons of previous wars, and reports from operations like WAR BONNET (commencing 3 January) and WAR BONNET II (28 January) cite numerous examples of poor coordination between infantry and their supporting tracked assets.

Near the end of 1965 Ray Stewart was transferred from 1st Tank to 3rd Tank Battalion in the S-4 section. "There I got to see how the tanks were being used, because we had to resupply them." Some units were operating in support of infantry in the field, but all too often, "They were set on a hill in hull defilade providing long-range covering fire for patrols and H&I fires out into the valleys."

The tankers had been specifically trained in this role, but Ray Stewart distinctly recalled, "At tank school they would talk about tanks can do all this wonderful stuff including high angle fire. But they didn't spend much time on that, because they immediately came back and said 'That's not what tanks are for. Tanks are *not* for H&I fires, they're *not* for indirect fire.'"

In total, "They just didn't do much operating until we started moving north" in April and May of 1966. In that time frame Victor Charles began to go after the Marines with a vengeance.

Pat Rogers was a tank commander in the Third Platoon of Alpha

Company, 3rd Tanks, which had occupied the new logistics and operating base at Hill 55. On 21 May an infantry squad got into a firefight and the VC decided to stand their ground. The battles quickly escalated as two tanks and infantry reinforcements were called in. The tanks and infantry began to drive the VC *R-20 Battalion* back, smashing through hedgerows into the killing fields of open terrain beyond.[1]

At last the VC decided to break contact, falling back through the vegetation with the Marines in pursuit. As tank A34 advanced, its coaxial gun overheated and jammed. The .50-caliber cupola gun ran out of ammunition; with enemy infantry in close proximity, there was no time to reload the awkward side-mounted weapon. The loader stuffed an anti-personnel canister round into the main gun breech. The thin metal casing ruptured, spilling steel balls into the chamber and disabling the gun.

The harmless tank had by this time outrun its infantry protection, and was in the unique position of having the retreating enemy moving past the tank, headed in the same direction. Rogers grabbed an M14 and shot several VC who fired at him and the tank. The new driver, Gene Whitehead, was standing out of his hatch firing away at other enemy who were rushing the tank. Rogers shouted at him to move the tank forward. Whitehead dropped back inside.

The rifle ran out of ammunition and Rogers shouted for another magazine, but received a pistol magazine. He threw it at an enemy soldier and grabbed for a grenade. He pulled the pin and threw the grenade at an enemy soldier who was rushing the front of the tank, only to have the tank roll over the grenade. It exploded underneath the tank.

By this time the grunts had caught up and began to clear a VC trench line hidden in the underbrush. Rogers watched grunts and VC in the trenches, killing each other with guns and even entrenching tools. Whitehead was moving down the trench, doing neutral steers (reversing one track) to crush the trench and the enemy in it. The VC had suffered enough, and desperately tried to fall back across the Yen River under punishing fire from helicopters. The seven-hour fight had cost a dozen Marine lives, and an estimated 50 to 130 VC. It was not unique.

All these were relatively small battles, but just as vicious as larger ones. For troops in the field conditions were no better than in other wars. At one point Dan Wokaty could no longer stomach the monotonous C-ration diet, and like many he began to high-grade the boxes and eat only the canned fruit. “This lieutenant walked by, and there’s pieces of bodies laying around. He said 'You probably gonna be eating them flies,' and I said 'If he gets in there, he'll get eat, too.' I was just out of it, you know."

Even this early in the war the officers were "out of it" with frustration trying to satisfy MACV's rapacious demand for larger body counts. Wokaty recalls one particular incident. "He (an infantry company commander) said that those people sitting back there in the rear say that we ain't killing nobody. What he was doing was picking up the pieces of the torsos of the bodies and throwing them on the armor plate on the back of the tank, (and) on the fenders. He said 'I want you to take that back in there, and I want you to drive right up in front of the Three, and unload that right in front of the Three.'" Wokaty dutifully unloaded his grisly cargo right in front of the infantry battalion's S-3 tent.

Even as DuPuy was advising Westmoreland that the Marines were not pulling their weight, both Westmoreland and the North Vietnamese leadership were laying the foundation for an expansion of the war. Wary of the American successes in the I Corps region, the North Vietnamese began to commit regular troops of the NVA to stiffen the lightly armed indigenous VC. Within months the NVA came to dominate the battlefield. American intelligence quickly identified two Communist divisions, the *2nd NVA Division* (*3rd* and *21st NVA* and *1stVC Regiments*) in Quang Tri and Quang Ngai Provinces, and the *3rd NVA Division* (*18th* and *22nd NVA* and *2nd VC Regiments*) in Quang Ngai and Binh Dinh, with the *95th NVA Regiment* identified later. MACV's appetite for troops seemed limitless. By March only the 5th Marines and the artillery of 2/11 would remain outside Vietnam. Within six months the entire 1st Marine Division would be committed to the battle.

John Bartusevics had more of a personal stake in the Vietnam War than most. His family, including his parents and six sisters, had fled Latvia just ahead of the Soviet takeover near the end of World War II. After living in several refuge camps the family finally relocated to Philadelphia. He grew up in the city where the Corps was founded, and like many future Marines his fate was sealed very early. One of his brothers-in-law was in the Marine Reserves, and John went hunting and camping with him in the mountains. "Being a Staff Sergeant in the Marine Corps, he had me singing the Marine Corps Hymn when I was thirteen years old. He started me off in judo and jiu-jitsu. Everything was geared toward the Marine Corps." Bartusevics signed up for the delayed entry program, and was sworn in four months before high school graduation. He graduated on June 11, and reported to Parris Island on June 26. Bartusevics described it as "the best move I ever made. I tell you the truth, I had nothing going for me. I didn't like school, I was learning English. If I stayed on the streets of Philadelphia it would mean trouble, because that's where a lot of my friends were going."

Bartusevics was originally designated a tank maintenance man, a shitfister in tanker jargon. He never attended a training school, but learned by OJT—On the Job Training.

Bartusevics's original plan was to serve a tour in the Corps and then get a job as a Philadelphia policeman. He kept extending for one more short tour, studying martial arts in Okinawa, and marrying a native of Okinawa, until 1965. He had only eight months to serve on his enlistment when Robert McNamara extended all tours by six months—making Bartusevics eligible for a tour in Vietnam. He was assigned as vehicle commander for the M51 retriever that would accompany 3rd Platoon, C Company, 1st Tank Battalion afloat. "One January of 'sixty-six, we loaded our tanks aboard Del Mar, and went right on to Battalion Landing Team with One-Five to Vietnam."

The Corps had not used draftees since World War II, but the increasing demands of the war outstripped recruiting. Most of the tank platoon enlisted men were draftees. The BLT was designated as one of Seventh Fleet's Special Landing Forces, which meant that they could be employed anywhere at the discretion of the fleet commander, not MACV. The BLT was assigned to Operation JACKSTAY, an amphibious raid in the Mekong Delta, where VC units were ambushing ships in the river channels below Saigon. Vehicles were useless in the Delta, so the members of the infantry's H&S Platoon, the tank platoon, the Motor Transport Platoon, and the Amtrac platoon were organized into a Provisional Rifle Company to fight ashore.

The Provisional Company destroyed VC facilities, including a mine factory, before withdrawing. The BLT made one more landing, Operation OSAGE, near the DMZ. "It was hills, straight up, and none of the vehicles would be able to operate in that area," so the odd assorted platoons again fought as a Provisional Rifle Company. The BLT went ashore to stay, joining C/1st Tank at Chu Lai in March 1966.[2]

For the units ashore, tank operations continued every day, day after day. On one such routine operation, grunts, supported by an Ontos unit and the 2nd Platoon of A Company, 3rd Tank paid another visit (their sixth or so) to an area called Hill 163.[3] The mission nearly had to be aborted when A24 struck a mine, ripping away two road wheels. The explosion threw three grunts riding on the fender high into the air, and one came down across the gun tube, injuring his back. A25 moved around to protect the blind side, but tore up the vegetation on the steep, slick slope, which prevented other tanks from passing.

While they waited for the retriever, the tanks and Ontos took the target village under fire, which the grunts said resulted in 440 enemy dead. On A25 a white phosphorus round misfired and the tankers followed the standard procedure, trying three times to fire the round. Finally Sgt. T. J. Siva ordered the crew to remove the round.

The late Thurlow J. Siva was another of the legendary tankers. He was a colorful Marine of the "old breed" who did not fare particularly well in garrison, but excelled in combat. He served multiple tours in Vietnam with both 1st and 3rd Tank Battalions, and consequently appears in many stories of the tanks in Vietnam.

Larry Roalson gingerly pried the damaged round out of the breech with a special tool, and passed it up to driver Robbie Robinson, who carefully carried it some distance away. The tanks resumed firing.

It would be a memorable day for the platoon. The retriever hooked up and dragged A24 away, but en route it ran out of fuel, and both had to be rescued by a tanker truck. The misfired WP round could not be left in place. The crew of A25 reversed the process and loaded the round back inside, then hooked up to the broken track from A24.

As the tank towed the broken track behind it (a fairly common practice) down the shoulder of Highway 1, they overtook a Vietnamese civilian riding a bicycle. Robinson veered out and passed. Forgetting the length of track, he started to pull back onto the shoulder when Siva screamed at him from the turret. Robinson overcorrected and the 5,000-pound length of track neatly clipped the bicycle wheels from underneath the rider, who was otherwise unhurt.

In early December 1965 MACV had issued orders for a joint operation along the boundary between I Corps (Operation DOUBLE EAGLE) and II Corps (Operation MASHER), a complex undertaking that would involve Marine, US Army, and ARVN forces. It would also require complex coordination across a corps boundary. The putative mission was to clear the enemy from the region around the new base at Phu Bai, but the implicit mission was to seek open battle with the NVA. The plan was an enlarged and more elaborate version of STARLITE.

Reconnaissance units would fix the location of enemy forces, and amphibious landings along the coast would press the enemy inland. The major change was that B-52 ARC LIGHT strikes would bombard the enemy, driving him inland onto blocking positions emplaced by helicopter.

Sam Binion's platoon from Charlie Company, 3rd Tank was assigned to a force including BLTs 2/4 and 3/1 that would land along the coast on 28 January. "We left our tanks on ship, and they sent us ashore as grunts, which was a fiasco. We weren't trained as grunts. We were tankers." The tankers carried their assigned weapons—pistols—and were hastily supplied with M-14 rifles. The platoon served as a provisional rifle platoon. The tankers thought that the platoon commander (1st Lt. "BB" Warner) had volunteered them, because like most young officers, "He was gung ho. He wanted get in action so bad he could taste it.

"Unfortunately, he was the first one to get killed.... He got killed by a sniper. They had us on this LV (Amtrac) out there, and every day about noon this sniper would come out.... For some reason, we still can't figure out why, Warner stood up, took off his helmet, laid it down, laid down his grease gun, and that's when the sniper shot him.

"The corpsman went over to work on him, and the corpsman got shot twice." The corpsman was shot once while working on Warner, and again through the floor of the medevac helicopter. Warner was critically wounded and evacuated, but died two months later.[4]

Warner's act may have been bravado of the type so common among the young, since another tanker was shot by the same sniper. Sergeant "Smoky" Crittenden, the platoon character, "stood up, beat his chest, and said 'Here I am VC! Come and get me!'"

About a half hour later Crittenden and another tanker went down to a nearby stream, intending to cool canteens by immersing them on a rope. In the Philippines Crittenden had bought a large machete. "When the sniper started shooting, he started running up the hill. Well, the sniper shot that machete on his side, and he thought he was hit, so he hit the ground. He wasn't hit, and he realized it. Then (he) got back up and started running again, and the sniper did get him then, but it was through the calf. He made it back to the top of the hill.

"They medevaced him, but at the same time the sniper had killed someone else. They got it mixed up, and notified Smoky's brother that he had been killed."

The sniper killed or wounded nine Marines in three days, and was never located.[5]

After DOUBLE EAGLE Binion's platoon landed at Danang and went to 3rd Tank. Binion's section was sent out to protect the helicopter facility near Marble Mountain, which was "a picnic. We sat there. I listened to Hanoi Hannah talk about us. She specifically mentioned us on the radio." After about a month the entire company was assigned to the new Phu Bai base. "There was an Army base right across the road, and I don't know what that thing was, but they had swimming pools, air conditioned trailers, and all that over there. Naturally, they stuck us on the other side of the road, in the sand, and we had to put up tents and what have you. They had hot chow in the mess hall, and we were eating C-rations. I didn't appreciate that, either."

The platoon John Bartusevics was attached to replaced Binion's at Marble Mountain, "playing a hopscotch game. They stayed with us for about a week, showing us the area, and dos and don'ts in that area."

Shortly thereafter Bartusevics and another sergeant were drinking beer in the maintenance shop. The other man, Sergeant Funkhauser, had a new child and was burned out from being in the field, so he and Bartusevics worked out a deal to change places. "I said 'Hey, let's go see the XO right now. I'll take your tank, you take my retriever. I'm tired of fixin' ... I'd rather go break them.'"

After Bartusevics had been a tank commander in the 2nd Platoon of Charlie Company for three months, the official paperwork came through. Bartusevics was legally a tank crewman. At this point the company was averaging two mine incidents a week, but Funkhauser was in his element on the retriever, with 'Funk's Junk' painted on the lifting boom. "He had plenty of business.... Every time he came on the air after we called for the retriever, he'd open up the air in the net by saying 'Abadabadoo,' and we all knew he's on his way. It was a great morale booster."

At this time in southern I Corps, "They had plenty of NVA advisors. They were trying to train the local Viet Cong. We were pretty well full time against the local Viet Cong. It was all mines, a lot of booby traps, lot of sniping, a lot of ambushes when they thought they had the upper hand. That included RPGs."

The 1st Cavalry commenced MASHER (later renamed WHITE WING) as scheduled on 24 January, followed by amphibious landings by BLTs 3/1 and 2/4 near the coastal town of Duc Pho on 28 January.

Bad weather and poor visibility limited the utility of the B-52 raids (which MACV refused to delay) on 30 January, and delayed the emplacement of the blocking force until the next day. Though the 1st Cavalry and ARVN fought major battles to the south, the Marines' efforts to fix a major enemy force were in vain. A hastily organized follow-on, DOUBLE EAGLE II, also failed to locate the *2nd VC Regiment* in the Que Son Valley.

Like most Marines, Binion said, "When one operation would end and another operation started, we never knew. We were just doing the same old stuff." A recurrent theme among those who served in Vietnam is the inability to precisely place events in time.

One event that did stick out in Binion's memory is the time a company commander was so intent on his mission that the company was caught by the first monsoon rains. "Everybody kept telling him the rains are fixing to come. We're out here in rice paddies. We'd better get the hell out of here. He waited just a little too long. We had the whole company stuck. Took us three days to go four hundred yards.

"They had to fly in timbers. We'd lay the timbers in front of the tracks, roll up, bring them from the back, put them to the front. That's how we got all those tanks out." It was brutal labor, with a shortage of rations, and under constant threat of attack. The misery was compounded by the weather. Normally the crews slept on the engine deck or top of the turret but the crews of the trapped tanks slept inside. At night, "all that steel would cool off, and get cold. But come about nine, ten o'clock in the morning, boy it was an oven. When it rained, the damned thing leaked."

Oddly, the stuck tanks proved to be the least vulnerable to the enemy. Two tanks that were not immobilized were sent ahead with a squad of infantry, moving into a position about 500 meters away. That night "They got hit. We could hear it, we could watch it, but we couldn't do anything about it." Several tankers and grunts were killed in the attack.

Operation UTAH was another attempt to utilize the superior mobility of the airmobile 7th Marines and ARVN airborne against the *21st NVA Regiment*. It resulted in heavy but indecisive fighting, mainly the result of ARVN units balking at heavy fighting.

One of the duties of the tanks at Phu Bai was to provide security at blocking positions at each end of the sprawling base. Bob Embesi: "Right outside of our one blocking position was the ARVN boot camp.

There was a hundred stories going around about ... NVA and Viet Cong going to get trained by the ARVN. Then right after graduation, or before graduation, they'd go UA [unauthorized absence]—take their rifles and uniforms and go UA, go back to the village where they came from. Occasionally at night ... we'd see them take off through the boonies and head off. Of course we'd take them under fire.... Of course most of them stayed there.

"We made friends with a few of the ARVN. Officers would come over to the tanks and talk to us, and there was of course a tank outfit down in Hue City."

Gene Hackemack joined the Navy in 1963, "To get out of the cotton patch, the hay field, and I was guaranteed to become a medical corpsman. That looked like the thing to do. There was no future in this little town of Burton, Texas." He grew up in a poor area, with no running water, so "boot camp was a breeze."

Hackemack completed his specialty training as a corpsman, and had orders for a naval hospital at Iwakuni Japan. "They gave me the option of going into the Marine Corps, and I guess that just sounded more adventurous." He reported to the Del Mar sector of Camp Pendleton, near the tank school, in February of 1964. "That's where we went through two weeks of, I would say intensive, Field Medical Service School. To a limited degree we fired the same weapons the Marines used, mainly the M14 and the forty-five. Corpsmen typically carried only a forty-five after they left Field Medical Service School, and went to their assigned unit.

"There was lots of physical training. It was focused toward rescuing a wounded person, and either treating them on the spot or trying to get them to safety using Marines for litter bearers.... Also we did some first aid instructing." Hackemack's first assignment was to 3rd Medical Battalion at Camp Schwab, Okinawa, an assignment he considered uneventful but "very educational. I learned a little of the language, and that was the first time I had been exposed to a different culture."

He returned to the 1st Tank Battalion, and spent five months at Las Pulgas, another sector of Camp Pendleton, before being given a thirty-day leave in December, 1965. In February 1966 he boarded ship at San Diego with H&S Company, 1st Tanks. After stops in Hawaii and for training on Okinawa, "We finally hit the beaches at Chu Lai."

The tank battalion was assigned to a sector of the base, and lived in small two-man tents until larger tents with wooden floors were erected.

"The hill we relocated to happened to have a small cemetery. Before we moved in the Vietnamese came, and they dug up remains of their ancestors. We were observing this. All we saw was sacks of dirt ... there was nothing even close to resembling body or bone parts. I guess in that humid jungle the body decomposes quickly, but they still would take the dirt out of that site and relocate it."

All medical personnel belonged to the Medical Section of the H&S Company, and were parceled out as needed. Corpsmen were assigned to be on call for emergencies at the battalion tank maintenance facility, to hold daily sick call to treat minor ailments, to provide emergency medical services for anyone in the battalion's sector which included the airstrip, and occasionally to accompany the tanks on training exercises.[6] "There were some gunshot wounds. The most major injury I saw was a Vietnamese boy who was flattened by a large vehicle. Of course there was no treating him." The battalion was responsible for security in a sector of the division base area, so "I did pull lots of patrol operations. When a (foot) patrol went out at night ... they always took a corpsman along. At nighttime a small squad of Marines would go out and patrol a certain area, scouting for enemy...."

One of the first steps the Marines took when moving into a new area of operations was to establish COUNTY FAIR operations, and the new division assumed this responsibility. The Marines would cordon off a village, and American personnel would provide medical, dental, and other services while South Vietnamese police and soldiers screened the population for VC operatives or sympathizers.

Gene Hackemack: "We set up numerous medical treatment facilities where we treated mostly kids. Ninety-five percent kids. I remember there were dentists operating next to us."

The battalion was also responsible for providing a MEDCAP (Medical Civic Action Program) corpsman to provide for the local populace in a nearby village; for Hackemack it was Tic Tay. "I would be given one Marine driver and a jeep, and then maybe several guards. It was usually a pretty secure area. I really never felt threatened at any time. One time I went out by myself, and some Vietnamese friends said 'Don't ever do that again.' It was probably one morning when there was no driver available and I just sort of shrugged it off, and said 'Well, hell, I'll just go myself.'

"I would go into a village, usually in the morning from about eight until noon. The mama-sans would bring their kids in and they were usually covered with sores, especially on the scalp and around the ankles and feet area....

"If there were sores on the scalp, which a lot of them were, they would bring them to us and the scalp would have like a cap made of water buffalo manure, made into a paste. They'd be wearing this like a skullcap. Of course the first thing we'd do, we took all of that off, scrubbed it, treated it with Bacitracin,™ and bandaged it up. A couple of days or a week later they'd bring the same kid back, and he'd have a fresh layer of water buffalo manure on it. It was kind of a frustrating situation there."

Hackemack vividly recalled that "There was this old man. He looked like he was ninety; he was probably not nearly that old. I had a ten year-old interpreter, his name was Phu. He spoke pretty good English, so he came along with me one day and said to come see this old man.... His foot was all bandaged up, and when I started to unwrap it, the entire foot started to fall off. I saw it was gangrene set into it. The next day I brought out our doctor, and he said we could amputate it. But the old man said no, he'd rather die because something about being a Buddhist, you try to take all your body into the next world, next life."

Hackemack was also treating an older woman who had the bubonic plague, giving her daily massive doses of penicillin. One day "She offered me a Tiger Beer, which was a great big warm bottle of beer with sediment floating around in it. So I drank the whole thing to be polite. Boy, I weaved my way through the rest of the morning. This was one big bottle of beer, and I'm sure it had more than just alcohol in it, the way it affected me. In the heat. I never did that again."

The big battles that MACV sought created a flood of refugees that overwhelmed both the civil authorities and the Marines. The Marines for their part resented the refugees for the disease, sanitation, and administrative problems they caused, as well as for the inevitably of VC included in the mass of people. The condition was exacerbated by the continuing instability bordering on civil war among the non-Communists after the Saigon government removed the popular General Thi.

THE WAR SPREADS NORTH

In early 1966 the Marines expanded their operations to the north in response to the NVA threat. Third Tank was shifted north, with 1st

Tank left to fill the increasing void. For 1st Tank the war would remain one of mines and ambushes. Dan Wokaty: "The only thing I really remember about that (period) was hitting a mine down there in that area." Wokaty was standing in the tank commander's hatch when "It blew our tank probably about eight feet in the air. It hit right underneath the hull of the tank, and it drove the hull up, they figured about twelve or thirteen inches."

The tank had been back to the rear to replenish ammunition and perform minor maintenance, and on the return trip hit an unusually powerful device. The blast actually bent the massive cast armor hull, and "Anyway, that was the first tank that had been surveyed[7] out of Vietnam.

"Probably what they were using was one-oh-five rounds, probably a command-detonated mine. The driver was bleeding at the ears, and that was the first time I ever saw anybody bleeding at the eardrums. The batteries sat underneath the (turret) basket, and it dissolved the batteries. The electrolyte was all over everything on the inside of us."

When the hull distorted, "It jammed all the gears wide open" and the tank rolled onward, the wounded driver unable to change gears or stop. "The driver couldn't hear me and I got out on the side and I was pointing at a hill," a mound about ten feet high. "We stalled it into that hill." The tracks continued to churn.

"What we had to do was take the plate off the inside to get to the engine compartment where we could disconnect the fuel from it to stop it from running." The access plate for the disconnect was awkward to get to in a hurry. "It was on the front end of the engine. What you had to do was in the fighting compartment, inside the turret, you had to turn the turret basket around and take this plate off. That's where your wires connected, your wiring harness and all that on the front of the engine, and it faced the inside of the turret.

"It's got a fuel quick disconnect. It finally just ran out of diesel."

The incident was to have lasting impact for Wokaty, injuring his hips and back.

Bob Embesi's platoon was sent north to Dong Ha as part of the 3rd Tank advance party. "We offloaded at Dong Ha. I left two tanks there, and I took three tanks to Cam Lo. That was the second group of tanks up there. There was another group up there prior to me getting there, and they loaded onto the U-boats when we got off. I didn't know who they were.... By this time we're now Third Tanks. We changed designations. One morning we woke up and we wasn't First Tanks any more, now we're Third Tanks."

The original runway at Dong Ha was constructed of pierced steel matting used for temporary runways. After some use the material begins to bend and the rough edges damage aircraft tires, so it is typically replaced by paving. Gibson recalls that at Dong Ha the tanks were used as heavy 'deconstruction' equipment. "They went out there with cutting torches and cut it all up. We hauled big sections of it out of there. We threw cables on there and drug that Marsden matting out of there in big sections after they cut it up."

The platoon's mission at Cam Lo was to provide indirect fire into the DMZ. Embesi: "Our tank guns could reach farther than the artillery guns. We sat up there with the artillery and fired at night, hundreds of rounds into the DMZ."

Engineer tractors constructed ramps to raise the noses of the tanks to get adequate elevation. "At the right elevation we could shoot twenty one miles.... One night we fired 250, 300 rounds in one fire mission. We just continually fired. I wondered where all the ammunition was coming from. I looked out the hatch between reloads, and they had everybody in camp standing out there with a round in their hands.... A helicopter would bring the ammunition in in pallets, and drop it. They never re-supplied by truck up there."

The Soviet-made NVA artillery pieces outranged the Marines' longest-ranged guns, the 155mm howitzers. The NVA fully realized the power of the American artillery in support of infantry actions, and made every attempt to use their superior range to neutralize the American guns. American artillery doctrine at the time emphasized the use of self-propelled artillery, which could quickly move into position and open fire in support of mobile operations. The Marines in the I Corps Tactical Zone (ICTZ) had only a few 155mm M109 self-propelled howitzers that could be rapidly deployed to forward firing positions. In the constant struggle to range in on the NVA artillery hidden in the hills and within the DMZ, the 90mm guns of the tanks substituted for mobile artillery.

Gary Gibson said that in emergencies "We could move out there two miles and run up on rice paddy dikes, set up aiming stakes, and we were ready to fire in six or eight minutes." The tanks were also trained to provide indirect fire with their .50-caliber machine guns, using spotters to adjust fire.

One night the tanks were providing indirect fire, and Gibson's tank was the base gun. On an indirect fire mission the base gun fires single rounds for the observer to adjust fire onto the target. When the spotter rounds strike closely enough the order to 'fire for effect' is the signal for all guns in the battery to open fire.

"We're ramped up on a paddy dike, and I leveled that bubble and set the azimuth. I always fire manually. I never, ever, used those electric triggers, because you have to activate the controls to use those and you can drift off.

"I pulled the handle. Boom! We waited and waited and waited. Finally they said 'End of fire mission. Secure mission.' So we all hit the rack.

"Next morning this Army captain came tearing in there on a jeep with a case of beer, wanting to know who fired that shot the night before." The initial registration round had gone through the roof of the target, an enemy bunker.

The tanks also learned to shoot artillery killing crosses, firing rounds center, over, under, left and right to trap enemy infantry in the open. Just as in the artillery, there was always competition to see who could get their rounds out faster. Gibson and his loader, Martin, worked out a system to fire very quickly. "One of the FO's said 'Man it's amazing how you shoot. You shoot the preliminary killing cross, then you shoot the big one.'"

Infantry support was an around the clock task, and Embesi said that "we'd set up in a defilade position in the daytime and watch the area. Of course if the grunts went on a sweep, out to the front or anywhere else, they normally didn't want to take tanks. But they weren't gone more than two hours, and they'd call for us to come get them out of the hole.

"Some of these grunt people thought that tanks were not any good, they didn't need them. They all thought that until they got pinned down."

These were the opening battles in what was to be a prolonged struggle for control of the strip south of the DMZ, from the coast west to the mountains. "The grunts always took a beating…. Their wounded they'd medevac by helicopter, and the dead, we'd either put them on an Amtrac or a tank and carry the dead for them.

"When we got up to right below Hill 888 … there was an area there that there were shallow graves—mass graves—just dug everywhere.

There must have been maybe a thousand NVA killed in there. They were just buried, like dirt. We were right on top of them. Smelled like a sewer, just dead bodies everywhere. It's a smell you never forget."

The remainder of the company displaced north into the Cam Lo area at about the time Embesi finished his tour. "They radioed to me to get on a helicopter that was coming in with my relief. They sent a Staff Sergeant up there to relieve me. He got off the helicopter. I got on. They said go straight to Danang, get on a flight, and come back to the United States." So rushed was Embesi's departure that when he arrived in California, he still had most of his 782 gear, and his pistol, that should have stayed with the unit in Vietnam.

Sam Binion thought it very different from the fighting in the south. "We weren't fighting VC, we were fighting the regular NVA. They had new uniforms, new equipment, everything." The Marines had an odd way of assessing their enemy's condition. "We knew that, because every time we'd go out on an operation it was usually after the B-52s had come through. You'd see bodies laying in the trees, and they had new boots, the whole bit."

By mid-year the NVA was operating openly and in strength in Quang Tri Province, and American planners feared a major conventional assault. Operation HASTINGS beginning on 15 July 1966 was designed to abort the suspected NVA plan. Because of the rough jungle terrain in the operational area the tanks played little part. As part of the supporting Operation DECKHOUSE II along the coast, tanks were landed with BLT3/5, but were left behind to secure landing zones when the force moved inland.

Operation PRAIRIE grew out of reconnaissance contacts on 6 August, when enemy fire drove away helicopters attempting to extract a forty-man patrol from E/2/4. An attempt to reinforce was driven off after only three men were able to get off the helicopters and another helicopter crashed. The commander of 2/4 ordered a section of artillery and a light section of tanks from C/3rd Tank to displace and be ready to support an infantry attack the next morning. The NVA had no intention of facing the tanks and artillery, and were gone by morning.

As the Marines expanded their operations to the west, new bases were established along the main east-west transportation axis, the infamous Route 9.

On the morning of 17 August, 2/4, supported by the guns of 3/12 and a platoon from C Company, 3rd Tank set out on a reconnaissance in force from Cam Lo, along Route 9 along the south bank of the Cam Lo River. The final objective was The Rockpile, a distinctive high hill that dominated the surrounding terrain and served as an observation post for recon detachments. Shortly after noon F/2/4 was crossing the bridge over the Song Khe Gio, a smaller river that flows northward into the main stream, when they were raked by automatic weapons and mortar fire from nearby Hill 252 that dominates the bridge. Foxtrot Company was pinned down, and the battalion's efforts to outflank the hill were driven down by heavy fire from well-built bunkers in the hillside that dominated the landscape. Air strikes and artillery failed to dent the defense.

At about 1600 the two tanks from C Company were brought forward and engaged the bunkers with direct fire. The fire slackened and the trapped company was able to make its way out. The next morning the bunkers were abandoned, and 2/4 set out toward the Rockpile, with the tanks (reinforced by a third tank that night) in the column.[8] After reaching the objective 2/4 searched the surrounding countryside while the tanks returned to Cam Lo on 19 August. The operation continued through 7 September, when H/2/4 and the tanks left Cam Lo to return to Con Thien by road, while the balance of the battalion went by helicopter.

Most of the subsequent fighting in PRAIRIE would center about the capture of the inaccessible ridges north of The Rockpile. The NVA was determined to resist the expansion of the Marine operations west and north.

Sweeps to the west were accompanied by ever larger tank forces. On 23 August one large sweep included all of C Company, 3rd Tank. On 9 September H/2/4, supported by a platoon from C Company, 3rd Tank moved north from Cam Lo toward an obscure, muddy hill called Con Thien. When the enemy resisted, the battalion commander credited the tank fire with carrying the enemy positions.[9]

Binion recalls one of many such operations when the infantry was abruptly ordered to break off after an ambush killed an infantry company commander who was riding on the back of a tank. One of the tanks hit a mine on the return, near Con Thien. The tank could not be repaired before nightfall, so most of the force departed, leaving two other tanks and some grunts to guard the crippled tank. "We knew there was a regiment of NVA around us. They were making noise like you wouldn't believe.

"We buttoned up in the tanks, and we called artillery all night long. Shrapnel was actually bouncing off the turret. But that's what kept us alive that night." The next morning "I had a mortar squad riding on my tank, but they had no mortar tubes. The other two tanks had remnants of grunts that they had left with us."

The officer in charge misread the map, "so for two days we're wandering around Con Thien, can't find our way back to Cam Lo. We found the right road. He put me in the lead, and we were batting it back there. I hit a mine on the left track. Blew a bunch of grunts off my tank. Luckily no one was hurt." The tank was disabled and night was approaching, so the wayward patrol spent yet another night in hostile territory.

The next morning the Charlie Company commander came out to collect his lost sheep, and was riding behind the turret of Binion's tank, leading the column down a narrow road. "Damned if I didn't hit a mine on the other track. I thought he was going to die. He yelled and jumped off that tank. There was no fixing that thing then. We hooked up the cables, and they dragged me into Cam Lo."

That night Cam Lo was attacked, and the enemy broke into the base. "I sat there with my tank. It was blown up and I couldn't move. Couldn't shoot it. So I just sat and watched the battle." The next morning Binion walked about a hundred yards in back of his tank, and "there was a foot laying there. So I guess they did get close. There were bodies everywhere. The problem was we didn't know they were inside the perimeter until they killed the cooks in the (mess) tent. I think they killed about ten (Marines) that night." The next day bulldozers buried seventy-eight NVA bodies.[10]

It is pretty much impossible to explain to civilians the feeling that Marines have when they are left safely behind and their comrades are in trouble. Binion missed another operation because of a mechanical malfunction, and the other tanks were hard hit, losing several killed. "I felt bad about that. I never did consider myself lucky on that one, because I wanted to go."

The battles along the DMZ occurred in a variety of terrain, from the low, sandy knolls along the coast to the rugged forested mountains inland. Most fighting would occur along the patch of country around Con Thien. This region was covered with rolling hills and coastal plain, scrub forest, and ancient farms and villages. Hedgerows that had accumulated soil around their bases to form earthen berms several feet in height separated individual fields. By burrowing into these walls the NVA could easily build sturdy bunkers, with the open fields forming natural fields of fire. Thus each field became a compartmentalized killing zone. It was much like the hedgerow country of Normandy that had provided the setting for one of the most brutal campaigns of World War II in Europe.

The NVA brought with them anti-tank weapons in abundance. The original RPG-2 was soon replaced by the more powerful RPG-7. Usually neither would actually destroy the M48A3 tanks, though the shrapnel created by a penetration was deadly to the crew. The bigger crew-served Chinese-manufactured recoilless guns were far more deadly, but also less common. Heavy mortars and artillery rockets were seldom a threat to the tanks. C. W. Casey, who would command the tank units in the fighting for Hue in 1968, recalled one tank that took a direct turret hit from a large rocket. "All it did was knock the gun out of synch, and we had to repair that thing. It gave the crew a headache. Fortunately they were buttoned up when the thing hit."

PRAIRIE and the struggle for control of the ridges north of The Rockpile continued, and by late September the enemy again controlled the area. The Marines were determined to take possession of the critical terrain.

On 22 September, 2/7 attacked up the western slope of The Razorback, the rugged, cave-ridden ridge north of the Rockpile. Artillery and tanks supported the attacks by fire, but the rugged terrain presented unusual problems for the worn-out and patched-up tanks. Embesi and many of the others from the original platoon had completed their tours, and Gary Gibson volunteered to go out with another platoon. "We were constantly maneuvering around there, trying to get shots in. One time we were going up the side of that frigging mountain or the side of some slope that was real steep. We had taken an RPG round through the fuel tank, the right fuel cell, and it was empty. All we had was the left fuel cell. A tank draws fuel from the front of the left fuel cell and the rear of the right fuel cell. No matter which way, up or down, you're drawing fuel." As the tank tried to climb the steep grades, the limited fuel remaining in the left cell sloshed to the rear and the tank stalled.

"They flew in a helicopter with a fifty-five gallon drum of diesel fuel, and what they call a horse-cock. (We) Stuck that in the thing and we're trying to manhandle this thing on a forty-five or fifty degree slope on that armor plate. Of course as soon as we spill some diesel fuel we're on a skating rink. That was almost as dangerous as getting shot at, getting that fuel into there."

The NVA redoubled their efforts in response to the Marines shifting forces north, and had no intention of avoiding contact with the tanks. On Operation PRAIRIE, Gibson was driving for a new tank commander, Sergeant Tews, in C Company, 3rd Tank, with an inexperienced gunner and loader.[11] The mission was a rather routine sweep and the tanks were returning with the grunts riding on top. Gibson retraced his same path, concerned about mines. Suddenly the ground gave way, and the tank began to plunge into a large rectangular eight-foot deep pit dug as a tank trap.

Gibson reflexively slammed the transmission into reverse, and the tank recoiled off the bottom of the pit and back out again. The main gun had been damaged by the impact with the ground at the bottom of the pit, and the left track damaged, but no one knew. Gibson stood up in his driver's seat to see Tews, the loader, and all the grunts in a pile at the bottom of the hole.

While the mess was being sorted out, Gibson noticed freshly turned soil far out to the right, and asked Tews if he could see anything from atop the turret. In response Tews shouted "Ambush right!" as the NVA fired a volley of RPG rockets. The tanks had already begun to move in response to Tews's warning, but one rocket struck the front of the third or fourth tank, decapitating the driver. The stricken tank accelerated and crashed into the tank ahead, jamming its main gun into the bustle rack and trapping the column behind.

A mass of NVA infantry rushed out of concealment in a ravine to assail the tanks. One of the TCs was an NCO and veteran of the Korean War who had improvised a sky mount for his .50-caliber. When he opened fire, "There were body parts flying everywhere."

Tews directed his tank out of the column and around to the front, and fired a canister round into the onrushing NVA. The damaged cannon recoiled, and then failed to go back forward into battery for the next round. Then the coaxial machine gun jammed after a half-dozen rounds.

Tews dropped down into the turret to help the inexperienced loader clear the jam. When the loader raised the feed cover on the coaxial gun the inexperienced gunner depressed the main gun, smashing the feed cover against the turret ceiling, permanently disabling the tank's main antipersonnel weapon. Gibson grabbed for a reworked M1 Garand rifle that he carried stowed behind a headlight. He had acquired the old but reliable relic in trade from a Navy Seabee. Gibson fired on several NVA before he was noticed, and killed two more who had taken him under fire. The old M1 ejected the clips as they were emptied, so Gibson had to climb outside to retrieve the empty clips and reload them, then climb back into the tank.

When a message came over the radio that F-4 Phantoms were inbound with napalm, Gibson threw the transmission into reverse—and the damaged left track broke. Shouting "Abandon Tank!" Gibson started out. The new loader was hung on the hatch rim by his pistol holster. With the strength imparted by adrenaline, he simply ripped the heavy steel wire holster attachment loose and dove off the tank.

"He got down near the fender and reached down and grabbed his belt where his pistol was at and he started to turn around. I ran right over him. I grabbed him and we ran off over where the grunts were at."

The NVA attack broke off in the face of the air strike, and the tankers were able to repair and recover their vehicles. The grunts were understandably reluctant to ride.

On 12 October, during the extension of Operation PRAIRIE, the enemy ambushed 2/5 and its supporting A Company, 3rd Tank vehicles. The site was carefully chosen in close terrain to minimize the efficacy of the American firepower while playing to the strengths of the short-range RPGs. Three tanks were hit. The platoon commander was killed and four crewmen wounded. Additional tanks from C Company were sent to the aid of the ambushed unit.[12]

On another sweep, probably in December, Binion was serving as the gunner because two lieutenants wanted to go along, and of course one had to be the tank commander. The other officer was made loader. The tanks found themselves in dense underbrush, and "then they come out with the RPGs. It was Sergeant Matthews' tank they hit." Matthews, Embesi's replacement, was apparently riding with his clamshell hatch partially open for visibility, and a hit on the hatch killed him instantly. "I believe it killed the other people in the tank except the driver. The driver was calling for help, telling us he was the only one alive, and he needed help. There was absolutely nothing we could do. We had to listen to that on the radio.

"The grunts got him out. It was a matter of probably a half hour. Wasn't that long. Probably seemed like years to him." The disabled tank was left behind with infantry protection as the operation moved on.

By this time Gibson had ended up in the battalion rear back at Dong Ha, which he did not much care for. The unit was short of tankers, and called for volunteers to replace losses in the field. When Gibson went to the helicopter, "They took a guy off on a stretcher, and he was laying on his stomach. His back was all chewed up. Somebody said that's the gunner off that M48 out there."

Gibson was the only passenger on the helo. "I get off and walked over there, and I said "Where's this tank that got shot up?'" He was directed to a tank with the cupola blown off. The cupola ring, which raised the cupola and incorporated vision blocks for better all around vision, was covered with blood and bits of flesh. "There were a couple of water cans on there, so I found me a rag, and started cleaning up. I cleaned everything out of the cupola ring." The right side and floor of the turret was soaked in blood and debris. Gibson unbolted all the machine gun ammo deck boxes from the floor, and dumped them. He cleaned the turret deck, and raised the battery access door to clean it out. "It was a hundred and fifty degrees in there. I used diesel fuel." He washed and reinstalled the ammo boxes. "I'm just a little bit testy by now."

Gibson wandered over to some grunts and asked, "What happened to the crew of this tank?" "I could see there were a lot of body parts, pieces in there. I could see where a guy might not want to get back on the tank. He said 'Oh, they joined the grunts. Pulled the thirty.'"

Gibson started walking down the line, "And there's the thirty sitting there. There's this guy, this Corporal sitting behind it with glasses on. I guess he was the driver and the loader was over there." Gibson confronted the shaken crewmen, who flatly refused to get back into the tank. "Something snapped in there somewhere. I think I was only a Lance Corporal, E-3. Anyway I whipped my forty-five out and cocked the hammer back... and I pointed it at his face."

For a few seconds the two just stared at each other. The crewman let out a long sigh. "All the air went out of him and he goes 'F-u-u-uck!' Soon as he started getting up I let the hammer back down, and stuck it in my holster." Gibson started gathering up the machine gun and ground mount. "I'm his assistant. I went from his assassin to his assistant in just a second."

The men remounted the tank, with Gibson taking the spot occupied by the dead TC. A couple of days later the tank, with its missing cupola, was dispatched on a hasty road march back toward a rear area loaded with the less seriously wounded. Gibson grabbed a walking grunt with one eye missing to substitute as a gunner.[13]

Like most Marines, when his tour was over Binion was jerked out of the field in mid-operation, and sent down the line for his trip to "the world." He was flown to Okinawa, and then boarded a ship for a thirty-day voyage to California. Now "I hate a ship with a passion."

Gibson volunteered for the Combined Action Company program and was assigned to a CAC squad to learn Vietnamese. After training he was set in a place between Phu Bai and Danang. "Thua Thien Province was Indian Country. We had no troops in Thua Thien Province at the time and we were kind of breaking trail up through there." The local force was a squad of Marines, a corpsman and two squads of Popular Forces militia armed with surplus World War II vintage weapons and a huge language barrier. The village was isolated in an area where the mountains came down to the sea, near Highway 1 and the old railway line. It was "Six or eight miles to Phu Loc District Headquarters. There was no way in to us by helicopter or anything without somebody shooting down on you from the hills."

The small garrison was supposed to build their own outpost around an old French position, using sandbags and a dump truck load of sand left at the base of the hill. "There was a concrete hexagon bunker on top of the hill, with RPG holes in it. Looked like the last occupants didn't do too good."

Gibson would go on to be wounded in one particularly memorable fight with an NVA sapper, and was sent home after suffering a relatively minor wound.

THE WAR SPREADS SOUTH

Down south around Danang the tactical task remained to try and isolate the population from the VC, so most of the year was a dreary and debilitating repetition of patrols and sweeps through the various TAORs. Bartusevics said that "We used to get hit a lot, but he wouldn't stay around and fight. It would be a short firefight. Knock out one or two guys, the point tanks open fire, secure the situation, and call in the medevacs. Numerous times that happened." The name of the game was hit and run. "I've seen battalion commanders crying because he kept losing his troops to booby traps, to snipers."

The Marines steadily expanded their operations south and west in the densely populated coastal region. On 4 July Liberty Road connecting the forward logistical base at Hill 55 with An Hoa was opened to ground traffic. Keeping the roads open would be a major task for years. On 6 July small groups of tanks supported Operation WASHINGTON in the Do Xa region, but infantry officers were still unsure of how to utilize tanks, and they were used as adjunct artillery firing H&I missions.

On 7 July, 3/9, accompanied by tanks and Amtracs, crossed the Thu Bon River south of Hill 55 to commence Operation MACON, a major sweep that would last until late October. On 20 August, 3/9 and tanks crossed the river and began the advance into an area that would become infamous as the Arizona Territory.

Operation COLORADO followed a pattern similar to WASHINGTON, with the tanks underutilized as artillery and mobile pillboxes.[14]

In 1966 Ken Pozder transferred to a line company. "Guys were going on R&R and stuff, and they wanted to know who wanted to fill in for them, because they were out in the field. I just said 'I will,' and that's where I went." He had always wanted to be a crewman, and "That was the opportunity, so I took it." He was assigned to B Company. "Finally I got transferred into the letter companies—that's what we called them. From then on I just fell in love with 'em. That's where I stayed."

Pozder eventually became a tank commander, then a section leader, and eventually a platoon sergeant, and began to see things from a different perspective. The tanks required a major service interval at 250 hours of running time, so the tank's instruments included not only an odometer to measure mileage, but an hour meter to record engine running time. The long-interval major maintenance was not always popular with the tank crews. "You went in for a 250-hour check, and that means you went in to battalion (the H&S Company Maintenance Section). They made you stand guard. Nobody wanted to go back to battalion." It was a chance to get a shower, better food, and a bit of a break from constant danger, "but not if you stand guard all night.... You come out of the field, dog-tired, and ... that night you got half your crew on guard duty."

Pozder's light section from Bravo Company, 1st Tank was stationed at a typical position to interdict potential infiltration routes across the flat coastal plain. The position overlooked a river, probably a major VC transportation route. The tank searchlights, artillery, and flare ships could illuminate the river and interdict traffic. In turn, the VC proved unusually willing to contest the position. Though they could not hope to assault the position in the face of entrenched firepower in the open terrain, they harassed the Marines with mortar and sniper fire. The Marines settled in for a siege.

"Out on a place called BOP-1, Bravo Observation Post, we'd been getting sniper fire, and we had a couple of people killed out there. Tankers. We had two squads of infantry, and a corpsman." Life above ground was hazardous. "We had a ditch dug that went out in front of the tank into a bunker.... You dropped the escape hatch, and moved it over to the side, and that's how you got out of it.

"They had a dinger over there. God! That old boy could shoot."

One day during a mortar attack "They threw in probably, I don't know, ten, fifteen rounds. I was trying to peep around the cupola because I had a sky-mounted fifty caliber, and was trying to see where the rounds were coming from. I saw this thing explode right out of the corner of my eye. My peripheral vision.

"Boy, it felt like somebody kicked me right in the head."

The aftermath was "Kind of comical, if you want to know. When I got hit I dropped down into the tank commander's hatch, and I keyed my intercom, and said 'I'm hit.' My gunner turned right around, he's right between my legs, and he said 'Yeah, you are.'

"I thought 'Jeez, I gotta get out of here, you know,' because I didn't know. I was choking because the blood was running down and all that. So I crawled up on top of the tank, and I fell off the tank. Hit the ground, banged my leg. That hurt worse than my neck.

"This corpsman comes running over, and he didn't know what to do. He's saying 'Oh my God, you're my first casualty, and bleeding and all this other stuff, and what am I gonna do?' He was a little shook up.

"He tied this field dressing around my neck, and he cinched it down. I couldn't even breathe then, because he was choking me to death. So I pulled it up on my ear. I thought 'You know, crap flows downhill,' so if I get my butt higher than my mouth, then I can get rid of it. So that's what I did.

"By this time it was dark, and they brought a medevac chopper in. They were popping these Matty Mattel's™ (infantry flares), they only burn for fifteen–twenty seconds, and then they go out.

"The choppers couldn't get in of course. They were drawing fire and whatnot. So they took the tanks, and the Lieutenant says 'Cross the searchlights on the tanks.'" This made an X of light to mark a landing site. "The bird came in, and I had a guy underneath each arm, and they were propelling me towards this helicopter. The adrenaline was punching so hard that they threw me. Now I weighed two hundred thirty-six pounds. They tossed me like a rock up onto the floor of that helicopter, and if it hadn't been for a pistol belt, I would have went out the other side.

"I'm serious, that's the gods' truth.

"The door gunner grabbed my pistol belt in the back, and stopped me from sliding out. My head and shoulders and stuff were out the other side." Pozder was flown to the hospital at Marble Mountain. After several days he was flown to the Philippines, then to the Naval Hospital in Oakland, California.

Corpsman Gene Hackemack had by now been attached to Bravo Company, where one of his monthly duties was to track down the tankers and give required inoculations. "You know how Marines hate to get shots. I would follow the (payroll) disbursing clerk. That's the way I got hold of the Marines who might want to get out of shots."

As the only corpsman attached to a company, "I probably went beyond, in some cases, what a corpsman in a Battalion Aid Station would do, because in a Battalion Aid Station you've got a doctor right there. Out in the boondocks, you have to make some decisions on your own."

Invisible to either the American public or the troops in the field, there was bitter dispute among the high commanders. Despite early and continuing successes, Westmoreland resented the Marine emphasis on pacification, feeling it diverted attention from the conventional battles he was planning. The Combined Action Platoons were the major tool in the program. Small squad detachments of volunteers lived, fought, and worked alongside the Vietnamese villagers. These groups were of course both a thorn in the flesh of the VC and all too vulnerable to attack. On occasion the enemy would concentrate forces to eliminate troublesome CAP outposts. In turn, the CAP unit could call for help from local garrisons of Marines.

John Bartusevics: "We came across this one CAP Platoon, where I think there was eleven members, eight of them got killed. We got there and caught the whole squad that attacked them going across the rice paddy.

"At first I thought it was friendlies, but then I said 'Wait a minute.

That's after a firefight. Friendlies are gonna be going toward the firefight....'

"The wind was blowing the right direction. If the wind is blowing, because of how loud a tank is, you're not gonna hear.... You bring your tank up on a dike, and you're just about rocking back and forth as you balance yourself. You got a good driver that knows how to feather that accelerator, and you sit up there, and all of a sudden you got a shitload of Charlie going across the rice paddy with his guns. And he never even seen you, or heard you."

For the VC, caught in the open in broad daylight by a skilled tank crew, it was a slaughterhouse. The driver would balance the tank against the recoil. The range was too great for canister, but "I had my tank gunner who could hit Charlie, running sideways, at I'll say five-hundred-fifty meters .... That's a human body, a small target, with the ninety. Give him a little practice."

The tanks went on toward the CAP compound, which was still taking sporadic fire and the medevacs refused to come in. "This sergeant that survived from the CAP ... he called the helicopter and said 'If you don't come down, I'm gonna shoot you down.' We just started shooting three-hundred-sixty degrees around, and they came down."

The medevacs, old UH-34s with limited capacity, were for the living, so "We had to load guys on the ponchos in bits and pieces, and put them on the back of our tank to take them back to Charlie Med."

By the last quarter of 1966, III MAF was stretched thin as most of the 3rd Marine Division was shifted to the more conventional war along the DMZ. The burden of the war was being felt in ever-larger circles. Personnel shortages caused the implementation of stop-loss orders (involuntary extensions of service), commissioning of experienced NCOs as temporary officers (which depleted the critical NCO ranks) and another of McNamara's pets, "Project 100,000," which forced the Corps to accept 18% of its incoming manpower from the ranks of men who previously would have been considered unacceptable for mental or physical reasons. The Army had also seen the light, and was demanding such specialized Marine equipment as heavy-lift helicopters. All the services were competing for dollars and equipment.

Heavy rains hampered even minimal tank operations as the river systems flooded.

The infantry conducted most of the village pacification programs, a fundamental part of the Marines' strategy, although the tank units participated on a regular basis. The tanks were typically involved in the ongoing COUNTY FAIR operations.

In December, 3rd Tank participated in a major program to distribute seeds and livestock in Phong Bac, in coordination with the Army's 28th Civic Affairs Company. The 3rd Tank CO, Lt. Colonel William R. Corson, poured considerable resources into the Civic Action Program, developing a marketing plan for livestock, constructing a fish processing plant, and other economic developments. Phong Bac was considered a showcase for the program.[15] The charitable efforts of Sergeant William F. Keyser of the 1st Tank Battalion were widely publicized when he solicited contributions from Waukegan, Illinois and distributed Christmas gifts to the villagers in Tic Tay.

Westmoreland continued to deride the pacification program since it did not contribute to his favored metric for success, the body count. Corson eventually expressed his disgust in a book that drew extreme censure from the military command structure and nearly cost him his career.[16]

Bob Embesi recalled, "Things were getting different toward the end of '66, because of the Viet Cong being downplayed and the NVA being up-played, coming in there."

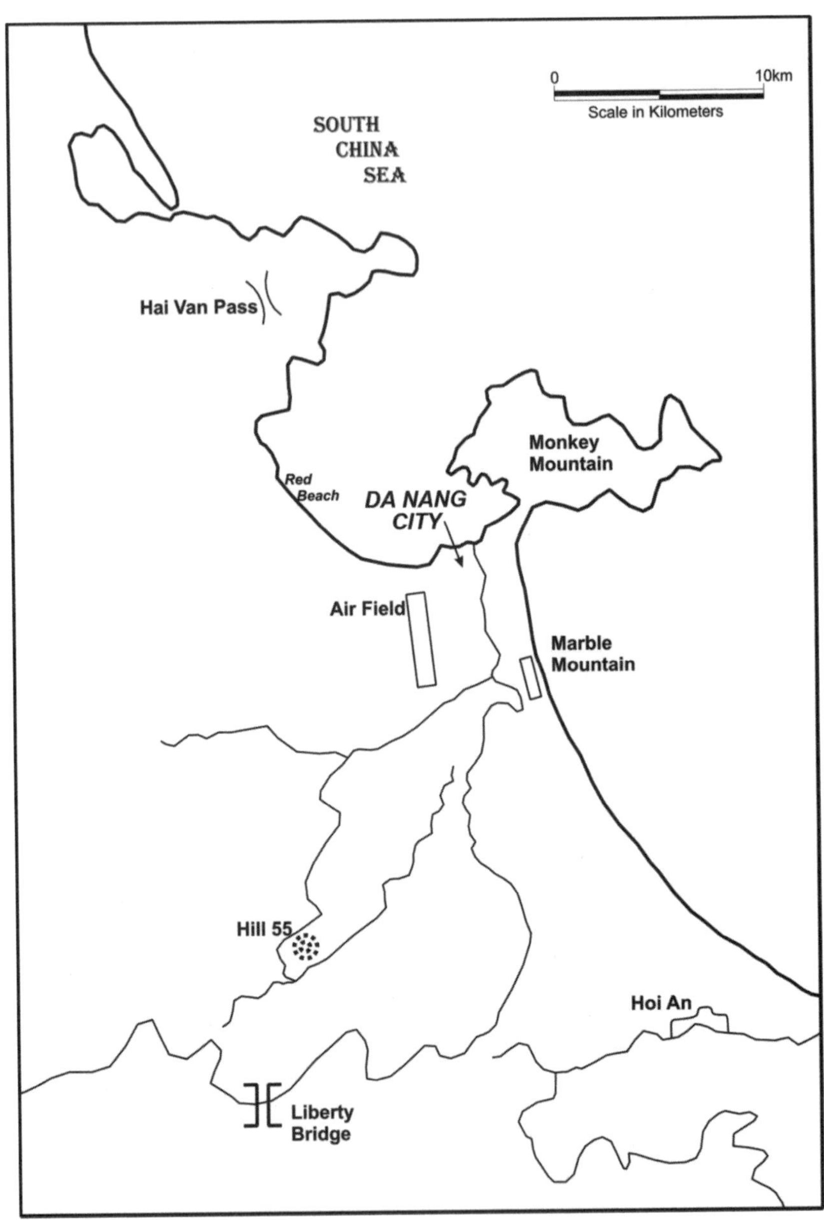

Operation Liberty, 7–30 June 1966, was designed to expand the Marines' Tactial Area of Responsibility (TAOR) inland from the densely populated coastal region around Danang.

CHAPTER 4

1967: A GROWING MOMENTUM

"I think Vietnam was what we had instead of happy childhoods."
Michael Herr (journalist)

The beginning of 1967 marked a fundamental change in the strategy pursued by III MAF in Vietnam. Under pressure from Westmoreland, the Marines progressively surrendered more of the pacification efforts to the ARVN, and assumed responsibility for tactical operations against major NVA and VC units. This of course contributed to the increased body count metric that Westmoreland was determined to pursue, but it also negated the hard-won gains the Marines had made in the pacification program. VC activity in the coastal zone south of Danang increased.[1]

In northern I Corps, the first month of 1967 passed relatively uneventfully as both sides gathered strength for the decisive battle that their leaders had planned. The NVA now deployed four divisions along and immediately south of the DMZ

The I Corps region was clearly evolving into one of the critical areas of the war, and there was as always disagreement among the commanders. Logistical traffic along the Cua Viet River was the lifeblood of units along the DMZ, but the river was under constant artillery attack from within the DMZ. III MAF feared an NVA offensive through the A Shau Valley to the Hai Van Pass that could sever critical overland communications as well. MACV, however, was fixated upon a potential NVA offensive through the Khe Sanh area to outflank the "defensive line" along the DMZ. MACV's fixations would set the stage for some of the bitterest fighting of the war.[2] Repeated sweeps in the PRAIRIE operational area were designed to bloody the NVA and forestall any possible enemy offensive. The Marines continued to shift operations westward, toward the rugged hills and mountains that were an NVA sanctuary.

Farther to the south around Danang the pace had not slackened. In the predawn hours of 15 January, a pitch-black night in the dark of the moon, a battalion of elite NVA sappers reinforced by local VC attacked positions held by a platoon from Kilo 3/1. The new NVA arrivals were assigned an easy target to introduce them to local combat.[3]

On most nights the tanks would be out in the field, but Bartusevics recalled that the 2nd Platoon's heavy section happened to be back to the rear. "Here it was, an opportunity to take a shower in cold buckets of water, raid the mess hall, and relax for a night.... We're waiting for the next (infantry) unit to go back out. Normally they're ready to go back out in an hour or two, and we would refuel, reammo, raid the mess hall, and go right back out with a new unit."

The infantry was not ready to leave for the field. "We're sleeping in the tent, and I think it was about like two or three in the morning when the shit started off in the distance. Mortars and artillery and crap like that.

"Here comes a guy from the COC [Combat Operations Center] running in. Said 'We gotta have the tanks. Get your tanks ready. We're going to have a company of grunts on there, and you guys need to go out there and take care of that problem. They're getting overrun.'"

The senior NCO was indisposed, so Bartusevics rousted out the heavy section and had them ready to go in about five minutes. "I'm going to take charge and do what I gotta do. We're not going to worry about where the Gunny's at. I grabbed the three tanks, and we're waiting for the grunts to show up." The firing was growing heavier by the minute, and "You could see the sky lighting up."

Forty years later you can still hear the frustration in his voice as Bartusevics recounts the fifteen or twenty minutes spent waiting for the infantry force. "I ran to the COC. I said 'Hey, give me one of your radio operators so they can operate that crypto stuff.'" The tanks did not have encrypted radios, and had to carry a separate radio unit. Bartusevics loaded up the radioman behind the turret, and left instructions for the grunts to follow aboard Amtracs.

"I took off.... I knew exactly where they're at, and I said 'If I go my normal route, easy for tracks to maneuver, I have a feeling Charlie might have an ambush for us.' He's known for that. He sets a beautiful attack.... He expects reinforcements.

"You get seasoned to that kind of stuff, and I'm not going to let Charlie outthink me.... I'm going to go out there the quickest way possible, because those boys look like they're getting hit, and hit hard."

The direct route would be to take the Main Supply Route (MSR), which ran fairly straight before taking a hard left turn before reaching the besieged patrol base. The tanks would have to slow down to make the turn, which lay in a row of coastal sand dunes. Bartusevics reasoned that the MSR would be mined. He led his tanks cross-country parallel to the MSR, plowing through rice paddies and vegetation and over the dunes, driving only short distances on the road, "Jump back on, jump back off, cross over it. Just like a cat and mouse game." Just before the turn, they veered off into the countryside, and could see the firefight ahead.

"At that moment I saw a green flare being popped right in that general area where if we would have went up that normal channel across the sand dunes. It was most likely they had an ambush set for us. The flare came from that area."

Bartusevics noted that all that had saved the base was faulty NVA intelligence. The new garrison platoon had been sent out a day early, and there were two infantry platoons inside the tiny patrol base.

Three belts of barbed wire surrounded the base. "I had no choice but to go straight into the concertina wire. As long as you don't do turns—you learn this from experience—you're not going to get the concertina wire caught in your tracks, and maybe spin off your sprocket. Just make a straight line, and don't turn and don't stop in there."

The three tanks plowed through, and "It was a madhouse in there. Green tracers coming and going. Red tracers going. We had sappers running across the compound with five-pound satchel charges. All they wore was shorts. They're slicked down, and all they had was like little jockey shorts, five pound satchel charges, and AK forty-sevens." RPGs were arcing through the night on all sides.

There were Marine bodies on the ground all over the compound, so Bartusevics gave instruction not to use the 90mm cannons. "Use your machine guns. Don't button up, because I don't want you running over any wounded Marines."

Amid the carnage, training and instinct took over. "You're almost like in a trance. You're just trying to keep yourself alive, trying to keep your tank running, keep firing.... We were running them over ... guys were trying to get around the side of our tank.

"I think some of them were on dope, to tell you the truth. Some of them would stand in front of the tank and fire at will, and wouldn't move. Some of them tried to get on the side of the tank while the tank's moving, which is a stupid mistake." The tank commanders were firing with heavy machine guns mounted on top of the commander's cupola, and "The loader was out of the hatch with a rifle, picking off guys that were trying to get on the tanks."

The tankers turned on the big searchlights atop their gun tubes. "I figured that the searchlights would blind them, and when they're shooting at the searchlight, they wouldn't be hitting us. They would be shooting high or low, which is normal if you're being blinded." The ploy seemed to work, since there were no tank crew casualties.

Bartusevics spotted a structure near the center of the compound. "It was the most reinforced with sandbags, and I figured that was the command CP. Nobody was moving, I don't see any other Marines." An enemy machine gun was laying down heavy fire on the command bunker from a nearby structure made of tents and metal. "I headed straight for that baby. I told my driver, not (to) button up, but get your head down and floor it." The enemy gun began to rake the tank and Bartusevics laid down a return fire from the sky mount.

"We ran right over that, and knocked out the machine gun crew there.... They weren't moving. Who the hell in their right mind is not going to move when there's a tank moving down on top of you?"

When the fire slackened, an infantry sergeant ran out of the bunker and "jumped up on my tank real quick. He said 'Hey, there's an observation post outside the wire that got overran before they hit our position. I think they're all dead. Can you go take care of them?'"

One of the tanks was sent out. "Thank God, two were alive and two were wounded.... You never saw guys as glad as they were."

More Marines were emerging from the CP and regaining control of the base. A green flare went up from outside the perimeter "... and you saw guys disappearing, taking off. I think that was the pullout (signal)." Bartusevics thinks the enemy commander was uncertain how many reinforcements were coming, and would have fought on if he knew that the entire relief force was only three tanks.

When the enemy began to break contact the tanks began a pursuit, "Chasing them, and starting to let loose with the ninety millimeters. Canister to start out with and then some HE.

"It was a real vegetated area on the northwest side, the rest was sand dunes, but that was the critical area. We started securing the area, around the perimeter. We took a chance, but it worked. Because I had no grunts sitting on my tank watching my back, we had to kind of watch each other's back. We swept the whole perimeter outside."

The medevac helicopters would not come until dawn. The radio operator told Bartusevics that two companies of grunts aboard Amtracs were lost. "That's our reinforcements. A day late and a dollar short."

He decided to leave two tanks to secure the base and take one tank to go and search for the lost column, "Which is a no-no.... You never go into Indian Country just by yourself. If you get stuck you got nobody to pull you out and all that. But hey, it's one of those times when nobody's around, you're in charge, and you gotta make a decision."

Bartusevics set out into the dark, suspecting that the Amtracs were somewhere around the site of the abortive ambush. He radioed the Amtracs and told them he would shine his searchlight into the air. "You tell me which direction to travel. I had to do that four or five times, and they walked me into their positions." The reinforcements cleared the compound, capturing one NVA in hiding, and waited for the medevacs.

At the end of the fight seventeen Marines were dead and thirty-three wounded. Many were found in their positions with their boots off and rifle safeties still on, taken completely by surprise. There were over sixty enemy bodies left behind (the count varies by source), and Bartusevics estimated that the tanks accounted for about a third of the enemy losses.[4]

Despite such attacks the Marines were by and large on the offensive. In January and February the 1st Division resumed major sweep operations, extending operations into the troublesome Go Noi Island region.

Like many others before and after, family played an important role in Robert "R.B." English's decision to join the Marines. His father was a farmer in East Texas, and it was "a pretty rough life, out there picking cotton and corn and all." His older brother, Max, had served in the Army horse cavalry for two years, and "he knew he didn't want to work for this old man on this cotton farm, so he joined the Marines." Max fought in the Pacific War and in Korea, and two other older brothers were in the Marines and Navy. R.B. saw Max only about once a year. "After I got out of high school, I worked for a year down in Beaumont (Texas) doing construction work, driving a truck. Max told me 'Get the hell out of there and come in the Marines.' So I went in. That was 1955."

In March of 1964 English was assigned to the 3rd Marine Division on Okinawa. "Vietnam was heating up then, and we made a couple of floats, and down to the Philippines. They cut short our Philippines float one time and sent us out to float around the coast of Vietnam." One such float in late 1964 and early 1965 lasted fifty-nine days. Despite the extra income from a regulation that exempted their pay from income tax if serving in a war zone, "We would have given all our money to get off that damn ship and land *anywhere*!" As luck would have it, "We were too short for a landing and when we got back to Okinawa, that's when the 3rd Marine Division was landing (in Vietnam)."

English went back to California. In late 1966 he boarded ship, spent Christmas back on Okinawa, and "I can remember ... being there at Danang on New Year's Day, at the Staff (NCO) Club, partying on New Year's Day." Third Tank headquarters was at Danang, but English was sent to Charlie Company at Dong Ha as a platoon sergeant. The platoon was led by a mustang, Lieutenant Beck, with S/Sgt T.J. Siva and S/Sgt Roberts as section leaders. English had unknowingly been sent to the eye of a growing storm. This was a "gypsy" platoon, an extra platoon within the company.

When the NVA chose not to fight, most sweeps could be routine. English said that they would stay off established trails and roads, but run the tank down hedgerows to detonate booby-traps before the infantry went in. "Most of the time it was just a nice ride in the sun. We'd keep our C-rations back on the engine compartment, back on the transmission, keep them hot."

Barnett Person also arrived in January. He had joined the Marines in 1947, in Montgomery, Alabama. He was checking out the recruiting station when the recruiter said, "'Sure, by all means, come on in. How old are you?'"

"I told him a lie. I told him I was eighteen when I was only sixteen. Went on in and took my test, passed it. About four days later I was off to Birmingham for a physical." After a day in Birmingham a group of sixteen or so recruits boarded a train for Monford Point, North Carolina where black recruits were trained in the racially segregated Corps. Recruit training was integrated in 1948 but by that time he was in an anti-aircraft artillery unit, a common assignment. In 1950 Person transferred to tanks, and spent the year 1951 fighting in Korea with D Company, 1st Tank Battalion. "I said 'Twenty years old, shoot, ain't nothin' out here could kill me.' I was kind of looking for the action."

Person, a Gunnery Sergeant, was assigned as the platoon sergeant. "When I got to Danang, they flew me up to Dong Ha by helicopter.... I went from there to Gio Linh and Con Thien, up in that area, where I picked up my platoon," 2nd Platoon, A Company, 3rd Tank.

As a lowly Lance Corporal, William "JJ" Carroll's route was more roundabout, but not entirely unusual. "I saw the movie 'Sands of Iwo Jima.' I used to watch that thing, like, forever. I was going to be a Sergeant Stryker one day. That and I had a cousin who was a Marine in the Korean War and he always came around and I was fascinated. He was a cannon-cocker[5] in Korea. He gave me a Marine Corps emblem one time, and I was just in awe. I said 'Man,' like a young kid, 'this is really cool!' Between that and Sergeant Stryker, I was sold." He said that about two thirds of the kids he hung around with joined up. "No electronic geniuses, it was all tanks and infantry, and that kind of thing, which was fine with us."

Carroll was assigned as a 2141, a tracked vehicle repairman, or shitfister, with a secondary MOS of 1811, basic tank crewman. He served in 2nd Tank in North Carolina, then "We show up at Camp Hansen (Okinawa) and there's three hundred people. They call my name out, and another guy who was a shitfister named Aguilar, and say, 'You guys are going to the brig.' We haven't done nothing!" They were assigned as guards at the "Kawasaki Monkey House," a red-line maximum-security brig that held serious offenders from both the Navy and Marine Corps.[6] "They had two riots, storming the gates, while I was there." He went on to explain, "We had some real bad-asses that came up from Vietnam, waiting to go to Portsmouth (Naval Prison)."

Most of the guards were combat veterans who had been wounded in Vietnam, and were awaiting transfer back to the US. Their final assignment was often to "chase," or escort, prisoners to a Stateside prison. Many prisoners were violent. "I took one out to empty the trash one time, and he picks up an old busted mop handle and says 'Carroll, I'm going to cave your head in.' I stepped back and chambered a round—remember we had double-ought buck shotguns with brass shell casings—and I said 'Go for it, because I'm trying to get transferred.'"

Carroll submitted weekly requests for transfer, and "Finally after a couple of months, they said alright...." Carroll was sent to 3rd Tank at Danang.

Corpsman Gene Hackemack left Vietnam in March, and after a short leave was sent to Sand Point Naval Air Station near Seattle. "They were supposed to discharge me when I arrived in country, but somebody messed up on my orders.... I was glad, because this was gravy duty. When I arrived the Chief up there at the dispensary was highly pissed because of this mix up." Hackemack spent the rest of his enlistment drawing blood and working in the lab.

A COLLISION OF PLANS

In the grand plan that General William Westmoreland intended to impose upon the enemy, in 1967 the ARVN would assume the primary task of pacification, while American forces would bring the Communists to bay and crush them under overwhelming firepower. The plan was approved by the NVA's primary strategist, General Vo Nguyen Giap. Thwarting the inept pacification efforts of the South Vietnamese "puppets" would be simple. His great strategic goal was to draw the Americans into the mountainous terrain west of the coastal plain, and "bleed them without mercy" as he had done the French before them. The generals were in agreement, and it was time to set the pawns into motion.

Company A, 3rd Tank spent the month of January in tents at Dong Ha, and Person said, "I think in February we went out and made a little sweep north of Cam Lo." The 3rd Marine Division was extending its sphere of influence over a broad expanse of northern Quang Tri Province, and on 19 March Highway 9 was opened to traffic as far as the site of a new combat base at Khe Sanh. A platoon of tanks from B Company and some Ontos tank destroyers were among the units dispatched to the isolated valley.

After a few weeks at Danang, repairman JJ Carroll was sent north to H&S Forward as a crewman on the retriever. In February he had one of those run-ins with authority that are so familiar to veterans. After an argument with a maintenance officer, Carroll was given Office Hours, a non-judicial punishment hearing conducted by a senior officer. "He made me dig holes for two weeks. Slit trenches. Dig them up, fill them in, dig them up, fill them in. Some one comes down and says 'JJ, Skipper wants to see your slimy ass.' I go in and he says 'You be in formation tomorrow morning. I'm promoting you to Corporal.'"

As the war heated up, English's platoon was split. "At the end of February or the first of March, Lt. Beck sent my section in U-boats up to the mouth of the river. That's when he took the three tanks (Siva's heavy section) and went out in the Cam Lo area for that sweep....

"They were out on a sweep with, I'm sure it was the 9th Marines.... They were just out on patrol, between Cam Lo, up in Leatherneck Square, and close to a little place called The Rocky Ford.

"I was listening to the radio that morning, and Lt. Beck says 'Siva's tank blew up.'" An RPG struck the turret face at close range. The heavier armor there "was supposed to be about fourteen inches of homogeneous steel, counting the gun shield. Went through there and killed his gunner, Corporal (Walter) Heuling, and T.J. and his loader Hamby and the driver were all wounded but they got out of the tank. Of course the tank burned up. That was the first casualties we had in my platoon."

JJ Carroll: "It was March sixth, and T. J. Siva ... his tank took an RPG that killed the gunner. The tank catches fire, Siva's greasing the gooks that are trying to get on the tank. That tank burned for twenty-something hours.

"Of course, knowing the Marine Corps, they're going to go scrounge for parts, right?" Carroll commented that the Army would probably have written the tank off, but the Corps could "maybe find an extra bolt...."

Carroll's retriever was sent out to drag the wreck back, and the trip provided an insight into the brutality of the infantry's war. "It's rainy and muddy. Here comes the grunts back, and they got like eleven prisoners, and they got rope around their necks, using them as pack mules. They had ammo on their backs. I'm on the tank retriever, and there's a couple of tanks there.

"I'm looking at these gooks, and I guess the corpsman had broken off a C-ration cracker and given it to one, but he gives it to another. It pissed the corpsman off, and he smacks this guy right in the head with his barb-wire gloves,[7] and I'm going 'Oh, this is going to turn bad.'

"They're getting them out of there and this one gook is playing sick. So they drag this dude through the mud, his face is plowing up the mud, and they stand him up and started pushing him around. I'm standing up on top of the tank retriever looking down on this. I said 'Somebody better get these dudes out of here....'

"Some lieutenant comes running up, yelling at the Marines, saying 'Marines! You're maltreating this prisoner!' I looked over and there's a bunch of dead Marines laying there with ponchos flapping on them. They said 'Lieutenant, there's the guys got maltreated today!' Then they got them on a six-by and got them the hell out of there.

"One minute you're getting your ass shot off, the tank's still out there burning, in flames, and you're (supposed) to just turn it off. That's just not reality ... I just said 'Jesus Christ, son, let's get outta here.'" The retriever left without the burning tank.

"About three days later," said English, "they came up and got my two tanks and brought me back down. For the rest of that year the only time we ever went back to Dong Ha was when a tank had to be serviced or something, and we were right back in the field. We went from Con Thien, in May we were up at Gio Linh, and before that ... at Camp Carroll. So we were just switching all around. I would say that I spent a good six months of my one-year tour at Con Thien. Up there for two or three weeks, out on a sweep, back to Con Thien....

In April Carroll joined R.B. English's platoon. "Then in May, we went to Gio Linh." With the tanks operating in small, often isolated, groups, each platoon had its own maintenance man. Carroll became both a crewman on one of the tanks and the unit's dedicated mechanic.

The platoon's communicator, responsible for maintenance and operation of the radios, normally would have ridden in the platoon's jeep from which he could manage long-range communications with higher headquarters, but he also typically served as a tank crewman. English made no bones about the fact that "I was a terrible guy on the radio, so my communicator was usually my gunner or something. AN-GR3! ....the hardest radio to work in your life! We had the Prick-25 (PRC-25, a man-portable radio), the platoon sergeant and platoon commander (each) had one inside his tank, that we could talk to infantry with. That old AN-GR3 we just used that for communications between tanks. Horrible communications.

"We didn't ever have a corpsman, unless we were at a stationary place. We used infantry corpsmen. We had a truck driver and a jeep driver, and he was usually back in the rear with the gear with the First Sergeant. We didn't need a jeep or a truck, either one out in the field."

In May English's platoon was back at Gio Linh. As at most permanent bases, the blade tank would scoop out a tank slot, simply a pit "as deep as the top of the fenders. Pretty good." When it rained "Of course it filled full of water. I used to always try to figure out some way to build a bunker underneath one of those tank traps, but I never could figure it out. They had little bunkers right next to the tanks. Most of the time there at Gio Linh we got those little eighty-fives ... The bunkers would stand those. Later when they started shooting one-five-fives and stuff ...

when they started shooting that big stuff in, we stayed in the tanks. Especially at night."[8]

The tankers quickly learned that no time or place was safe, and that death could come from many sources. English: "They had trenches dug completely around it. The tanks were spread out all around it, and I would go visit with them all the time. You would hear that little eighty-five, 'Boop!', you'd hear him shoot over there and you had about fifteen or twenty seconds. You could go a long ways in fifteen or twenty seconds, right? We'd just drop down in that ditch. You didn't have any idea where it would hit. Soon as that one landed you would hop up."

One struck the ammo dump and "That stuff fell down for hours." JJ Carroll backed his tank out to a safer position, but found an infantryman wounded in the face and body. "I threw this guy over my shoulder and ran through the fire down through the trench lines, and then made my way back to my tank. The guys in my tank said 'You're about a dumb fuck, Carroll.' But it's one of those spontaneous things. You don't think about it, you just do it." Carroll never found out if the man survived. "To this day I don't know who the guy was. Some grunt."

The entire area was littered with unexploded rounds, said English, so that "They had to bring the EOD up there to try and recover what didn't go off."

One Sunday in May, Carroll "was walking down to the tank, shooting the shit—you know how Marines do—and I said 'What are you doing, asshole?'" to Ron Knoski, another tanker in the platoon.

"He says 'What's it to you, JJ?' I said 'Ahhh, just curious, guy.'

"He says 'Well, if you must know, I'm writing to my mom.' I said 'Tell mom I said hi.' He says 'Why should I do that,' and I said 'Mom's got the hots for me' and started laughing.

"I turned around and walked to my tank, and boom-boom, here comes artillery.... So I dust myself off and get on up to my tank. A couple of grunts start yelling 'Hey, tanks! Your tank got hit down there.'

"I go running back down there, because I'm like senior guy of my tank. They're flipping over Knoski, the whole side of his face was sheared away. Otto, the other guy I was talking to, it blew off the back of his head and he had dropped inside the turret."

English: "We were there for a good month and we wanted to get out of that place so bad because that's where Knoski and Otto were killed."

The two tankers were killed by what Carroll thought was a recoilless round, but what English suspects was friendly artillery fire.

"Corporal Knoski was the tank commander there at the gate of Gio Linh on Mother's Day, of all days. Lance Corporal Otto was with him, and they were both killed by an airburst, right over the tank. Otto was standing up in the TC hatch looking around. Had his flak jacket on but no helmet. Of course we always wore our tank helmet. Knoski was next to the tank shaving, and that round went off right over the tank. Killed both of them.

"Ron Knoski, only son of a family back in Elizabeth, New Jersey. Tragedy." Otto was from Minnesota, which seemed to provide a disproportionate number of casualties from the 3rd Battalion.

Carroll said that a day or two later a replacement came into the platoon, distinctive because "You could always tell the new guys. They got brand new Stateside utilities." In the distance Carroll heard the distinctive booming sound of artillery firing from inside the DMZ. "I said 'Get under the tank! Get under the tank!' and he's looking at me like I'm crazy. I drag him under the tank." Seconds later the shells impacted nearby and "You hear this whipping through the air, and about six pieces of shrapnel landed like two feet, right in front of us.

"His eyes were big, and I said, 'Welcome to Gio Linh, bud.'"

The platoon was sent to Con Thien, "Which wasn't that much better," said English. The platoon was acquiring a reputation. As Carroll pointed out, "You see that platoon roster, I mean in this platoon, you're going to get whacked."

The protracted presence of the tanks in the region led to brief periods of settled life. For a brief period English's platoon guarded the Cam Lo Bridge. "We had a heavy section on the north side of that bridge and a light section on the other side. We stayed there for a long time. We put little hooches up next to the tents, with our tarp, and that was it. We didn't have any reason to build any bunkers, because bunkers get you killed. We didn't have enough material to build them in the first place.

"At Con Thien I (would) forbid my people from sleeping anywhere but inside the tank. We sat outside next to the tank, on the leeward side, away from where the artillery would hit, and cook our rations, and then get back in the tanks."

The bridge guard mission was distinctly unpopular among the tank unit leaders. Captain (later Colonel) C.W. Casey had enlisted in 1957, then ended up in a Reserve tank unit and was enrolled in a commissioning program that allowed him to graduate from Florida State University. He started his tour in Vietnam as CO of the H&S Company,

1st Tank at Danang, and became the CO of Alpha Company, 1st Tank in the southern ICTZ. "The primary responsibility was guarding damn road bridges! Bridges! They were using those doggone vehicles ... a mobile pillbox. They would run that thing out there and set it on a bridge."

The use of small isolated groups of tanks meant that many tankers and their officers never met. JJ Carroll said, "You never knew who you belonged to anyway. I must have had three or four battalion commanders in Third Tanks, and I never saw a one of them."

For the crews, guarding bridges was not all bad. "We called that R&R" said Bartusevics of his tour at Liberty Bridge, south of Marble Mountain, during the monsoon. "You went out there for twenty days." With the river in flood, "Charlie was sending down logs with NVA flags on them. In many cases they would be filled with explosives. Which one is explosive and which one is a dummy? I wasn't going to take chances. We were going to shoot the hell out of them." The tank rounds would ricochet off the water surface. The next day the battalion operations officer came out demanding to know who was in charge, and as a result "The next day I was back out in the field."

The Marines established another position five kilometers south of Con Thien, officially known as C-2 but more commonly known at the time as The Rocky Ford. The tanks frequently occupied positions there. About three kilometers farther south was C-3, with large bunkers, safer from artillery. It was the location of a regimental CP.

Nothing was ever truly safe. JJ Carroll described an incident during one Bravo Company H&I mission, in which the loader failed to properly seat the round and it misfired. "You're supposed to tap it with your rammer-extractor tool. Well, he gets pissed off and he swings at it. That rammer-extractor tool has a quarter moon shape on one end. In those days the nineties were percussion ... He hit that damn thing, and that shell went out the front end and that shell casing buried him into the radio rack." Propellant gasses venting into the turret, and the heavy shell casing, killed two men and left body parts scattered throughout the debris. The tank was towed back to the base at Dong Ha, and the turret had to be removed to clean the gore from inside. "I was one of the guys who washed it out."

Part of the tank unit assignment was to cover the daily engineer road sweeps. The NVA used anti-vehicle mines, pressure plate mines which would blow the road wheels off a tank, lavishly. English: "Every day, from Con Thien back to The Washout[9] (close to C-2), they would have a sweep detail. They always sent a couple of tanks along with it.... The Washout people would take care of it back to whatever that other Charlie was (C-3). Charlie -3 would take that road sweep all the way back to Cam Lo. It wasn't that far; seemed like it was a long ways back in those days."[10] The process could take hours, as the engineers had to dig up mines, old cans, and other suspicious metal objects buried in the road.

The individual tank companies usually had defined areas of responsibility, but would occasionally be assigned to other areas. English's platoon was sent up the road to The Rockpile, where the Army had emplaced a battery of long-range 175mm guns that fired missions around Khe Sanh, 25 kilometers to the southwest. "The first time I took my tank platoon up to A Company, one of my tanks had its muzzle cover on. Of course if he'd have got in a firefight he'd have just blew the goddamn thing off, no big deal. We got up there, ol' Cap'n Burns just chewed my ass out. 'Ah, damnit English, you coming up here with muzzle covers on! This is a combat zone!'

"I said 'I know that, Cap'n. I'm aware of that. I'll take care of that.'

" 'Ah, blub-blub-blub', he chewed my ass out. So I got him back about an hour later.

"We got the tanks to the tank park, got whatever maintenance we had to do on them, and got them ready to go the next day in case we went anywhere. I went back down to the staff tent and nobody was there. I went in and got me a beer, because that was the Old Corps. You drank a beer if you wanted to.

"I was drinkin' me a beer and the First Sergeant came in. Then Cap'n Burns came in. He was all apologetic but he wasn't talking to me. He was giving me these mean looks. About that time those big ... things, those one-seventy-fives—I had never heard of them before—fired. The tent shook, and I yelled 'Incoming!' I took off and run out, and there was a trench right out in front of that tent. All those goddamn assholes followed me out there and jumped in the ditch with me. Ol' Fuji Fox (Burns) got buried in the mud. He was all muddy and shit.

"Everybody got up and said 'English, you stupid bastard! That was those one-seven-fives.' Hell, I didn't know anything about this goddamn place. We all went back in all muddy and got us another beer. So I got that Fox back. God, those things were noisy. They were a good seventy-five yards back from where our tents were."

Still down around Danang, operating in the Arizona Territory, John Bartusevics "felt obligated and felt responsible for the kids. I was an old man at the age of twenty-four, twenty-five years old, while the rest of the kids were young draftees under twenty years old." He extended his enlistment for a year, but was rotated back to Okinawa in April.

THE DMZ WAR HEATS UP

One of Secretary of Defense Robert McNamara's pet projects was the construction of a physical barrier intended to block infiltration of troops and equipment across the DMZ. Westmoreland eagerly embraced the idea, and so in April the decree went out that the Marines would construct the Strong Point Obstacle System (SPOS) from the coast, passing north of Gio Linh and Con Thien, and ending six kilometers west of Con Thien. The Marine commands resisted the project in vain, pointing out the difficulties of construction and maintenance, and the probability that it would not succeed. The project would be remembered as the McNamara Line, an obvious play on the Maginot Line of the 1930s.

In the initial stage a battalion of Marine engineers, protected by two battalions of infantry and tanks, would clear a broad strip. Later the cleared trace, as it became known, would be widened and sown with mines and seismic sensors to detect movement. Artillery, aircraft, and a reaction force of infantry would render intrusion impossible, or so went the plan.

Person's tank platoon helped clear the path for the engineers from Gio Linh to Con Thien, "blazing away ... cleaning out, making sure there were no NVA, trying to get them out of there." It was a two-stage process. "They cut one strip down one way, and then they went back up the other way. Kept widening that place." The force did not meet much initial resistance, but "When we finished the first strip going through, and we set up at Con Thien we really caught hell up there." Another tank platoon protected the engineers as they widened the strip back toward Gio Linh. Person's platoon went out on local road sweeps and helped the infantry search the local villages, at first without much resistance from the NVA. "First time we started going out it was pretty good. You could go out, make a sweep, five or ten thousand meters, nothing. But later on they kind of built up around there. You go out about a thousand meters or less, you're going to meet some resistance."

English recalled, "The first time I went up in there, they still had the marketplace on the north side of that strip." As predicted by the Marines, the NVA was not about to let the plan be implemented. "Once they started that strip, that's when the gooks were mining everything up there. You couldn't get on a road.... If we had to go down this road, we'd put one track over the ditch and one over the edge of the road. If we didn't, we got out in the middle of that road, man you were done because you were going to hit a mine. We hit them all the time up there."

The North Vietnamese were determined to resist the construction of McNamara's barrier. Two battalions from the *812 NVA Regiment* were to annihilate the Americans and South Vietnamese forces occupying and enlarging the old Special Forces base at Con Thien. The ARVN garrison had been replaced by A and D Companies of 1/4, plus engineers and tanks. The east end was still held by Army Special Forces advisors and Nung mercenaries of the CIDG, whom the Marines did not trust. "Soon as we finished cutting that strip through there, setting up there about a week or two weeks, 8th of May, we got overrun up there on Con Thien," explained Person. He had only three tanks, as the Platoon Commander had taken the other two back to Gio Linh. The tanks were positioned on the more exposed northern side of the perimeter. The infantry commander in that sector, Captain John Juul of D Company, wanted direct control of the tank and its firepower. "He told me, said 'Gunny, I want your tank right here. Back right up in front of the CP here.'

"The (infantry) company I was with, we were on the north end of the hill. Battalion was set up all around the hill.... Just about a whole company went out on LPs and ambushes. Them doggone NVA, some way they got around our patrols out there, our company, and hit us right on the hill." Person remembers that the perimeter was thinly held, only one or two Marines in each bunker.

The attack commenced with a stunning artillery and mortar barrage. A wave of sappers rushed in under the artillery bursts to blast holes in the wire barriers, and infantry flooded in.

"They went right through on the north side. I was at the northeast side, and they hit me right on too ... and they came right through my perimeter. They surrounded us completely. They came in from all sides of that hill. How they did it I don't know. They missed the CP, which was located on the southeast side."

The attack struck at about 0300 hours, and "They hit two of my tanks right off the bat, put the crews out of action and everything. I know one thing, they were all over the top of my tank, and they hit me in the rear and the back there, but they didn't hit me with no RPG, thank God!"

The tank to Person's right was not so fortunate. An RPG slammed into the side of the turret, spraying the interior with hot shards of metal. The platoon maintenance man, Sergeant David Danner, was sitting in the gunner's seat. Though severely burned and riddled with steel fragments, he dragged the other wounded crewmen out of the tank to the aid station. He climbed back into the tank, and stripped out the coaxial machine gun and all the belted ammunition. Positioning himself with some of the surviving infantry, he began to lay down a heavy fire on the attackers.

The commander of the third tank, Corporal Charles D. Thatcher, was asleep under the vehicle when the attack began. The gunner, Lance Corporal David Gehrman, took the enemy under fire with the coaxial machine gun, but an RPG slammed into the side of the turret. Gehrman stood up in the commander's hatch, and another RPG blasted him out of the turret and onto the ground. Lance Corporal John Young and PFC James Lester lay mortally wounded in the floor of the turret.

Bullets struck the badly wounded Gehrman in both legs before he could reach safety, but nearby infantrymen dragged him into a trench. Thatcher climbed onto the burning tank to try and rescue the men still inside, only to be struck in the back and neck by shell fragments.

Finding the men in the tank to be beyond help, Thatcher returned to cover and cared for Gehrman while fighting off enemy infantry. An hour later Thatcher climbed back into the wrecked tank and fired the coaxial machine gun until the ammunition was exhausted. He climbed back out and grabbed a rifle, then scurried about carrying ammunition to the grunts.

Gunnery Sergeant Person: "Small arms. They jumped on top of my tank and tried to set off satchel charges, which didn't do any [significant] damage. Did do some damage. I couldn't traverse my turret, because they kind of messed up my cargo rack back there. Bent them up.... It just had me where I couldn't traverse it all the way around. I could only traverse it about twenty-five degrees each way.

"I was firing all in the front. Fifty, thirty, ninety. This captain who was in charge of the infantry company there, he was sitting right up in back of my tank, his CP. He finally killed about three of the NVA who were trying to sneak right up on my tank.

"They took over the trench line. We only had about one squad in the whole perimeter on the side we were on. They killed quite a few of the guys there.

"I killed the ones who set off the satchel charges on my tank. I killed those. When they jumped on top of my tank ...I stopped firing at that time. I guess they thought they had me knocked out. They had flares going up.

"They jumped down off my tank and they went out about twenty-five yards in front of my gun.... Looked like they were making up some more explosives, whatever. There were six of them.

"They jumped up and headed back toward my tank, and when they did I just let them have it. Killed all of them with one shot. Canister. I had that gun just leveled right down, firing point blank out there. Canister, HE, anything I could get ahold of."

JJ Carroll was at Gio Linh, and "We saw the attack that night. The gooks were actually using flamethrowers on them. From Gio Linh we could see the flames shooting out down the (cleared trace)." Gio Linh was under artillery attack, and any attempt to send a relief force was an invitation to an ambush.

Person's tank was unable to climb out of the tank slot, the pit in which the tank sat, or to back up because of the infantry CP behind. The bunker beside him had been destroyed, and his two other tanks—on his right—were knocked out of action. Person was also one man short on his own crew. "All the tank commanders got wounded.... I had a maintenance man on there, Sergeant [David J.] Danner, was on the middle tank. He finally got out of that tank." Danner and his machine gun were still fighting alongside the infantry. "He sat there with a few infantry guys in the bunker, with the thirty caliber machine gun, fired here, fired there." At one point Danner rushed out to recover a badly wounded Marine caught in the open and dragged him to the aid bunker. Then he returned to his machine gun.

The engineer platoon sprinted across the open aircraft runway and helped D Company contain the breach. A platoon from A Company, on the south side, boarded two Amtracs, and with an Army M42 "Duster"[11] started across the runway. The Duster was ripped apart by an RPG. One Amtrac was disabled by a satchel charge but the crew and passengers escaped. The second Amtrac became entangled in barbed wire, and was hit by an RPG. The blast inside the thinly armored tractor wounded many of the men inside, and ignited the gasoline fuel. The screams of the men inside lasted only minutes, but the blazing vehicles added to the eerie light cast by the constant artillery illumination rounds and flares dropped by a circling plane.

Person: "Then that morning I guess about five, five thirty, we were still fighting, everything was in chaos. Kind of quieted down, and I saw these NVA had all the bunkers occupied on my right flank.... We just started up and moved right around the perimeter, blowing up everything in the bunkers. HE and canister. Wasn't nobody in it. Nobody friendly."

In the last minutes of the fight, chance intervened again to save Person's life. "When I moved out on the side and turned a little corner, my doggone cargo rack blew up. One of the NVA was over on the side. Fired an RPG and hit it. If I wasn't traversing the turret, he would probably have hit me dead in the center. I was traversing turret so he hit my cargo rack and it went up in a fireball. My tank commander [Thatcher], who had got out of his tank over there, because all his crew got killed.... He had an M14, he was laying in a little trench over there.... When that guy jumped up and fired that RPG, he jumped up and shot the guy—killed him. Then he crawled out there and grabbed the RPG."

Thatcher jumped up onto Person's tank and started pounding on the hatch. "I looked through my scope there, my little window, and saw him out there.... He said 'Gunny, this is Thatcher.' I opened it up. He said, 'That sonofabitch hit your cargo rack, so I killed him! But that bunker up there is full of NVAs too.' He was kind of ... crouched over, and I could see them in the bunker, the NVAs. So I just moved right on up front.... I said 'Just move right on up a little bit, Fisher, we'll load the ninety on it.' Wipe that bunker out, went on up, wiped that one out, went almost up to the CP (on the south side), wiped out every one along there. Wasn't any infantry left on the perimeter. They all got killed and wounded."

The NVA had moved systematically down the trench lines "killing everything in the bunkers. I never will forget we had this little black kid, he was in one of the bunkers all the way around on the right.... He was blown to pieces, but we found about three or four, five NVAs in that bunker, dead as a doornail. He had cut them from A to Z. He had a Ka-bar. He was always sharpening that Ka-bar. The only way we figured they killed him, they must have run in with some kind of explosive on and just hugged him. Blew themselves up with him." Then the tank turned and worked its way back around, double-checking every position for NVA survivors.

When morning came Person helped recover the dead and wounded from his platoon. Three men on the middle tank were wounded. Two men were killed and another wounded on the third tank.[12] At dawn a relief force consisting of B/1/4, with two tanks and two Ontos, started down the trace from Gio Linh. The commander had the artillery fire protective boxes on either side of the advancing column, as well as having the armored vehicles rake the vegetation. They disrupted an expected ambush, killing more NVA.

Person: "The next morning I was setting up there picking up what wounded we had, and the dead. Lo and behold there's a mortar round come in and hit right down by the track, and hit me in the foot with a piece of shrapnel. I guess it was about eight o'clock. I was doing fine until then." Person was evacuated back to Phu Bai to recuperate. He rejoined his reconstituted platoon at Dong Ha after a week. Danner and Thatcher were each awarded the Navy Cross for their actions that night.[13] The small unit would be perhaps the most highly decorated tank unit in the Marine Corps.

When he was young, Lloyd "Pappy" Reynolds's parents rented out an extra room to a former Raider and veteran of the 4th Marine Division in the Pacific. "He was on Saipan and Tinian, and I got influenced by him a lot, plus one of my high school buddy's fathers was in the Raiders in World War II.

"Third day of my high school senior year, I was gone. A buddy of mine that graduated the year before me came by my second period class, and he had a gallon of wine. He said 'Let's go get drunk' and we did, and we signed up." After an infantry assignment in Hawaii, he was sent to the 1st Marine Division at Camp Pendleton. He and another Lance Corporal reported to the personnel office. "This sounds like a joke, but it's actually true.... There was a Corporal behind the desk, and he said 'Well, what do you guys want to do?'

"I said 'I don't give a shit, I just don't want to walk anymore.' Two years in the grunts. And so the guy said 'I got openings in Motor T and tanks.' My buddy popped up and said 'Thanks,' so he said 'Okay, tanks,' and he put us down and we both wound up in 1st Tank Battalion." Reynolds attended the battalion tank school. "The tank barracks were at Las Pulgas ('The Fleas'), and the tank ramp was out at Las Flores, and just down the road was where they had their tank school."

Reynolds has determined, with greater accuracy than most, the precise sequence of events in which he was involved.

Historically, one of the most confusing aspects of the Vietnam War was that the fighting might commence before an operation actually started. Operations were often somewhat arbitrarily defined by start dates, and thus fighting might commence as the troops maneuvered into position. In addition, one operation might end and another start on some specified date or when troops crossed some map boundary, with no actual break in the action. In the memory of the troops, "preliminary" fighting already in progress would simply be included in the "official" named operation.

In mid-May, 2/26 was sweeping an area south of the Trace, and the actions of that day blended imperceptibly into Operation HICKORY.

On 16 May, F/2/26 advanced into the abandoned hamlet of Phu Oc, and straight into a massive ambush. Foxtrot called artillery and air strikes down on the bunker complex, and G/2/26, with its supporting tank platoon, moved forward to counterattack.

Pappy Reynolds was the driver for B-11, the command tank of 1st Platoon, B Company under Lt. Fred Rivero. The tanks advanced behind two platoons of G/2/26 grunts following one of the typical narrow trails, too narrow for the tank to traverse its long gun.

> There was a company of grunts in front of us and I was in the lead tank. I heard one shot and a grunt in front of me did a cartwheel to the left. Immediately all hell broke lose, like that shot was a signal. We tried to traverse right but couldn't because of the trees. We just stayed there for what seemed like a long time but was probably only a few minutes. We did a hard right and broke through the tree line into an open field. Across the field was another tree line and I could see NVA moving around. By now I had the hatch over my head but not locked down as I had a fear of being trapped if I did.[14]

The tanks opened up with all weapons, moving out into the open ground. The peculiar ochre smoke trails of numerous RPG rockets sought the tanks. One hit the number five tank.

> There were RPG smoke trails all over the place. I never saw Staff Sergeant Reed again. I found out later his tank had taken

> an RPG in the turret side and he had a leg taken off. He was on Bravo 15. I don't recall seeing Bravo 15 again until after the operation.[15]

As the tanks advanced, an NVA rose from a spider hole and fired an AK-47 burst that severed an antenna from B-11. Like most tank commanders, Rivero was riding with his hatch open. Another round missed him but hit the inside of the clamshell hatch, shattering into metal shards that tore into both of Rivero's arms.[16] With the enemy so close Reynolds drew his pistol and laid it in his lap.

The tanks began to slug it out with the NVA in the tree line. Sometimes the war could be quite personal. Reynolds: "There's an NVA, and I could see him through the driver's periscope. It's hard to judge distance in there, but I guesstimate he was maybe a hundred yards out in front of us. He got behind this log, and he had an e-tool digging a hole, because we could see the shovel and the dirt flying up. Every time he'd pop his head up and look over the log, we'd fire a burst at him with the thirty, the coax.

"We did hit him eventually, but it took quite a while. When we did hit him, it blew him plumb out of the hole, and he wound up behind the log. So the gunner hit him again. Everybody in the tank started yelling 'Hit him again! He's still moving!' He was moving because of the rounds hitting him. We must have put a thousand rounds into this poor bastard."

After several attacks, the Marines pulled back so that an air strike could be brought down on the hedgerow.

Reynolds described how you frequently lose any sense of elapsed time in battle. "The NVA was right out in front of us. We were firing up quite a storm. I thought we were out there maybe five, ten minutes. When it was over and we started to pull out, I got two packs of Pall Malls, and all the cigarette butts were in the bottom of the driver's compartment. I said 'How long were we here?' and they said 'We were out here about three hours.'"

The "fast movers" incinerated the tree line, and the tanks pulled back from the ghastly mess of burned men and trees.

Operation HICKORY was to be the first real incursion into the DMZ, involving over 10,000 troops. A previous foray by 1/9 had resulted in heavy losses when the Marines were ambushed near a bunker complex. On the morning of 17 May, one of the heaviest artillery barrages of the war, followed by air strikes, pulverized the complex. Other units were not so lucky. A mortar barrage wounded virtually every member of 2/26's command group, and that night over 150 artillery rockets fired into Dong Ha destroyed critical supplies and inflicted heavy losses on 3/4 even before they could be airlifted into the field.

The next morning BLT 1/3, supported by a tank platoon, landed by helicopter and boat along the coast, against heavy resistance.

The blocking force was airlifted into the DMZ. The main force consisted of 2/9 and 2/26, supported by four platoons of tanks from Alpha and Bravo, 3rd Tank. This larger force swept into the DMZ west of Con Thein. For the main force, the operation would commence when they crossed the start line, the Trace.

As usual, losses occurred before the fighting started. A mine disabled English's tank before it could go into action. "We hit one on Hickory, just before we went across the strip. We had to sit there and patch that tank up. If (more than) the road wheels were blown off, we were screwed, because we carried an extra road wheel strapped on each side of the tank, and track blocks. If that's all the damage was, then the crewmen, with the help of the maintenance man, could put that thing back together. If anything else was damaged, a (torsion bar) or the (drive) housing was ripped off, we couldn't deal with that. They'd have to send the retriever out with some parts, which they could get out there pretty soon."

Pappy Reynolds recalled advancing across the Trace, to become part of HICKORY:

> The next thing I remember is crossing the trace and almost driving into a very large bomb crater. Probably from a B-52 Arc Light raid. The terrain seemed pretty flat. At least what I could see of it through the periscopes. The brush was fairly heavy except where it had been cleared by Arc Light strikes. Just after that our own helicopters strafed us. I remember Sgt. Hambelton in 14 coming on the open net and yelling, "You fuckers strafe us again and by god I'll return fire." We got, or at least knew we would get, some return fire, so I was driving buttoned up.
>
> We were not far above the trace, maybe about two hundred yards. When I hit the mine I was looking out the right periscope just in time to see a grunt get hit by one of my road wheels. He

> was at about 1 o'clock and maybe 50–60 feet from the tank. It probably killed him. I don't know. The next thing I recall is L/Cpl. Fornwalt, (or Cpl. Boil) the TC of 12 in front of the tank. I opened the hatch and he said, "Looks like you got a flat Pappy. Hang on and I'll get the auto club." Kind of broke the tension. I was told to stay in the tank and the rest got out to hook up the tow cables. We were maneuvered off the broken track and it was hooked by cable to the front of the tank. The escape hatch had been shaken off by the blast also and was put on the fender.[17]

In addition to wrecking the wheels, the blast of a heavy mine could twist the large steel torsion bars of the suspension system. A dragging arm would jam the track and make it impossible to move the tank. The tankers had developed a quick, though dangerous and highly unofficial, technique for removing the massive bars. You removed the end cap from the opposite end of the bar, packed a little plastic explosive onto the end of the bar, and detonated it. The explosion forced the broken bar out of the housing.

> We'd lost the first two sets of road wheels on the right side. The first one was not a problem because it was gone. But the second road wheel arm was still hanging on and we had to get it off. We rigged up a C-4 charge to blow out the torsion bar. Yelled, "fire in the hole" and set it off. When we went around to the other side of the tank, there was a grunt just standing up in his hole with about six feet of torsion bar staring him in the face. If he had not ducked he might have gotten hit by it.[18]

After a night sitting in the damaged tank, a helicopter loaded with correspondents landed nearby. One was a French photographer named Cathy Leroy. Later that day Leroy was talking to a group of Marines when a single mortar round killed two of the men she was interviewing, and wounded her and another grunt.

With two tanks damaged by mines the only way to recover them was to tow them out with other tanks. In the confusion amid the narrow trails one of the tow vehicles collided with Reynolds' tank and ripped away the heavy drive sprocket on the right side. Eventually the two crippled tanks were dragged away.

Reynolds's tank was being towed backward, dragging its broken track behind. One of the grunts assigned to accompany them for protection decided to ride the track "like a surfboard," according to Reynolds. Reynolds was stricken by one of the by-products of the C-ration diet. The hole from the missing escape hatch was too good to pass up. Reynolds was crouched over the open hole, holding a conversation with the surfing grunt, as the bizarre convoy made its way back toward Con Thien.

> Just about the time I got my trousers back on and the seat back up all hell broke lose again. We were receiving a heavy volume of fire from my left. The north side of the trace. The grunt had disappeared. The crew was yelling at me to turn on the master switch as they were traversing by hand. I did. I may have even started the engine. I don't remember. One RPG trail went by right in front of me. The two guys in the turret were yelling for me to get up in the turret. We were not moving then and somehow I got into the turret and took over as the TC. I tried to get the .50 to fire, but it would only put out about three to four rounds before jamming.[19]

The combined fire from the various tanks and the infantry drove the NVA back, and the firing died down somewhat. As always, water was a critical commodity in the intense heat, which rose above 100 degrees Fahrenheit.

> It was hot as hell and the grunts had not had a water resupply. We had seven five-gallon water cans on the tank. Some of them had shrapnel holes in them but what water we had we shared with the grunts. We kept one can inside the tank down by the gunner's feet for us.
>
> This I remember very vividly. The firing had died down. I heard a banging/rattling on the outside of the tank. I stuck my head out and there was the track-riding grunt. Banging on the water cans. I said, "What the hell you want?" He told me his buddy had been gut shot and he needed some water to put on his intestines as they were hanging out. I told him we were out of water. We'd given it all to the grunts yesterday. Then I remembered the can down by the gunner. I got the gunner to

> give it to me, and I gave it to the grunt. I ducked back down and watched him through the vision blocks. He crawled about fifty feet away dragging the can. When wham. A mortar round must have hit him right between the shoulder blades. Just a dirty black and pink explosion. His body did a little flop and just lay there from the chest down. I'll never forget that.
>
> I must have been in shock because I don't remember the rest of the trip until we got to Con Thien. We were towed around to the back of the hill and put into position overlooking the helicopter landing area. A bulldozer pushed dirt up around us and we were told to watch the area. L/Cpl. Brown's tank was about a hundred yards away and bulldozed in too.[20]

Reynolds had given away the last of the water. By his own admission never among the most tolerant of men, he was still somewhat irrational from the heat and stress.

> I saw a water trailer about two hundred yards away. From one of the tanks I got a water can without any holes in it. I went over to it to get some water. An engineer Lieutenant came running out of a bunker and started yelling at me that the water was his and I couldn't have any. I was hot, tired, and hungry, probably in shock and now pissed. I pulled out my pistol and pointed it at the water buffalo. Told him that if I couldn't get any for my people I'd shoot that thing full of holes and nobody would have any. By then there was a S/Sgt. up on the buffalo looking in to it. He told the Lt. that there was enough that they could afford to give me some. By then I was already filling the can. He probably saved me from another office hours.
>
> Sometime later that day Lt. Rivero with two tanks came over the hill. The tanks were covered with wounded and dead. They went to the helicopter-landing site. We all went down to help. One of the wounded was that blond French correspondent Cathy Leroy. About all we could do was hold ponchos over them to keep the sun off them. When the choppers came in we loaded them aboard and went back to the tanks.
>
> The next morning while we were waiting for the retriever, I went over to L/Cpl. Brown's tank. We were sitting on the tank just bullshitting when an artillery round landed about two hun-

> dred yards away. Near the water buffalo. Blew a lot of holes in it. Retribution? A little piece of shrapnel hit the tank, bounced off. Hit Brown's helmet. Fell into his flack jacket pocket, burned through and landed on his leg. He wasn't hurt, but got a little burn on his leg. We decided to wait in the tanks.[21]

The NVA had detected a certain tendency of the Marines to conduct routine sweeps of the terrain north of the cleared trace at two week or longer intervals, so the *90th NVA Regiment* began to infiltrate the region between sweeps. For Operation BUFFALO the commander of the 9th Marines ordered his 1st Battalion, supported by tanks, into the area north of Con Thien only a week after the previous sweep. There was concern that the NVA might attack Con Thien, so English's platoon, now transferred to Alpha Company, was hurriedly brought up to the base to augment the B Company platoon there, along with a platoon from SLF Alpha.

On the baking hot morning of 2 July, B Company advanced northward along Route 561, actually a narrow dirt track through a broken terrain of ancient hedgerows and fields. At about 0900 the lead elements came under sniper fire. The fight quickly escalated, with one platoon surrounded. When A Company tried to come to their aid from the west, it was also pinned in place by heavy casualties from mines and enemy fire. Artillery fire struck the B Company command group, killing most of the leadership, and the Forward Air Controller assumed command. NVA flamethrower teams moved in to ignite dry underbrush that concealed the Marines.

The battalion commander dispatched four B Company tanks and a platoon of infantry from D Company overland along the cleared trace from Con Thien. Charlie 1/9 would come by helicopter from Dong Ha, where it was serving as base security.

When the tanks turned north onto the "highway" they were hit by heavy fire, and as luck would have it the helicopters carrying C/1/9 landed smack in front of the column. Artillery fire began to fall upon both. In the confusion the battalion S-3, Captain Henry Radcliffe, grabbed a still-organized platoon from C Company and headed up the trail with the tanks.

There was little the small group could do for the ravaged B Company, but the Marines tried to evacuate the dead and wounded.

First Lieutenant Gatlin Howell, the battalion S-2, had until recently commanded one of the trapped platoons, and he made repeated trips into the flames and gunfire to bring out twenty-five wounded. Casualties were heaped onto the tanks until there was no more room, and some had to be left behind.

One platoon from A Company was cut off and forced into the underbrush. It stumbled into the carnage at B Company, and the column, burdened with dead and wounded, moved slowly back down the trail. Artillery and mortars fell on the wounded and those still moving. Two tanks struck mines, killing and wounding men nearby and temporarily halting the column. When the survivors reached C Company, more enemy artillery fire fell among the wounded. In the chaos, walking wounded started back down the trail and turned toward Con Thien. A scratch column from the base, which included English's platoon of A Company tanks, gathered them in.

By 1800 three companies and a command group from 3/9 landed east of the fighting and attacked the NVA flank, and the 1/9 units were able to withdraw down the trace. The next day English's tanks supported an attack by 3/9, which ran into even heavier fighting. "If you see all those tanks hauling bodies around, that was my tanks. I didn't have any on mine.... But they were hauling bodies back up to Con Thien, or out on the strip where they had a helipad set up to get them out. That's what we did there for several days."

Carroll said, "We had bodies all over the tanks ... the blood is draining into our engine compartment, I mean just nasty, nasty...." At Con Thien, "The reporters smelled blood. They're all over the place.... They had some good lookin' babe, she was a French reporter[22].... Then they had some big dude, this guy must have weighed four hundred freakin' pounds or some shit. They're going to put them on the tanks, and let them ride out because they can't be humpin' all the way out here.

"Well, this guy gets on my tank ... I looked at him and I started laughing. He says 'What's so damned funny, Marine?' He had a chrome snub-nose thirty-eight, with pearl handles. It just struck me as funny as hell.

"I said 'What are you going to do with *that*?'

"'Whatta you mean, Marine?'

"I said 'Where we're goin' they're givin' Purple Hearts out by the gross'."

The reporter explained that it gave him "a sense of security," to which Carroll replied, "You'll need it today, bud."

The tanks rumbled up the Trace, carrying infantry reinforcements as well as the reporters. "We go in counterattacking, and we lose two tanks in the first twenty minutes. One from my platoon hit a mine." The crews tried to remove the damaged torsion bar by blowing it out, but failed. Carroll was detailed to tow the crippled tank back to Con Thien, escorted by the dead officer's tank. They closed the damaged tank up, short-tracked it, and began the cross-country tow.

The locked road wheel was dragging against the track, and the friction soon had the rubber smoking. Carroll had volunteered to stay in-country, but the headquarters was calling for him to go home. He thought, "This is an opportune time, because I might die out here this damn week."

At Con Thien the Company Gunny began to berate Carroll for burning up the road wheel, but "I says 'Hey, Gunny, last time I saw it, you got your tank ... no track, but you got your tank.' He looked at me, shook his head, and said 'Good job there, Marine,' because he realized I made the only decision I could."

That night English "... used my canister rounds to clear me out some field of fire, because that's some pretty thick stuff down there."

The infantry of BLT 1/3 (SLF Alpha) was brought in by helicopter, but delays in unloading slowed the arrival of their tank platoon. When those tanks arrived English pulled back into Con Thien. "The lieutenant that landed with that 1/3 got killed that night. I'm sure it was an RPG. They were set up in the same place where we were." The infantry of BLT 2/3 (SLF Bravo) also was committed. Ferocious infantry fighting with stunning casualties on both sides continued through 8 July as the Marines pursued an enemy who chose to stand and fight, even counterattacking and shelling Con Thien. BUFFALO was finally suspended on 14 July.

At the 3 July roll call only 27 Marines from B/1/9 were present out of an authorized strength of 217 men. The little group of tanks had in reality done little to decide the outcome of the fight, but their ability to move through enemy fire to evacuate the dead and wounded had likely saved the company from complete annihilation. Unknown to the young Marines, it was a long tradition of protection dating back to the Pacific War.

It was not only the tanks and infantry that suffered brutal treatment at the hands of the NVA, but the vulnerable support vehicles as well.

Carroll recalled that Alpha Company lost two retrievers. “We had one tank retriever called ‘Jolly Green’ or something like that. It got RPG’ed at The Washout” and another was also lost to an RPG. “Remember tank retrievers had gasoline engines in them.... It’s bad enough to get a tank on fire with all that diesel. An M48 held 360 gallons of diesel, a lot of burning, and then the rounds start cooking off inside there.”

The enemy shelled the Marine positions with guns and rocket launchers emplaced inside the DMZ, where the Americans were forbidden to retaliate. English: “That stuff was coming in all the time. Some days we wouldn’t have anything and the next day they would fire rockets and everything. Rockets, they would always go over the hill and scare the poop out of everybody.[23] They would usually hit down on the gate side, on the south side of the hill.... They hit on the CP around in there a lot, but most of the time they went over.”

In late July Person’s platoon headed back out to Con Thien to replace English’s platoon, which was scheduled to go out on an operation with 1/9.

JJ Carroll was sent on a thirty-day leave before returning to Vietnam. On leave in the US he ran into two women he knew from high school. Their brother had just been killed in Vietnam, and they had a letter from him. “We passed each other in transit. He replaces me in that platoon, from what I’m told. He gets killed. He’s only here two weeks. Now he’s dead. That one day, July 27th, our platoon had ten or eleven casualties.”

July 27 was the day luck ran completely out for his old platoon at Con Thien. The tanks had been in almost constant operation, and were badly in need of maintenance. English: “The tanks were worn out, the tracks were completely shot. We’d go out on an operation, and we wouldn’t do anything, just make a sharp turn and the track would break.” English and the Platoon Leader, 2nd Lt. John Brock, decided to pool the crews and assemble the tanks in an open area near the dangerous south gate for maintenance. Normally this would have been a relatively safe area, but after long practice the NVA artillery observers had virtually every inch of the combat base plotted. Still, the NVA artillery was hardly good enough to hit a pinpoint target, so sheer bad luck would play a role in what happened.

The three tanks were drawn up in a triangle on the hard-packed lateritic clay with the crews hard at work, when a single artillery round whistled over and impacted well to the south. By some accounts an artillery officer warned them that the NVA had the site plotted precisely, but English does not recall the warning.[24] Some of the new men dove under the tanks, but the more experienced kept working, made blasé by the continuous shelling. The sheepish younger men went back to work.

Seconds later a salvo of artillery bracketed the tanks, and every man in the group went down in a fraction of a second. Three men were killed outright, and another died the next day. English was thrown under a tank, and Lt. Brock and six other Marines were wounded. The heavy section had been eliminated as a functional command.[25]

Barnett Person's platoon replaced English's in the sweep into the DMZ, west of Con Thien. The sweep was the end phase of Operation KINGFISHER, destined to go down as another of the bloodiest episodes of the DMZ war. On the morning of 28 July, 2/9, accompanied by the tank platoon, three Ontos, three Amtracs, and a platoon of engineers, swept toward the Song Ben Hai, the border with North Vietnam. The column guided along another typical national road, Route 606, which Person said "looked like a little old bicycle trail" sandwiched between the main river and a tributary. Somehow the staff planners had overlooked the large tributary.

The initial plan was to turn east and follow the south bank of the main river. Ominously, infantry flankers noted bunkers and spider holes scattered about the terrain. "Going up it wasn't bad at all.... After we researched the bridge, and the bridge wasn't able to hold tanks, we had to set up out there all night.... I knew something was going to happen because we were getting artillery and air strikes all night long, right outside where we were. That morning they came and told us we were going to have to go back out the same way." This violated one of the fundamental rules of the war: never return by the same route lest you fall into an ambush. As the Marines set into their night perimeter near an abandoned hamlet, the NVA were already filtering into the area athwart the return route, occupying positions prepared even before the Marines swept through the area.

At 1000 the next morning the column moved back along a trail toward the cleared trace. Person, with two tanks, brought up the rear of the column, with Hotel Company. At about 1115 the enemy detonated an aircraft bomb buried in the trail, halting the column. Heavy fire split the column into several small perimeters, and the vehicles were restricted to the narrow trails. "The first bunch (E/2/9) went out, they did pretty good. They got through. But the second one, they caught the devil up there. From there on back they had to fight every inch of the way."

The tanks bulled through the mayhem on the road. "I met this Ontos commander coming back with some of his people laying across the hood of the Ontos, after they got killed. He stopped and he said 'Gunny, you better be careful. They're throwing RPGs up there like they're goin' out of style.' I just kind of waved and said 'Okay Lieutenant, thanks a lot. Don't worry. We'll do it.'"

Tank commanders almost always fought their vehicles with the cupola hatch open for better visibility, as seeing the enemy provided better protection than any armor. Person was riding with his cupola hatch ajar, looking out and gripping the hatch rim with his hand.

"About that time I caught an RPG right in the front, 'WHAM!' It didn't do no damage because it hit the front slope. Caught a little shrapnel in my hand and stuff.' The blast also wounded the driver. "The Lieutenant took off in the lead tank. Number One, Two, and Three, they finally got through there.[26] Four and Five, I had the fifth tank, we caught hell, so I called the fourth tank and I told him 'We're going to clean this road.' I told him take the left flank and I'd take the right flank because we had Hotel Company right with us. I made sure there was no infantry out in the bush." The tanks moved forward shooting machine guns, canister and HE blindly into the dense growth and hedgerows. "We cleared that bush for about a hundred and fifty yards up, just firing, firing."

Person then turned around and went back to Hotel Company. "I told the [Hotel] CO 'Well, I know it's clear for a hundred and fifty yards,' and it was." The tank moved back along the road again, and after they reached the end of the cleared zone "Good God A'mighty! Got nasty again. It was nasty the rest of the evening. And the night."

Over the radio Person could hear the battalion commander calling in repeated air strikes and artillery fire from Camp Carroll on both sides of the road. "They called and said, 'How close do you want it, Colonel?', and he said, 'Close as you can get it.'"

Shrapnel was flying across the road from both sides. "I heard the Colonel call and say, 'Hey, move out a little bit right and left! I want it close but that's too damned close!'"

Person's brother was a Gunnery Sergeant with the 105mm artillery at Camp Carroll, and Barnett had visited with him to explain they were going into the DMZ. Camp Carroll was being shelled by the NVA in an attempt to suppress artillery support for the Marines in the DMZ. The brother told Person, "He said 'Oh, hell!' and broke for his gun. Some of the people said 'Where are you going Gunny?' He said 'I got to get to my gun, my brother's out there.'

"I got hit two more times with an RPG.... I got wounded a second time. That's when I really got wounded on that one.... I got caught in the neck, and back, and everything."

Person was standing in the cupola with the hatch open when the tank hit a mine, but it did no significant damage. After a second strike from an RPG "[concussion] blew me completely out of the tank. It just went up, Boom! The hatch came forward and hit me in back of the head. I caught shrapnel in the hand, I caught shrapnel in my leg, because it came right through the side of my turret.

"It killed my gunner. Hit him right in the middle section." The hit also sprayed hot metal into the loader's eyes, and wounded the driver again.

The extra man who was the acting tank commander when Person was away was riding on the Platoon Leader's vehicle. "He told the lieutenant, 'I got to go back there and get on that tank with Gunny Person, because I think everybody back there is either dead or wounded.' He jumped off the tank and ran back there and jumped in my tank. He replaced the loader, because he was hit in the eyes and face." The driver was already driving with one eye.

Despite the damage and wounded crews, the tanks managed to fight their way out to the landing zone to the south. Hotel Company had no chance of making it through the maelstrom with the tanks, but established a defensive position for the night. Person's two tanks were loaded with ten or fifteen dead and wounded, including a "good friend of mine, he was the First Sergeant of Hotel Company... named Mike Dial. His leg got shot off out there."

Much later an infantry officer told Person that once the tanks departed, the enemy fire died down, "and they laid in there all night. The next morning Colonel Kerns told them 'Mount up. We're going to walk out of here.' They put the rest of the company, and the rest of the battalion, whatever they had left out in the road, and they walked out. Didn't get a round fired at them."

Despite Person's wounds, "When we got to the landing zone I helped unload the dead out of my tank. My gunner. Got my loader out of there. With the help of one guy who came over in particular, helped me pull Lance Corporal Dewey out of my tank; he was my gunner.

"After that I kind of hopped off of there.... They got my name and shot me right on that helicopter." Everyone on Person's tank was evacuated, so the Platoon Leader assigned men from the other tanks to limp the damaged vehicles back to Con Thien. "I went to Danang, and from there to the [hospital ship] *Sanctuary*, and from the *Sanctuary* I went to Guam. That was the end of my tour." As for the hospital at Danang, Person said, "It was just like a vacation tour back there. People had picnics back there. Damn! They had a club and all of that junk. But they had to work back there. I know they were bringing in those helicopters, medevacs, were coming in right and left. I had to give them people credit back there, they definitely knew their job."

The lead element, E/2/9, fought through and linked up with a relief force, M/3/4, moving overland from Con Thien. Unable to move under the burden of numerous casualties, the isolated companies and platoons dug in for the night. The NVA launched attacks all through the night, advancing through the protective artillery fire, but melted away before dawn.

En route back to Vietnam in August, JJ Carroll ran into an acquaintance at Camp Hansen. "I said, 'Well, how's the platoon doing?' He says, 'JJ, there ain't no platoon. They split what was left of it up'." Carroll was sent back to Con Thien, arriving at the end of the month.

The NVA were determined to contest every sort of American activity, and every one of the routine truck convoys required to support daily activities had to run a gauntlet of mines and ambushes. Tank units stationed at points along the highways were tasked with both protecting the groups of grunts and engineers who daily swept the roads for mines, and responding to attacks on the logistical convoys.

On 2 September JJ Carroll and Ken Bores were in a three-tank section from 1st Platoon, Alpha Company assigned to escort the daily road sweep from Con Thien to Charlie Two and back again. India 3/4 was the assigned infantry force that day.[27] On the return trip to Con Thien the infantry found a command detonated mine in the road and began to follow the wire into the trees. As they approached the tree line, the enemy detonated another mine. Carroll: "Wham! All of a sudden we're moving forward. My tank driver ... [Bores] he had the presence of mind just as this one RPG came at us to put it in reverse and back up, and it landed short of us. Then all shit's going down, and we're making it to the tree line with these grunts.... Some of them got all shot up."

One badly wounded grunt was down in the fire-swept road, so

Carroll had Bores pull the tank up over him. Bores dropped his escape hatch, grabbed the grunt by the belt, and hauled him inside. They repeated this maneuver several times.

When reinforcements from M/3/4 arrived the tanks and infantry drove into the tree line. The grunts piled their dead and wounded onto the tanks and hauled them back out to the road where helicopters could land, then the tanks returned to launch a counterattack against several identified bunkers. Like many battles in Vietnam, both sides began to pile on. A new officer with Mike 3/4 assured Carroll that the enemy had no anti-tank weapons, which caused Carroll to conclude he was an idiot.

In the confusion, Carroll realized he had not put on his flak jacket, and pulled it on. "I put all the HE rounds on five-second delay so they would penetrate the bunkers and then blow. Air strikes were coming in so close on us that you could feel the air sucking out of the tank."

Two tanks went in with a frontal assault. The third could only provide covering machine gun fire. A canister round had broken open in the breech, dumping hundreds of steel balls into the breech and tube, disabling the main gun.

The loader was firing his coaxial machine gun by hand since the firing solenoid was broken. He had fired up all the ammunition in the ready boxes, and was stooping to recover ammo from the deck boxes. A ruptured cartridge jammed the coax, so he cleared it and pulled the charging handle back to chamber a fresh round.

From the driver's compartment Bores sighted an RPG team and yelled, "One o'clock! One o'clock!" Carroll grabbed the override and swung the turret. The main gun fired and vaporized the RPG team and nearby NVA infantry. The RPG team got their rocket away before dying.

Carroll: "They fired another RPG, and that hit right under the [coaxial] machine gun, and then came in and lit up the turret. I thought we were on fire. I'm lookin' up at the hatch, and I'm seeing like a red glow....

"I'm getting out of the hatch, and 'peoww, peoww'... rifle fire. I roll on back in the tank." It flashed through Carroll's mind that this was like a John Wayne movie. "Then I looked down and I'm soaked in solid blood. I had like forty pieces of shrapnel through me."

At first, "I didn't even feel it. I was stunned. But then when the pain set in they shot me up with morphine. Carroll was evacuated to Dong

Ha (which was under artillery fire), then to the big hospital at Phu Bai, where he developed a threatening blood clot in his right leg. "You could hit my leg, it was like tapping wood." He was sent to Danang and then to the hospital ship *Sanctuary* offshore. Rather than evacuate him to the US, the Corps thought "Oh, we can get some more use out of this guy."

On 7 September Pappy Reynolds, still driving B11, was stationed at a position called 'Payable,' on Highway 9 south of The Rockpile.[28] The platoon had a brand new lieutenant who had arrived only days before, and Reynolds did not even know his name. John Macovitch (spelling uncertain) was the gunner, and Jesse 'Grif' Griffin, the platoon mechanic, was the loader.

That morning a big convoy rumbled through, westbound toward Ca Lu and the new base at Khe Sanh. A short time later word came over the radio that the convoy was caught in a massive ambush. The reaction force raced west, not knowing that the ambush force had let the convoy fight through and was waiting for the reaction force.

Rounding a bend in the road the tank ran into the ambush zone, with Army M42 Dusters and grunts firing in all directions. Reynolds veered around a Duster to get to where the infantry was fighting up front. The tank's main gun fired one round to the left of the road, and the new officer called for canister.

As Griffin shoved the round into the chamber, he heard and felt the distinctive sound of the thin metal walls of the shell crunching, spilling steel balls into the chamber. The main gun was jammed, and several efforts to clear it by rapidly raising and dropping the tube failed.

The lieutenant told Reynolds to back the tank into the protection of a ditch, and the other three crewmembers got out, assembled the long cleaning rod, and ran it down the tube to clear away the steel balls. All the while Reynolds was watching a ground-level view of the fight. Grunts were being hit, and rounds were striking the turret above his head. A Duster pulled up and began to fire its twin automatic 40mm guns with their distinctive poom-poom-poom sound.

The crew remounted the tank and Reynolds pulled back up onto the road in front of the Duster, just in time to see three RPG rockets pass from left to right across his bow. They were coming from the 'friendly' side of the road. The officer stood up in the cupola to talk to a grunt, and an NVA hidden in a shallow hole on the right side of the road popped up and fired. One round tore through the back of the officer's flak jacket and came out the left side of his chest.

In the next few seconds a corpsman shot the NVA through both legs and the grunts dragged him out of the hole, throwing him into the road. The Lieutenant had a sucking chest wound, with air flowing uselessly in and out of his wounds as he struggled to breathe. Griffin stuffed the plastic wrappers of field dressings into the holes and closed them as best he could. Macovitch dismounted to tell the infantry what had happened and to advise them the tank was leaving.

Macovitch directed Reynolds to make a Y-turn, but when he started to back up the grunts started "yelling about a 'Gook' in the road." Watching the Lieutenant struggling for his life, Griffin yelled at Reynolds to keep going and the tank backed over the NVA soldier.

About a hundred yards from the ambush site the tank overtook a truck loaded with wounded, and the load of wounded was moved to the tank. As the loaded tank raced toward The Rockpile, Reynolds was driving with one hand and holding a wounded grunt onto the front of the tank with the other. When they came upon one of the numerous small bridges, and its bumpy bypass through the creek bed, Reynolds made a quick decision. The climb up the far side would probably cause some of the wounded to slip off the tank. Gambling that the narrow bridge might not collapse under the weight of the tank, he told the wounded man to hold on, grabbed the wheel with both hands, and floored the accelerator. It worked, as the bridge held.

When the tank pulled into Payable, other Marines began to unload its burden. Reynolds watched a truck pull in with another load of wounded. When it stopped, blood flowed out of the cargo bed onto the ground.

Blood and debris had flowed down onto the hot tank engine in the baking heat, and the stench was too much for Reynolds. He could not face the task of cleaning the tank. "I don't remember who did it, but I don't think it was the crew."

Even the fall weather seemed to conspire with the NVA. The monsoon was fast approaching, and everyone feared a major NVA attack under the cover of the incessant rains. Jim Coan was the brand new platoon leader for 1st Platoon, A Company, 3rd Tank that was helping defend Con Thien. Coan had six years prior enlisted service in the Reserves, and had arrived in Vietnam the previous month. He had replaced Lt. Tom Barry about a week earlier.[29]

One night in September it began to rain, a drizzle developing into a steady downpour. Coan had orders to take a light section and a squad of grunts out the next morning, 16 September, to protect the daily mine sweep to C-2, but was delayed when he could not locate the engineers. After being berated by a 3/9 staff officer, he located the sodden engineers, and they all set off down the road in the downpour. Coan was worried about the soaking rain, since it meant his tanks were for all practical purposes trapped on the narrow strip of road covered with crushed stone.

Near C-2, and just before the stream crossing called Rocky Ford, they encountered the grunts of 2/9 trudging north in the rain to reinforce Con Thien. The engineers had installed large steel culverts to carry the stream runoff so that vehicles no longer had to ford the stream, but the culverts were inadequate for the continuing heavy rain. Coan eyed the large lake that had formed on the western, or upstream, side of the causeway and the brown water jetting out of the downstream ends of the culverts.

On the return trip an hour later the grunts and engineers were riding on the tanks when they drew up at the stream crossing. Part of the fill had collapsed, but grunts from the long E/2/9 column were still crossing. A brief conference with the driver of the other tank, Ken 'Piggy' Bores, who had a year's experience driving in Vietnam, determined that it was 'now or never.' When Coan climbed back onto the tank and turned to grab his helmet from the gypsy rack, his passengers were clearly terrified.

Just before the tank started to move the fill burst in an explosion of mud and water, hurling the massive steel culverts that would support a tank end over end into the air. Where the causeway had been was now a hundred-foot-wide roaring flood. Coan realized in horror that some of the grunts had been swept away. Most were rescued, but a corpsman was missing and the grunts were frantic with grief.

The tanks returned to C-2 to sit out the storm as best they could, joined on 18 September by a blade tank that had been trapped on the wrong side of the flooded Cam Lo Bridge to the south. The Rocky Ford would henceforth be known as The Washout.

When the weather broke on 22 September a jeep bearing several officers, followed by a retriever, appeared from the south. The exhausted senior officer, a Captain Jacobsen, explained that Coan's tanks were to escort the retriever north. R.B. English's 5th Platoon tanks had gotten mired in flooded fields near Con Thien, and English medevaced out with an injured back. Despite major efforts, one was still stuck. Another

The first vehicles and infantry of the 9th Marine Expeditionary Brigade landed across the beaches south of Danang. The Marines landed in battle configuration, though it was an administrative landing, and were greeted by Army advisors and young women distributing flower garlands. The vehicle in the background is an all-terrain forklift of the Shore Party Detachment. (NARA)

Tanks A11 and A13 of the 3rd Platoon, A Company, 3rd Tank Battalion, which accompanied the 9th MEB landing in March 1965. Note how clean and uncluttered these early-war vehicles are. (NARA)

The M67A2 was the last of the flame tanks, and used only by the Marines. Though popular with its crews, its tactical utility was limited by the need for special support vehicles. (NARA)

The M51 VTR (Vehicle, Tank Retriever) could easily tow two M48A3s at once. They were sent into action alongside the tanks, and were often in the thick of battle. (NARA)

The "blade tank" was the tank company Executive Officer's vehicle, used for obstacle breaching and hasty construction. This vehicle is engaged in a Civic Action program, knocking down vegetation around a hamlet to reduce the fire danger in the dry season. (MCRC)

The Ontos tank destroyers of the Anti-Tank Battalions and the LVTP-5 amphibian tractors were the stable mates of the tanks. After 1967 the Anti-Tank Battalions were reduced to companies and included as a company in the tank battalions. (NARA)

Crews and tanks of Lt. Ed Mels's 3rd Platoon, A Company, 3rd Tank after the Danang landings. Mels is the man pointing with his arm. (NARA)

SGT. ROBERT EMBESI

The vision of the driver of the M48A3 tanks was often blocked by mud or dust that accumulated on the vision blocks, or by tall vegetation. The driver usually operated the tank with his head exposed, and sometimes drove standing up. (NARA)

Though the tanks could negotiate almost any terrain, few of the bridges in Vietnam could accommodate their weight. Streams too deep to ford had to be crossed by ferries or pontoon bridges until stronger bridges were constructed by the engineers at a few critical crossings. (NARA)

As in both World War II and Korea, mines were the primary threat to the tanks. The shape of the M48A3 hull made it more resistant, saving the lives of numberless crewmen. This 1st Battalion tank struck a mine south of Danang. Note the missing gypsy rack. (NARA)

Operation STARLITE was the first of the sweep operations that would become so emblematic of the war. This tank is from the 3rd Platoon, Alpha Company, 3rd Tank Battalion. It is operating with infantry from Battalion Landing Team 3/3 and helicopters. (NARA)

A tank from 3rd Tank Battalion fords a stream in Elephant Valley as the Marines extend their TAOR away from the populous coastal strip in April 1965. Note the unusual battalion marking, the 3rd Division's caltrop inside the yellow arrowhead. (MCRC)

By the beginning of 1966 General William Westmoreland was exerting ever-increasing pressure on the Marines to shift away from their pacification efforts to seek combat with the VC and NVA. His single metric for success was the body count. (NARA)

The lack of a clear doctrine for tank employment led to increased use of the tanks for local security duty, like this vehicle in a tank slot at Camp Carroll, south of the DMZ. (NARA)

The increasing number of sweep operations contributed to the deployment of tanks in detached two- or three-tank sections, like this tank and Ontos supporting Hotel Company 2/1 on Operation JAY in 1966. (NARA)

Operation PRAIRIE in February 1966 extended the fighting into the rugged and heavily vegetated foothills along the western DMZ. Helicopters were increasingly utilized for evacuation of wounded and re-supply. (NARA)

The rectangle bounded by Gio Linh, Dong Ha, Cam Lo and Con Thien became infamous as Leatherneck Square. Deserted by civilians, it was the scene of almost conventional warfare between the Marines and the NVA. (MCRC)

The region south of the DMZ contained centuries-old hedgerows that channeled the tanks and created box-like killing zones in overgrown fields. Overhanging limbs like the ones from this hedgerow east of Con Thien could conceal deadly booby traps. (NARA)

Operations along the DMZ were a continuing series of sweeps like Operation KINGFISHER, July 1967. (NARA)

First Tank Battalion adopted the practice of "sky-mounting" machine guns atop the cupola to replace the unreliable cupola gun. This is typical of the early improvised mounts, simply strapping and sandbagging the tripod to the cupola. (John Bartusevics)

A heavy section from 3rd Tank advances along one of the "roads" in the northern ICTZ during Operation RUSH. Tankers like driver Wally Young discovered the hard way that local wildlife could take up residence in objects like the tarps stored on the track guards. (NARA)

Blade tank were sometimes used to help recover other tanks, like this one that has become bogged in deep mud south of Danang. (MCRC)

Left: An engineer dozer drags two mine-damaged tanks out of a remote area south of Danang, September 1967. (NARA) Right: A burned-out ARVN tank on the outskirts of Hue City. In the background is the cemetery from which the unit took sniper fire that inflicted the first tank crew casualty of the battle. (Carl Fleischmann)

Tank maintenance tasks could be better accomplished by several crews working together, like this group unching out a gun tube in Operation INCINERATOR near Chu Lai. (NARA)

Casualties could be heavy when a tank with infantry riding outside struck a large mine. Marines and Navy medical corpsmen attend to the wounded after a mine strike. (John Bartusevics)

A medevac lifts off carrying the more severely wounded. After a mine strike, VC or NVA would often lay in wait to ambush the helicopters. (John Bartusevics)

Tank A51 of 1st Tank Battalion and infantry fighting along the walls of The Citadel in the old city of Hue. A51 was Captain Casey's "personal" command tank, but the Headquarters Platoon tanks were more typically used as replacements. (MCRC)

Tank C23 from 2nd Platoon, C Company, 1st Tank. The artwork on the spotlight cover, an ace of spades with DEATH DEALERS, was unique to this platoon. The tanks were named after the Horsemen of the Apocalypse, in this case DISASTER. (NARA)

C52, the dozer tank from Headquarters Platoon, C Company, 1st Tank leads a column of Amtracs toward Go Noi Island. (NARA)

The tropical vegetation had almost reclaimed Route 9 to Khe Sanh during the short interval during which it was closed. Vegetation encroached onto the roadway, bridges and fills were wrecked, and it was liberally sewn with mines by the NVA. (NARA)

Infantry and a tank caught in an ambush during Operation ALLAN BROOK, May 1968. The dense vegetation and minimal road network made Go Noi Island a VC stronghold for most of the war. (NARA)

This 1st Tank Battalion vehicle struck a mine on Operation MAMELUKE THRUST. The man at center is using the heavy lever bar with the socket wrench used to remove road wheel bolts. (NARA)

Two 3rd Tank vehicles negotiate a typical bridge bypass near Con Thien. The tanks were far too heavy to negotiate most of the bridges in Vietnam, and tanks crossed streams through such diversions. These were a prime location for mines. Note the angle iron fuel can rack and the loader's folding lawn chair on the closer tank. (NARA)

A tank from C Company, 3rd Tank leaves the Con Thien base for a daily road sweep south toward the C-2 combat base. (NARA)

Retrievers Bull (left) and Bandit pull Anthony Rogers's burned out tank from a huge mine crater. It was wrecked during an "Alice's Restaurant" re-supply run for infantry in late 1969. Two crewmen were killed, and two were wounded. Rogers escaped unscathed since an officer had "bumped" him from his normal position. (NARA)

Joe Sleger acquired M113s from the Army to mount a mobile command group. The M113s were also used as logistical carriers and infantry carriers in the dangerous Leatherneck Square area. (NARA)

A tank from C Company 1st Tank with infantrymen from G Company 2/5 during Operation BARREN GREEN, July 1970. The tanks were used to crush the standing corn crop in the Arizona Territory. (NARA)

section was mired up outside Gio Linh. The company's tanks were trapped or buried in mud all over the operational area.

The column started north, and debated how to bypass the washed-out causeway. Coan's A11 went first, followed closely by the retriever. On the far side the big retriever headed off parallel to the road, while Coan's driver, DuBose, cut toward the hardtop. Coan warned DuBose to follow the retriever, but it was too late. The NVA had been busy during the rains, and a mine tore off two road wheels. Then A13 crossed the stream, but despite following in the tracks of the two others, it too struck a mine, blocking the ford.

The retriever trundled off to attend to English's stuck tank, leaving Coan and two inexperienced sergeants (one was a former Amtrac crewman, the other was new to Vietnam) to effect repairs. A sniper interrupted the brutal work until a crewman cranked off a dozen rounds from the .50 caliber, discouraging him.

The retriever returned before dark with the recovered 5th Platoon tank to find Coan's tanks still stuck. For some reason one 5th Platoon tank decided to cross the stream, and plunged in upstream of the ford. It took water over the bow and into the driver's space, but began to claw its way up the far bank. Then it stalled and rolled majestically backward, coming to rest in a cloud of steam with the engine deck awash. All three tanks, and the retriever, were trapped.

Arrangements were made for a squad of grunts to watch the tanks through the night, but they found that an ARC LIGHT strike was planned for the area the next morning. The disconsolate Jacobsen told Coan to take his men to Con Thien on foot. The crews disabled and stripped the tanks and distributed their food, including a case of fresh apples scrounged at C-2. The ragged group of grunts and orphaned tankers set off up the road in the pitch-dark night, each man holding the belt of the man in front. After a harrowing march, they spent the rest of the night sleeping in the mud with 2/9's grunts outside Con Thien.

Two tanks came from C-2 later that night and managed to drag the 5th Platoon tank out of the stream, but could not cross over to recover the others. During the night the NVA pumped numerous RPGs into the abandoned vehicles. A13 was recovered. A11 was written off as a total loss but later dragged away. The enormous M51 retriever was burned out and never recovered, a monument to what the company came to call the Washout Fiasco.

At the start of the monsoon rains described by Jim Coan, Pappy

Reynolds was with 1st Platoon, Bravo Company, 3rd Tank stationed at a small outlying position along Highway 9 near The Rockpile. The tank crew was housed in a hole in the ground topped by boards and a leaky canvas tarp. On a night that it rained particularly hard the tankers took turns pushing up sags in the canvas to make the water run off. Eventually somebody on tarp watch dozed off, and about 0300 the whole thing collapsed under the weight of the water.

After spending the rest of the night shivering in the tank, the crew decided to build a more luxurious hooch. Reynolds, an inveterate scrounger from his infantry days, got a ride on the mail run to the battalion rear area at Dong Ha.

One of the interesting aspects of military life is that you can often steal anything so long as you have enough men to carry it away, and someone to be in charge. Reynolds looked up an old friend in a heavy Motor Transport battalion, and arranged for a truck and driver. Then he borrowed six new men—replacements—from 2/9, and a set of Master Sergeant chevrons from someplace.

The "working party" drove to the Seabee compound, where Reynolds presented an old trip ticket he found in the truck, and bluffed his way past the guard. The driver, another more experienced Marine, "has this all figured out and he's starting to get into it." As the working party was loading up plywood sheets, a young naval ensign asked if he could help and Reynolds replied, "No thank you, I have my own working party and Captain So-and-So is getting the paperwork processed now." The two parted with a salute. The group finished loading a large load, thanked the gate guard, and drove away.

A few sheets left at the 9th Marines paid for the working party, and a few more at Motor T sufficed for the rent of the truck. The truck joined a convoy headed for Payable, and dropped out at The Rockpile. The truck had to stay overnight, and the grunt company commander was irate at having a truck—a lucrative target—spend the night on his hill. More plywood soothed his temper.

The plywood was enough to build better accommodations with even more left over for the infantry. Unfortunately, the continuing rains flooded access to the position, and the whole group had to move on to Payable, on Highway 9, leaving most of the wood behind. Several weeks later Reynolds was sitting in a four-holer at Payable when a young Marine entered and addressed him as "Top." He told the baffled

Reynolds that he had been on the working party at Dong Ha. Thinking quickly, Reynolds explained that he was a thief, and since he [Reynolds] was working undercover with Counter-Intelligence, he had better keep his mouth shut. "I hope he survived the war."[30]

As the tankers settled in at Payable they grew tired of waiting for the occasional trip back to Dong Ha for a hot shower, since at Payable everyone had to bathe in a cold stream at the base of the hill. The platoon soon constructed a single-stall shower, including an immersion heater donated one night by an Army mess hall.

The infantry battalion commander asked the tankers to build him a shower, and they complied. Meanwhile the grunts were still hiking down the muddy hillside to bathe in the cold river. One night the officer took a nice hot shower and went to bed in the dark. The next morning when he started to shave, he was bright blue. Someone had dumped grape KoolAid™ into the hot shower water, and the dye had set permanently into his skin.

Reynolds was careful to point out that the tankers didn't do it. "Coincidence? Maybe, but by the time the color wore off there was a hot shower unit in operation down by the river for the rest of the Battalion."[31]

Also during the stay at Payable, Reynolds decided to try and make raisin jack, an alcoholic concoction that many tankers try to make—once. He somehow acquired the usual ingredients—raisins, sugar, and yeast—mixed it in a five-gallon water can, and let it ripen in the sun for about a week.

When they opened the bulging can, the stench was predictably horrible. When they strained the gruel through a coffee can lined with field dressings, they noticed that it had eaten the enamel lining from the five-gallon can. The crew quickly learned to mix the vicious product with C-ration fruit.

One night an infantry lieutenant paid a visit, cup in hand. The tankers shared about a third of a cup while they exchanged lies. The lieutenant excused himself and left, but when one of the others left the bunker, he came back in laughing. The officer was lying face down in the mud outside.

Reynolds said, "We took pity on him, picked him up and propped him up on the side of the bunker. He could sleep it off there without drowning in the mud. He was gone in the morning."[32]

A LOOMING STORM

After a juvenile scrape with the law in Montgomery Alabama, Wally Young appeared before a local magistrate. "The judge, I guess, was an ex-Marine himself. I went before him and he asked me, 'If I were to let you out of here today, how long would it take you to get down to there to the Post Office and join the US Marine Corps?'" He recalls the day exactly, since it was the day of the Selma to Montgomery Civil Rights march in 1965.

Young replied not long, since the Post Office was only about two blocks away. At the Post Office he asked the recruiter what he had to offer. "His name was Gunny John Smith. He told me 'Basically, I don't have anything to offer you, but: if you were to decide you were lucky enough to join the Marine Corps, and you were lucky enough to pass the exams and all, what I will offer you is one hour sleep and one meal a day.' Basically that's what I ended up getting up there on that DMZ."

Young was sent to Vietnam in October 1967 and, ominously, "Friday the 13th was my first full day in Vietnam."

After five weeks JJ Carroll was discharged from the *Sanctuary*, back to Con Thien to join R.B. English and his platoon. "I'm there like two or three days and arty comes in. I tried to get on the tank and I hit the light mount, it has a protector on it, and split my leg right open again. R.B. just looked at it and said, 'Pull your pants up.' Some of the wounds weren't totally healed." English sent him back with orders to tell them, "Don't send you back up here, because that's just going to get infected."

Carl Fleischmann was in high school when his parents received word that his older brother had been wounded in Vietnam. "They came to the school to get me, and the student counselor was there. I was pretty pissed, because my brother and I, we got along, we still get along pretty good. I left the school and I took off. I went to Danbury Connecticut. I was living in Newtown, Connecticut, to join the Navy." In his teenage mind, he chose the Navy "because they had the biggest guns. They had battleships. That's what I pictured. I was going to get someone with the biggest guns, and I was going to blow Vietnam up."

As in many such enlistments the Navy recruiter was out of the office, and the Marine recruiter offered to take him to lunch while he waited. The legal drinking age in Connecticut was twenty-one years of age, "but New York I believe was sixteen. So he took me across the borderline into New York [and] we had a couple of drinks. I got home the next day. I woke up from being sick. My mom said, 'Are you all right?'

"I said 'Boy, I feel horrible.'

"She says 'Are you happy?'

I said 'No, I feel sick.' She said 'No, are you happy? You joined the Marine Corps.'

"I went '*What?*' I said 'When is this all going on?'

"She said 'Your bus leaves in a few hours.' So that's how I got in the Marine Corps."

Fleischmann completed boot camp, ITR, and tank training, but he could not be sent to Vietnam. His brother had recuperated and returned to duty, and at the time all siblings in a family were not allowed to serve simultaneously in a combat zone. This policy dated from 1942, when the cruiser USS *Juneau* was sunk in the Solomon Islands, killing all five Sullivan brothers. He marked time in a .50-caliber machine gun school, interrogation school, and other training until his brother returned. In late 1967 the two brothers met at an airport in California and went to Disneyland. "I put him on a plane the next day for Connecticut. That following day I was ordered to El Toro (Marine Air Station), out of California, headed for Vietnam."

With the enormous buildup of manpower, the Corps had started flying troops to and from Vietnam on chartered airliners. Fleischmann traveled on a Continental Airlines charter, with a stop in Hawaii and an unscheduled stop in Okinawa caused by a typhoon.

Everyone on the flight was young and fresh to Vietnam. At Danang, "They shuffled us around from tent to tent to tent. They didn't give us any weapons. When we first landed, we had incoming rockets into the airfield in Danang." Fleischmann was the beneficiary of a two-day orientation and acclimation period. "A pamphlet, which I still have, and stuff like that. Then they assigned us where we were to go to pick up our ride to wherever we were going. I was assigned to Third Tank Battalion, Third Marine Division, which was in Phu Bai, H&S Company." Unlike most early arrivals, Fleischmann flew into Phu Bai.

Because of his extensive training, Fleischmann was assigned to H&S Company as a machine gun specialist, and to crew on H52, the battalion Executive Officer's tank. Tanks crewed by senior officers also had an NCO tank commander who ran the tank, supervised the crew when the officer was not aboard, and took care of daily maintenance and other activities. On the whole the battalion officers were occupied with administrative functions, and the two headquarters gun tanks were used as spares.

"We were held back for support of the bases, and if any of the other tanks in Alpha, Bravo, or Charlie Company had to come back for maintenance, our tank would go up and replace it. That was our primary function. But for some reason, H five-two, we never got any assignments like that." Many of the crewmen agitated for transfer to a line company, but even when a new batch of men came in, Fleischmann remained stuck in H&S.

PFC Fleischmann was at first a human spare part until two other men rotated back to the US, and he became a regular member of the crew, the driver. At six feet tall and weighing "about 110 pounds," it was a tight fit.

The other duties included bunker watch, night patrols and listening posts. "Phu Bai was very, very quiet. We had a couple of snipers and stuff like that." Fleischmann used a Super-8 movie camera to film one occasion when they located a sniper and blasted away with the main cannon.

"It was pretty fun back then, because again we were kids, and that was the first action we had. We were very, very excited. Nobody ever got wounded. We had rounds come in, but we never knew of anybody that got wounded. To us it was still like 'Wow, this is pretty cool.'

"Even though it was that way, we were still scared, but to us it was an excitement."

Dan Wokaty had extended his tour and stayed with B Company in 1966. After duty in Japan and an assignment in the US, he returned to Vietnam in November 1967, and was assigned to A Company, 1st Tank. The unit was assigned to his old stomping grounds in the same area.

Captain Conwill Casey had not yet taken over the company, and Wokaty was flabbergasted at what he found when he went to his platoon. "Each tank crew had their own woman in the bunker."

When he quizzed one of the leaders, he was told the men had had a hard time, and "'we're letting them relax here.'

"I said, 'Did you ever stop to think about how they could kill those people, you know?' As soon as I found out that, I ran them all out of there, which was probably the wrong thing to do." He told the platoon leader that "I was the Platoon Sergeant, and if he didn't want me for his platoon sergeant he could just tell me or send me back to battalion, and I'd go. But I said there wasn't going to be no females hanging around there as long as I was the platoon sergeant." Wokaty does not think his actions made him very popular.

In December R.B. English completed his tour. Long after, he thought that the only saving grace to repeatedly fighting over the same ground was that "We got used to knowing where we were going.... I had a map that when Lt. Beck left the first time, it had acetate over it. You could write, and put grease pencil marks on it. I had every spot we ever hit a mine, had all that stuff on there. Instead of bringing that map home with me, I gave it to this young Staff Sergeant that relieved me, Patterson."

The endless string of operations would enter the official history books, but for Marines like English the names were irrelevant. "I went down and went over and saw this clerk. He says, 'Okay Gunny, what operations were you on?' I says, 'You gotta be shittin' me!' So he named them all off, and I said yeah, I was in this one, and that one.... My service record book, I think it has Kingfisher, and Buffalo, and Prairie II through IV, and whatever."

The replacement and rotation system churned relentlessly. Karl Fontenot grew up in a small town near Lafayette, Louisiana and had served as a junior tank officer in the ferocious battles for control of the JAMESTOWN Line in the last days of the Korean War. He went to Vietnam in 1967 as a Major and was the XO of 3rd Tank before being transferred to the Division staff. As the year came to a close, he was scheduled to rotate back to become the CO of the battalion.

On 3 November Jerry Clark arrived to take over as Maintenance Chief for C Company, 3rd Tank at Camp Evans, near Phong Dien. He was quickly put to work recovering mine-damaged tanks. He also noted the confusion in the nearby ARVN compound. If firing broke out the ARVN were supposed to fire color-coded flares to indicate incoming or outgoing fire. Every time firing broke out the ARVN fired numerous flares of all available colors.[33]

Under the burden of the war, the Corps reactivated the old 5th Marine Division, which had fought on Iwo Jima. Component units would serve in Vietnam, as attachments to the two division commands already there.

The light Ontos tank destroyer, though armed with six powerful 106mm recoilless guns, was proving far from ideal. It was vulnerable to small arms fire and mines, and the guns had an inexplicable tendency to fire unexpectedly. In December the Ontos battalions were decommissioned, and the Alpha Company of each battalion was transferred to its partner tank battalion as a reinforced Anti-Tank Company. The new Anti-Tank Company had 20 Ontos and 101 men, with a special section in the battalion's H&S Company.[34]

At nineteen years of age Jim Carroll had landed with the 5th Tank Battalion on Iwo Jima, and participated in the occupation of Japan. He left the Corps, attended college and became an elementary school teacher, and joined the Reserves as a tanker in 1953. In 1965 he was a Warrant Officer. "I thought, well, Johnson will call the Reserves like they did in Korea," so in late 1965 he took a leave of absence from the school system and volunteered for active duty. In 1967 he arrived in Vietnam, assigned to H&S Company, 1st Tank Battalion at Danang.

"We had tank crewmen down there, that when they came in-country, they stayed down there until they were reassigned to a gun company. Division being the way divisions are, they tasked us with providing them with junior troops to man the perimeter of a huge ammo dump down there around Danang. We had a quota. Every headquarters unit in the area had a quota of people they had to send over there. We had young Marines who were tankers that wanted to get out in the field and get in a tank that were walking guard duty in this ammo dump. If we got a call from one of our three outlying companies for troops, we could go over and bring those kids in, and then we'd whine and snivel to the people running the ammo dump, and tell them to get somebody else over there to fill in."

John Wear's father had been in the Air Force for thirteen years, and he had gone to three years of military prep school as a teenager. He had always anticipated military service. In August 1966, after a year of college and that rite of passage, a dispute with his parents about career goals, "I said well the hell with it. I went down and the Army recruiter was closed, the Air Force recruiter was closed, the Navy recruiter had hair kind of over his collar, and that wasn't very cool. There was a Gunnery Sergeant leaning in the door of his office, and he said 'You man enough to be a Marine?' I said "Show me the papers.'" Wear joined the Corps about two weeks later on a two-year term.

Near the end of boot camp at San Diego, "The Senior DI called all the two-year pukes out onto the platoon street and said, 'You guys are all going to be grunts and going to Vietnam, because Uncle Sam needs to get his money's worth out of you.' I asked the DI how could you remedy that, and of course the ship over [reenlistment] NCO was right there." Wear had seen the tanks from a distance when he was at the Edson Range rifle training center at Camp Pendleton. "He said, 'Sign up for a year and you can get anything you want.' I said I want to go to tanks, and he said 'Gimme a year.'"

Wear enjoyed tank school, and spent almost a year in 5th Tank Battalion at Camp Pendleton. He was a Corporal when he received orders to Vietnam, so "I wasn't like a lot of the guys who come right out of tank school and go right over there, kind of cannon fodder."

Wear went through the four-week training program at Staging Battalion at Camp Pendleton. "We did some escape and evasion, fan-firing, some obstacle course and that kind of stuff. Kind of got ourselves, as you say, acclimated. They gave us a little bit of Vietnamese culture, one or two words to learn, that kind of stuff."

At the end of 1967, five of the seven Marine infantry regiments in country were deployed along the DMZ under control of 3rd Marine Division. To the south the 1st Marine Division was still laboring to conduct an effective pacification program, but was simply stretched too thin. MACV insisted that the Marines turn over the pacification program to the ARVN, and spend more "battalion days in the field." This played into the hands of the enemy, who were already infiltrating strong forces for the Tet Offensive.[35] The enemy was clearly planning something, as indicated by the detection of numerous large enemy units on the move.

Throughout the region the doctrine, if there could be said to be one, for the use of tanks now varied greatly. C.W. Casey, the CO of Alpha/1st Tank, thought that for Bravo Company at Hill 55, "The infantry out there used them a little bit better, and used them in a tank-infantry type team." He lamented the extensive use of his own tanks for bridge guards.[36]

Jim Carroll did not particularly care for the way tanks were channeled on the roads, and particularly the use of tanks as convoy escorts. "If they know where you're coming from, if they've got anybody that's got any balls, they're going to have them out there with these RPGs. That was an awesome weapon."

Casey too was disenchanted with the convoy escort mission. "Every time they would do that, we'd end up losing at least one tank, out of a section or out of a platoon, due to mines. What the infantry wanted to do was put that tank out there in front, put all the trucks behind it, and let that tank clear the mines. It'd clear them all right. Very expensive mine detector, but that's exactly what they wanted to do."

A lot worse was in store for Casey's tankers.

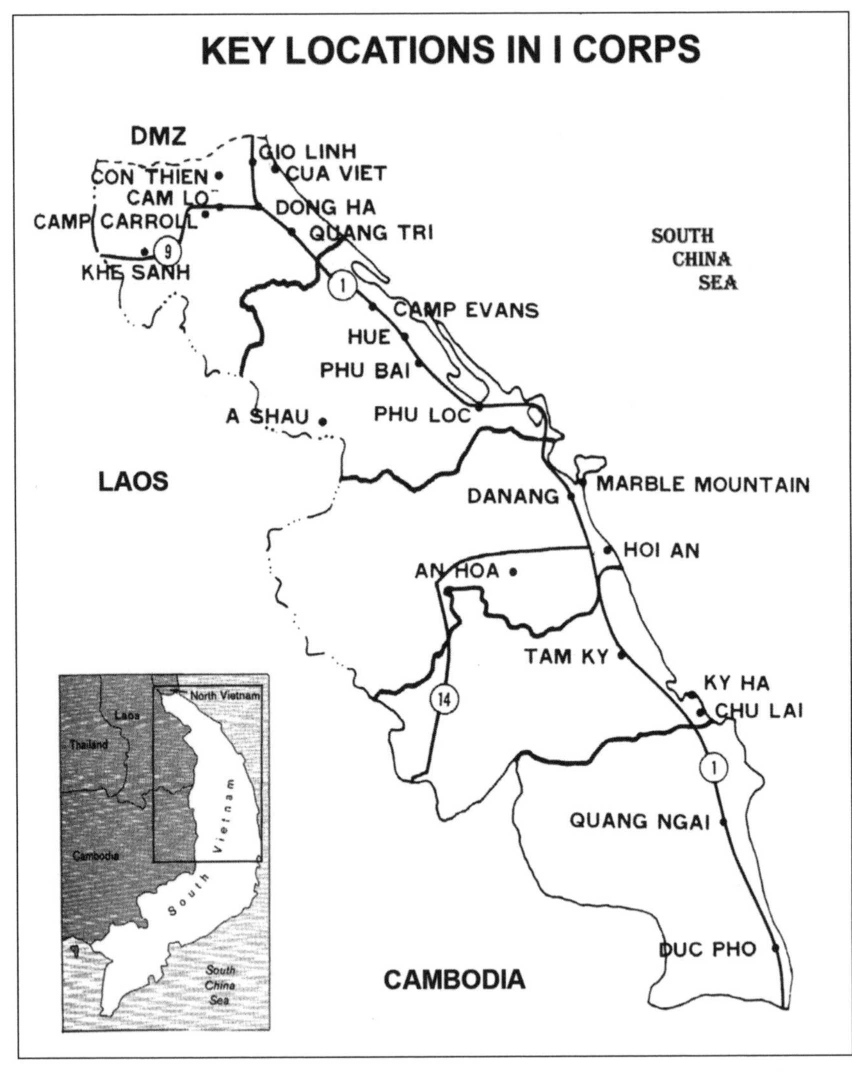

CHAPTER 5

1968: CRISIS AND DECISION

"Vietnam was the first war fought without censorship. Without censorship things can get terribly confused in the public mind."

General William Childs Westmoreland

Back in the world in January 1968, Gary Gibson was in the Oakland Naval Hospital recuperating from wounds suffered while he was with the CAC program. One day he walked into the head and remarked on the scars crisscrossing the back of a man shaving, that "it looked like he had been dating a mountain lion."

"He turned around and looked at me and says 'Well, I know it looks like that, but I was hit in the back with shrapnel when they blew the cupola off my tank." It was the man who had been carried off the helicopter in Vietnam.

As the war entered a new year the Marines were sweeping and searching, killing and being killed, over the same ground, month after month. MACV was still shifting formations northward (Operation CHECKERS) to thwart a potential NVA offensive that Westmoreland feared. The 101st Airborne and 1st Cavalry divisions were moving into the ICTZ as the Marines moved north to the DMZ and west into the isolated base at Khe Sanh. Westmoreland in particular had long been obsessed with Khe Sanh, which he saw as a critical blocking position that prevented a major NVA invasion. He insisted that the destruction of Khe Sanh, a replay of Dien Bien Phu, was a major enemy goal. Paradoxically, Westmoreland wanted a major battle at the remote site, seeing it as the climactic clash that would justify his plan to destroy the NVA in conventional battle.

Following an incident in which the Marines captured documents indicating a plan for the capture of the base, Westmoreland poured in more troops, filling the base to its carrying capacity. By mid-January the base held the entire 26th Marines, five artillery batteries, engineers, a reinforced tank platoon (1st Platoon, Bravo Company, 3rd Tank), two Ontos platoons, Army anti-aircraft vehicles (40mm and .50 caliber motor carriages, more suitable for ground fire) as well as logistics, air control, and other units. Then heavy rains caused bridge washouts and mudslides that closed Route 9. With all land routes severed, President Johnson, the American public, and the news media agonized over the fate of the isolated base. All eyes were firmly fixed on the western mountains. The Marines, in their usual stubborn fashion, refused to accept that the base could fall, but concentrated on how the base should be held.[1]

Westmoreland was playing to Giap's grandiose plan, called "General Offensive – General Uprising," to draw American forces north and west while large units slipped past ARVN units left to defend the cities and the densely populated coastal strip. The plan was for a coordinated attack to seize control of the population centers and incite a general uprising against the "colonialists." The Americans would have no choice but to withdraw.

NVA activity increased throughout early January, and intelligence identified two NVA divisions in the immediate area of Khe Sanh. The onslaught began with attacks against the critical hill positions that ringed the base in the valley floor, and a day long rocket barrage launched under cover of the monsoon rain and fog. The American response was to reinforce the base, with 1/9 brought in by helicopter. When the skies cleared somewhat in late January, American airpower began to punish the NVA in the surrounding hills, and the 37th ARVN Ranger Battalion arrived by helicopter.

There was already considerable friction within the command inside Vietnam, and Westmoreland felt that the Marines were thwarting his plan to bring the enemy to open battle by insisting upon fighting to control the population centers. He assigned General Creighton Abrams to establish MACV-Forward at Phu Bai on 9 February, to oversee the tactical activities of the Marines. Two additional Army brigades under the 101st Airborne Division moved into the ICTZ. XXIV Corps was established with an Army general in command of the 1st Cavalry, 101st Airborne, and 3rd Marine Divisions. One of the first activities of this new command was to plan for the relief of Khe Sanh; it was to be an Army showpiece, with airmobile forces leading the way.

For several months the force at Khe Sanh would continue to defy the NVA, but it would be almost entirely an infantry and artillery battle for control of the critical hills. The handful of armored vehicles never left the confines of the Khe Sanh Combat Base, and under the rain of NVA artillery that outranged the Marine Corps guns, mostly stayed in hide positions during the day. At night the tanks would emerge to occupy defensive positions along the perimeter, and for indirect fire missions.[2] Significantly, Giap never significantly reinforced his units investing Khe Sanh. Unlike Westmoreland, his plans lay elsewhere.

Meanwhile the never-ending cycle of ambushes and reaction went on. The NVA ambushed a large convoy on 13 January, between The Rockpile and Ca Lu. The convoy, with an escort of tanks and an understrength infantry company, was carrying heavy ammunition to Ca Lu. The tanks were supposed to stay on the road, and the grunts were to break up any ambush with support from the tank guns.[3]

Wally Young was driving the lead tank, followed by a flame tank. The two vehicles immediately behind were a six-by laden with tank ammunition, and a tractor-trailer with a large load of mortar ammunition. About a dozen more trucks followed, with two more tanks bringing up the rear. The infantry escort rode on the vehicles.

The NVA had planned the ambush meticulously, emplacing twenty men in spider holes close to the single lane road in the tall grass. "A good portion of the way that elephant grass was higher than the tank," said Young.

"They let both tanks pass, and then they hit both trucks when they initiated the contact, with RPGs in the engine compartment and the load. The ninety-millimeter ammo didn't go off, but the mortar [ammo] was going off during the entire five or six hours that we were there."

The infantry was hard hit, and "Half them boys never did get off the dadgum low-boys. They were just riding on the trucks. When they stopped, you know how dusty it is and all, the twenty men with full automatic AK-47s just jumped up out of the spider holes and ate them up.

"When the trucks blew up we stopped, and laid down a field of fire on both sides to protect ourselves. Then we started pumping rounds out there in any place where we saw, but basically we didn't see nothing."

There was considerable confusion, not only from the shock of the ambush but from clouds of dust that obscured everything. "There was a Marine FO, Forward Observer, up under that low-boy, and it was on fire cooking off ammo. He called the Colonel over the air and told him he needed somebody to come down there and get him. The Colonel says 'Yeah, we'll get you.' You could hear all the gunfire. 'But I damn sure ain't gonna run up there and get you right now! But we will get you.'"

The wounded FO continued to direct artillery fire from under the burning trailer, and eventually, "They did get him out from under there."

The disabled truck loaded with tank ammunition blocked the road. The tank commander of the flame tank, Thomas Yax, dismounted and hooked his tow cable to the truck. "Moved that six-by off the road so the rest of the convoy could come on by. That saved a lot of lives."

The tank commander requested permission to fire on a suspicious position on the nose of a commanding ridge some distance off the road. The company Gunny refused permission, probably to conserve ammunition.

Intense fire stripped away all the gear from the outside of the turret, and punctured all the water cans. Young dismounted to get a canteen from a dead Marine beside the road, then returned to the tank and stood beside the turret to give the others water. One of the other crewmen remarked that it was probably not a good idea to be outside, and Young started back toward the driver's hatch. "They opened up on us from out there, [with] I believe it was a fifty caliber." The heavy gun eventually did most of the damage to the stalled convoy.[4]

"Just looking back on it, he didn't have to move that fifty [muzzle] twelve to fifteen inches either way, and he was raking that whole convoy." The tank quickly took the machine gun position under fire, but most of the damage was already done.

As the Marines slowly fought their way out, "They started loading the wounded on my tank, and we just made a suicide run with them on to Ca Lu for medevac. They started doing the same thing on the other end of the convoy, taking them back to The Rockpile."

Young was driving, the tank was belching smoke, and the wounded on the back were yelling that the tank was on fire. The turret crew was firing machine guns to both sides of the road to break up secondary ambushes.

"We got down there about halfway to Ca Lu from where we were hit, about halfway from The Rockpile and Ca Lu, and I saw two choppers off to my right flank that were shot down by a fifty caliber on the right side of the road." Young watched both helicopters "Hit the ground and blow up. They said those were the ones that were coming to pick the wounded up that we had on our tank." The radio message came that more helicopters were on the way, and to proceed to Ca Lu.

The tank pulled into Ca Lu, belching smoke from the engine deck. "I was wanting out of that dadgum tank, bad." It was Young's first major ambush and "I was a little shaky." His personal dangers were not past. "I started to crawl out of that tank when we got stopped, and they had traversed the gun. It caught my head in there. It just happened that the intercom switch was pushed back to where I could talk to the rest of the crew. Just by accident, being pinned up in there.

"I hollered 'Hold it! Hold it! My head's in here!' They stopped and I got my head out of there." The crew traversed the turret and Young scrambled free. The crew had been firing the coaxial gun non-stop and "The thirty cooked off, and like to got me when I came out of there."

It was quickly determined that the heavy batteries had shorted out, generating the smoke. The tank headed back toward the ambush site alone. "I really had been pretty calm up to then, and before we got back to that ambush site, I just felt like I was shaking all over." Young literally did have his life flash before his eyes, like a fast-forwarded video.

The Marines began to unravel the wreckage of the convoy to drag it back to The Rockpile. "They took my tank, and they started hooking vehicles to it." Several wrecked trucks were pigtailed—hooked behind the tank with cables in single file. "Some of them didn't have any wheels. We were just dragging them. I pulled them through two rivers.

"When we got back they had one of the NVA we captured. It took all I could do to... I wanted him. But I didn't do nothing."

Young later read that total casualties in the convoy were 23 killed and over seventy wounded, and "ninety per cent of them had to be sent back to the States."

The tanks, with their speed and firepower, were typically a major component of the reaction forces sent out to rescue ambushed vehicles, a role that made their actions entirely too predictable. On 24 January the NVA ambushed a small truck convoy on Route 9 just south of Camp Carroll, and waited for the onrushing reaction force.

Harry Christensen was the tank commander of the lead gun tank, with two Army M-42s and a flame tank bringing up the rear. All the vehicles were loaded with grunts. Twenty-four-year-old Captain Daniel W. Kent, the CO of B Company, 3rd Tanks, rode standing beside Christensen's cupola with his pistol drawn.[5]

The relief column halted about 100 yards from the ongoing fight and began shooting at positions along both sides of the highway. Kent dismounted and ran back to coordinate the fire of the other vehicles, then returned to the lead tank. By this time the intense small arms fire had wrecked the tank-infantry phone on the rear plate, so Christensen and Kent began to try and coordinate the action by hand signals. The arm-waving brought down even more intense fire.

Christensen took a ricochet from the tank's armor above his right eye. Temporarily blinded by blood, he was trying to tie a rag over the wound when Kent and a corpsman jumped up on the tank. In a quick conference Christensen convinced Kent he was good to go. All the while the tank continued to blaze away with canister, HE, and the coaxial gun. Back on the ground, Kent ran to direct the infantry to fire on more positions that had revealed themselves. The reaction force had inadvertently tangled with elements of the NVA *48th* and *52nd Regiments*.

Kent remounted the lead tank just as Christensen and the commander of the M42 behind decided to charge into the ambush zone in response to desperate radio calls for help. By this time the tank was almost out of main gun and .30 caliber ammunition, and the ever-unreliable .50 caliber in the cupola was disabled when the cable that connected the charging handle to the bolt broke. The gunner passed the tank's grease gun and a bag of magazines up to Christensen.

Kent was riding on the left side of the turret, firing his pistol and pointing out targets to Christensen. Harry killed two RPG gunners and turned to look at Kent. Just then two rounds entered Kent's back and exited through his chest, splashing Christensen's face with blood.

Christensen grabbed for Kent and began to drag him across the turret roof, just as an RPG impacted, wounding both men again. He dragged Kent closer to the cupola, but another RPG sprayed both with more hot metal fragments. With his strength slipping away, Harry cradled Kent's head, tried to reassure him, and made one last desperate effort to drag him to relative safety. A round from a recoilless gun struck the turret roof, wounding Christensen yet again, and blowing Kent off into the road.

The recoilless gun round started a fire inside the turret, and Christensen ordered his crew to abandon the tank. As he climbed out, another RPG impact blew him out of the cupola and into the ditch on the right side of the road. From there he could see Kent's body smoldering in the road.

A relief force large enough to deal with the powerful ambush headed toward the site. Wally Young was driving one of the two tanks. He said that it was the fastest he had ever driven the tank, about forty-three miles an hour. Out of the corner of his eye Young saw something move. It was a big banana rat that had been hiding in the tarp on the left fender.

The huge rat ran onto the slope plate, stopped to look Young in the face, and ran to the other side of the tank. The rat, agitated by the motion of the tank, headed back across. "He stopped right there and looked like he was going to turn and come down there in that driver's compartment with me. When he did that I just stood up and took a hard, quick punch right in his side. He was as big as a small dog." The rat tumbled off the front of the tank. Young "dropped down real quick and turned it just a little bit. I looked at my tank commander, and he gave me the thumbs up and said, 'You run over it.'"

Just then the tank arrived at the ambush site. "There was a three-quarter ton [truck] that was on fire there in the middle of the road and there were some fifty-five gallon drums." Young drove right over the drums. "I hit it and it was just like running over a beer can with a pick-up truck. Just Poof! Oil or diesel fuel just spewed out."

The relief force arrived too late to aid the convoy.

While the American public was fixated on the siege of Khe Sanh, MACV was determined to respond to the perceived threat of an invasion from the north. The Marines of III MAF were in motion, shifting northward as part of MACV's realignment. Operation CHECKERS saw 3rd Marine Division shifting toward the DMZ, with 1st Marine Division assuming responsibility for those parts of Thua Thien Province west of Hue City. On 13 January the 1st Marine Division opened a forward headquarters, Task Force X-Ray, at Phu Bai, to coordinate the move.

THE TET OFFENSIVE

Between 29 and 31 January the Communists launched their planned Tet Offensive. In all, 105 cities and towns were attacked, including seven in the ICTZ. The old Imperial capitol at Hue was captured by seven enemy battalions (with another four in support in the nearby countryside), and would be held for over a month. The major Marine bases came under rocket attack.

The old Imperial capital and educational center of Hue had thus far been largely untouched by the war. The major north–south logistical routes—Highway 1 and a railway line—choked into the city, and the US Navy operated a large unloading facility in the city's center. The Citadel, a sprawling brick fortress dating from the earliest French colonial era, formed most of the north side of the city. The sluggish Perfume River separated it from the south side, the French colonial part of the city with wide, straight boulevards, open parks, and massive masonry public buildings and residences of the wealthy. The walled gardens of the residences made each a small fortress. The ARVN 1st Division headquarters was in the old city, but no significant combat formations. Most men were on leave for the Tet holiday (the Vietnamese New Year), and only the equivalent of an infantry company remained on duty. There were American advisors in the city, but no combat forces closer than Phu Bai, ten kilometers to the south, and that was largely a control and logistical center for units deployed in the region. The critical city was virtually undefended.

The original onslaught by the *4th, 5th and 6th NVA Regiments*, the *12th NVA Sapper Battalion*, a rocket artillery battalion, and local VC units gained control of the city within hours. The only holdouts were the MACV Compound (a converted hotel) on the south side of the river, and the ARVN 1st Division headquarters compound inside the old Citadel.

Karl Fontenot had just returned to be CO of 3rd Tank when the Tet Offensive broke, and his battalion was in the process of displacing north toward the DMZ. "We had four remaining tanks.... They were due to go into the city of Hue the morning that Hue fell, to load onto LCUs to go on up to Dong Ha." The vehicles included the two command tanks from battalion headquarters, and two additional tanks.[6]

Despite the holiday truce, Fontenot's CP had taken thirty or forty rockets the night before.[7] "We were shelled that night, but we didn't know any more than that. The four tanks left in the morning with the Division Embarkation Officer to go up there and boat in."

Fontenot went in to the Division HQ, where he found that "The G-3 didn't know that I had tanks on the road. I went in and told him, I said 'I've got four tanks going up the road, and I'm just going to tell them to join the first unit they find.'" The Embarkation Officer, an infantry officer, stayed with the tanks, "and I had a major, who was with the tanks, he was on leave from the United States. He took leave to go there and observe what was happening, and he ended up in Hue. He got a good look." Perhaps more than he had counted on.

Carl Fleischmann was with the small group of tanks. "We got orders to take an advance group to Con Thien. What they were going to do is that we had more personnel than we had room in the tanks, and we split the H&S Company up. We had a forward group go up, and I think Gunnery Sergeant Cornelius was the senior person that went up with the advance group. They went up weeks ahead of time. We picked up the convoy that was going to go up to Con Thien at the start of Tet. We picked it up on Highway One. We were the tank escort. We were the second tank in line."

The tanks were escorting a mixed convoy. "A bunch of trucks. Tanker trucks, personnel, it was a large convoy." The tanks were apparently supposed to report to the Navy Boat Ramp to be ferried across the Perfume River, because of weight limitations on the Nguyen Hoang Bridge, then continue the road march north.[8]

The Marines, in the process of the move north, were caught with parts of two regiments near Hue, and like Fontenot's provisional platoon, many units were actually in transit through the affected areas.

The local controlling headquarters was Task Force X-RAY, the advanced HQ of the 1st Marine Division at Phu Bai. Believing that the assault on Hue was a diversion, on 31 January Task Force X-RAY dispatched a single understrength company, A/1/1, to move into the city aboard trucks and assess the situation at the MACV Compound. Fontenot found that the infantry was on the road into Hue, "so I got on my radio and called the tanks, and told them to watch for his battalion, and lower their gun tubes and get ready to fight when they went in."[9]

The infantry unit's first clue that something was badly wrong was a total absence of any civilians on the normally busy Highway 1. Before they reached the southern margin of the city, they encountered Fontenot's tanks halted in the road. The first indication that something was very badly wrong was when the tanks came upon an ARVN tank. According to Fleischmann, it "was blown up, with bodies hanging out of it." Several charred ARVN M41 tanks and M113 personnel carriers partially blocked the road.

Just after crossing the Phu Cam Canal that formed the southern boundary of the city, the infantry climbed aboard the tanks, leaving the vulnerable trucks.

"We got to the outskirts of Hue City, and all hell broke loose. We

CAPT. GORDON BATCHELLER C.O.

started taking incoming rounds. Small arms, nothing big, just small arms. We all stopped to try and figure what's going on."

Without any prior experience or frame of reference, "We heard the shots, but we didn't know what they were, again, because we were actually not combat-experienced. We had no idea what was going on until we saw Hicks get shot with that bullet. Holy smokes!"

The tank commander in the lead tank, an NCO named Hicks, was as usual riding exposed in the cupola. "He got shot in the neck. He was our first wounded that we've actually seen, up front." The round entered his neck and came out his back. "They had to medevac him. I know he lived, but I never saw him after that.

"There was somebody there. They told us to get back to our tanks. When he [Hicks] got hit, we all ran to him. One of our friends was hurt. Even though he was a corporal and I was a PFC, he was a friend."

Hicks's evacuation was the first medevac the group had witnessed. "We were told 'Button up,' we were under attack.

"I remember that there was like a religious figure, like a large cross or something to that effect, where the sniper was. They told us to take our guns—I was the driver—and aim our guns out that way and take the snipers out. From that point on, we were stuck in the tank. We never left the tank."

The convoy turned back toward Phu Bai, and the tanks and infantry continued on into the city. "Once we buttoned up our hatches, we lived in the tank. We pissed, we shit, we ate, we did everything in the tank."

As the force attempted to barrel through a built-up area, the infantry was swept from the tank decks by fire from buildings alongside the road. Fleischmann: "We had people on the tank when we got hit with rockets, RPGs. People were actually blown off the tank." The deadliest problem was sweeping machine gun fire from buildings farther away which kept the infantry pinned in the roadside ditches. "We were in the tank. We were scared. I was petrified. It's something. Once you start seeing bodies, you start getting a little nervous about this.

"There was nothing we could do." The infantry was communicating through the phone box on the back of the tank. "They would tell us what to do. Stop the tank. They were loading people on, and they'd tell us where to go and stuff like that." Down in his isolated position, a tank driver could see virtually nothing of what was happening. "The tank commander would tell me to turn, straight, forward, and go from there."

All this was coming as something of a shock to Fleischmann. He had a camera, and was taking numerous photos, but "Don't ask me why I took pictures. I was born in Brooklyn, New York and raised in Connecticut, and the worst thing I saw was a dead deer. So I took a lot of pictures. It was the wrong thing to do, but I'm kind of glad I did, because it's part of me."

Task Force X-RAY dispatched Golf/2/5 aboard more trucks. The relief force reached the pinned company at about 1300 hours, and fresh infantry and tank fire were able to suppress much of the machine gun fire. The combined force slowly fought their way into the city, and "We worked our way to ... the MACV compound" by mid-afternoon. The tanks took up position in the street outside the hotel courtyard. "That was pretty much the staging area for everybody until somebody, whoever was in charge, started fighting back."

At first there seemed to be no clear idea of how to use the tanks. The tanks were shifted over to the other side of the MACV compound. "One street overlooked the water [of the river], and they had us sit there to make sure nobody was coming over by boat.... They had us on kind of guard duty there." The officers were still trying to make sense of the confusion.

"They were receiving recoilless rifle fire from the other side. They were shooting from underneath the bridge, and wanted to know could we shoot some rounds under the bridge? That was the big steel [Nguyen Hoang] bridge. We shot underneath the bridge, on the Citadel side. I guess we knocked them out. They came up and congratulated us, told us we did great. We didn't damage the bridge at all. We got what we were supposed to. That was our first action firing the main gun." It was to be the only time they fired across the river.

The first task was to expand the tiny enclave around the MACV Compound. Men were being killed and wounded transporting the wounded through the exposed streets to the landing zone east of MACV. Tanks were used to smash a path through buildings to make a narrow, protected path to the LZ.

Tank H52 was assigned to support infantry fighting their way west, parallel to the river toward the University. Fleischmann: "I remember sitting in the tank driving, and I looked out the right little hole [periscope] again, and I saw these infantry moving up alongside our tank.

"I saw this one guy kneel down, and he was shooting. The next thing I know he kind of slumped there, still in the kneeling position. Slumped, and he had a big smile on his face. It turned out he was shot in the head." Fleischmann says that for decades he has worried about and tried to grasp what went through the man's head as he was dying. "All anybody will say is, 'It had to be a happy thought.'"

The infantry threw the man onto the back of the tank for the trip back to the MACV compound.

Not long afterward, H52 was the first to be hit by enemy anti-tank weapons. The tank was working its way west, toward the University complex that occupied several blocks near the river. "I looked through the little portholes [driver's periscopes] that we had there, on the right hand side. I saw a gentleman step out, a Viet Cong, step out of a building and point the RPG at us.

"I took the wheel of the tank, yelled 'Incoming' or whatever I yelled. I turned the tank, and we got hit with the RPG. When that happened Robert Hall, the tank commander, took the full brunt of the RPG." The gunner was also wounded.

"We backed out of there, we backed away enough that we could get out of there. We got down to the end of the road. Robert Hall lost his face." The tank went back into a protected position. "We got him out of the tank. I got him onto a Mule," a small four-wheeled utility carrier used by the infantry, "that was there, and we got him back to the MACV Compound."

At the aid station that had been set up in the compound, "The doctor and the corpsman said there was nothing they could do for him, because he had no face. Robert was holding onto me. They said, 'Just hold onto him until he passes on.' He did. He passed on."

Fleischmann walked back to the tank, and "We got back into action. Even though we had the hole in the tank, and we were a mess inside, we got back into the action again."

Headquarters at Phu Bai, still ignorant of how bad the situation was in Hue, ordered the relatively fresh Golf Company to cross the river on the high Nguyen Hoang Bridge that carried Highway 1 and link up with the ARVN in the Citadel. They managed to cross the bridge after heavy fighting and several attempts, but were driven back to the south side before darkness.

With the roads under constant attack the first contingent of Conwill Casey's A Company, 1st Tanks arrived aboard Navy LCUs that came up the Perfume River and passed underneath the high Nguyen Hoang

Bridge, at the time still controlled by the NVA. "The doggone U-boats were just, I mean, devastated trying to come up from the sea, coming up the Perfume into Hue. There were two or three hulks, LCU hulks, all up and down that thing. They weren't so bad when they noticed there were tanks on there. But when those U-boats were coming in and they were loaded with ammunition, they could stand by. That was nothing but a death run up there."

The first platoon arrived on 2 February. "We steamed up from Danang aboard LCUs. First thing we brought in of course was the retriever, and a couple of gun tanks. Of course on an old LCU you could only put three vehicles on her. It took us a day or two to get the other vehicles up there." A communications jeep, his personal jeep, a three-quarter-ton light cargo truck, and three five-ton trucks made up the balance of Casey's small force.[10]

On 2 February the Marines fought desperately but in vain to enlarge their area of control around the MACV compound. In the early evening the NVA counterattacked, destroying one of the 3rd Battalion gun tanks. There is some disagreement about the circumstances under which the tank was lost, but the crew was not in the tank at the time. Fleischmann recalls, "They were by the University in Hue City. There's a wall around there. They were supporting the infantry, and I believe they were evacuating some civilians. The guys out of the tank came out there to help get the civilians out. The tank got hit with an RPG. It just destroyed it. It was a solid hit."

When the first contingent of Casey's Alpha Company arrived on the south side, a sobering sight greeted them. "When the thing first started, Third Tank Battalion I guess had a heavy section of tanks in there. They lost one due to sympathetic detonation, where it [an enemy round] hit those rounds in that turret, and that booger just went up. That old tank hull was still sitting there on the ramp at Hue City when we got in there." The wrecked vehicle was Karl Fontenot's command tank H51. John Wear later saw the vehicle, and noted that the destructive round entered the turret front below the gun mantlet.[11]

Only part of Casey's company was available to go into the city. Casey recalled that by the time his unit arrived, the Provisional Platoon from H&S, 3rd Tank had already departed the city, but apparently the Provisional Platoon was still there, just lost in the chaos.[12] Casey assumed control of all armored units in the city. "On the south bank was the regimental headquarters, along with one-one and two-five. I had my company headquarters there. I had six gun tanks there, and two flame tanks and a retriever."

On the night of 2 February, Carl Fleischmann's tank was positioned to guard the south end of the bridge to keep the enemy from launching their own attack across the bridge. The enemy had no plans to cross the bridge. "The whole ground just shook. There was dust everywhere. The first thing everybody comes on [the radio], 'What the hell did you do?'

"We did not do nothing. They didn't know if the gun went off, the ninety-millimeter went off, or somebody shot a recoilless rifle off, or somebody did something. We didn't do nothing. The bridge blew." Enemy sappers had dropped the center span into the river, ending any hope of a coordinated action between the Marines on the south bank and the ARVN holding out in the old city. The tank stayed for a short while. Soon, "They had some kind of boats down there, little flat boats. We helped them get them in the water, and they were doing something back and forth, and we just stayed on the banks." Marine and Army Bridge Companies were already constructing a small pontoon span to allow infantry and light vehicles to cross the river.

When the assault on the University reached its final phases, Fleischmann says, "I remember going into the college compound with our guns and shooting into part of the classrooms that the enemy was in. We were in the same compound, and that's how close they were to us."

The following morning the Marines attempted to fight their way toward ARVN forces at a prison southwest along the bank of the river. With air support blocked by the *crachin*, and prohibited by the senior ARVN commander from using artillery in the city, the Marines were able to progress only two blocks, despite supporting fire from the tanks. Later in the day the first reinforcements landed by helicopter at a park northeast of MACV, the first of several infantry companies that would slowly dribble into the city. Task Force X-RAY hastily organized an amalgam of available bits and pieces of units. The controlling unit was headquarters 1st Marines, and included 1/1, 1/5, and 2/5.

The NVA attempted to further isolate the battlefield. Truck convoys from Phu Bai had to fight through constant ambushes, including large command detonated mines that cratered the roads. The NVA had already destroyed the bridge over the Perfume River, and on the evening of 4 February blew up the Highway 1 crossing over the Phu Cam Canal. All reinforcements would now have to arrive by helicopter, or by boats that ran a gauntlet of fire on the Perfume River.

Casey's company would conduct this critical and brutal battle with only two of its three five-tank platoons, two of his three company flame tanks, his VTR, and the orphaned 3rd Battalion Provisional Platoon. Again, the problem was the use (or misuse) of tanks for local security. "That's the reason I never could get my other five tanks, my Third Platoon, up there. Because damn Division had them hung up on bridges down there, around Danang."

Dan Wokaty said that when Casey's A Company was sent north to Hue, "I got cut out of that, left there. They sent a young guy by the name of Parker, and Novak." Casey was particularly attached to Novak, whom he considered an exemplary tank commander.

Wokaty was given a rump platoon of four tanks at battalion headquarters, and assigned to any emergency duties. "We were down at the Tuy Long Bridge. Providing security at that bridge. It was just tanks there, no infantry or anything there." The Tuy Long Bridge was a weak spot on the critical resupply route between Hill 10 and Hill 37, two infantry battalion positions. Another platoon of tanks was assigned to the Cau Do Bridge, also in 1st Tank's TAOR.

The infantry guarding the bridge had been pulled out, leaving the tanks isolated on the two ends of the bridge. The tankers fired rifles at anything suspicious in the water, and tossed grenades into the river to discourage swimming sappers. "We were lucky we didn't get hit.

"We could see the rockets flying to the Danang airstrip. We could hear the explosions and everything."

In Hue City the tanks were proving a mixed blessing. The close confines of the street battle made it dangerous for the infantry to be anywhere near them, as they attracted intense fire from every enemy weapon in the vicinity. In return the diversion they created often relieved the pressure on the grunts. All too often they were driven back by clouds of RPGs.

The Marines were inexorably pushing the NVA and VC back, but even the secured areas were not safe from stragglers, holdouts, and snipers who had gone to ground in the wreckage. The south side was also still taking mortar and long-range machine gun fire from the Citadel walls across the river. The tanks frequently had to return to the vicinity of the MACV compound. The Navy Boat Ramp to the east, and a nearby landing zone were the distribution points for food, water, ammunition, and fuel.

Fleischmann: "We were outside the MACV Compound by a park (probably the nearby traffic circle), and we got out to reload supplies on our tank, the ninety millimeter, thirty caliber, fifty caliber, C-rations and stuff. We were standing there and a mortar round came and took us all out. We were all wounded.

"I guess I was the least wounded of everybody, but we were all wounded. There was a corpsman stationed in one of the buildings close by, and we got everybody down there. He wrapped me up, and everybody else was more wounded, and they had to stay." The corpsman gave him morphine, and Fleischmann stayed temporarily at the aid station.

The tank was left abandoned, so "I walked back to the tank, and stayed with the tank until the next day. By myself I took the tank from that position back to the MACV compound.... Then we picked up another crew. That's when I picked up John Wear."

John Wear had arrived in Danang at the end of January, and "I think I spent one night in the Transit Barracks, and was on an airplane up to Phu Bai." After a few days at Phu Bai, "They flew me on a chopper to replace one of the crewmen who got shot." He arrived shortly after the infantry had recaptured the University, and ended up in a flame tank.

"Landed at the boat ramp, got off the helicopter, and they were shooting at us from the other side [of the river]. All the grunts were shooting back, and the helicopter was in between the grunts and the gooks! They were shooting over our heads, and next to us... scared the hell out of me! I had never been shot at before that."

The relatively unscathed flame tank was now a primary vehicle. Fleischmann said of his tank, "It was still functional, the gun would still function even though we had holes in it. Unfortunately the brain matter and the blood and everything from Robert and from the other guy were throughout the tank. It was still a functional tank. We kept going.

"To this day it still haunts me on that one."

Fleischmann was moved over to the flame tank, "And that's where I met John Wear. He became my tank commander."

One of the toughest nuts to crack was the Jeanne d'Arc church and school complex. Even the 90mm tank guns were relatively ineffective, though canister rounds from one of the tanks were instrumental in breaking up an NVA counterattack that tried to cross the open streets on 5 February.

Casey: "The unit that actually saw most of the battle, the house-to-house type fighting, was one-five, on the north, though we saw a tremendous amount on the south bank also.

"Also under me, as the armor officer for Task Force X-Ray, I had two platoons of Ontos. There were fifteen Ontos in a company, three platoons of five each. On the north bank, with one-five, with that platoon of tanks, I think we had ... three Ontos over there with them. We had seven Ontos on the south bank."

The gun tanks would have to bear the brunt of the battle. The 106mm recoilless guns of the Ontos gave it considerable firepower, and the HEP-T round[13] proved very useful against the masonry buildings of the old city, but "The Ontos was primarily used as a backup for the tank. That Ontos is awfully vulnerable. If it's hit just right, a thirty caliber will go right through it. And if it's hit with an RPG, it's just mayhem. We primarily used them in a hit-and-run type of thing. We'd run them up there between the tanks. They'd run out and fire those six one-oh-sixes, and then turn around and be gone. It was primarily a building buster, just like we were doing with the tanks."

The flame tanks had been designed for just this type of fighting, but Casey said "We actually used those things very sparingly. We had none of course on the north bank. The two that we did have, we used them in pairs, in a section. We used them to guard lines of communications, in and out ... between the two infantry battalions. ... we would put at least one gun [tank] with them, and made dadburn sure we had some grunts around them. We fired those things in anger. We probably put out about a half a dozen rods. A rod is a shot of flame."

The utility of the flame tanks was limited by circumstance and policy. "We didn't have the mixer and the transfer unit with us. We had a compressor with us.[14] What we would do with those aggravating things was to load them by hand. We'd pump by the fifty-five gallon drum of gasoline. We'd pump five gallons into an old jerry can, then pass it up, and have a crewman up there dumping it into the tank. Then we'd dump in the thickener, and then fire up that compressor and get pressure on it."

The other issue was one that hampered Marine operations in general, the desire of the South Vietnamese government to limit damage in the historic old city.

The flame tanks made limited use of their primary weapon, fighting mostly with their coaxial machine guns, though Casey does recall some use of flame. "One morning I remember going back down there, and they had fired them at night. We had about eight or ten NVA out there that had gotten torched that night. But so far as a tremendous amount of use, no. Nowhere near what the gun tanks did."

Wear said, "You'd trundle down the road, you'd either catch some incoming mortars or RPGs, or something. It was almost like you waited until they shot at you, and you just shot ... wherever they were. I was in a flame tank, and we had already blown the load, and they wouldn't allow us to reload napalm because we'd burn the city down. So we were a machine gun platform, and we just fired the hell out of the thirty and the fifty. Non-stop."

The flame tanks "did fire one load, and it burned down a whole city block, and they said, 'That's it.'" Wear recalls firing only one rod.

Casey said that the tanks were used in different ways depending upon the tactical situation. Sometimes the tanks were bait. Tanks are largely blind, and very vulnerable in the close confines of street fighting. However, to infantry inexperienced in dealing with tanks they are still frightening things. The NVA would usually direct torrents of ineffectual small arms fire against a tank, revealing their positions and saving the lives of the following Marine infantry. "The platoon that was on the north bank, with One-Five, was actually used to clear the streets. As long as we could keep some form of infantry protection around them, we could run them down those streets. Where they were receiving fire, we could knock a hole in that building, and usually put a damper on that fire."

In the complex urban landscape, areas behind the fighting were by no means secure, as units from both sides maneuvered amid the rubble. One critical requirement was to limit the enemy's ability to move freely, to prevent him from flowing back into cleared areas, and to interfere with his efforts to shuffle men and ammunition about. The tankers learned to use the design of the city to aid them in the effort.

The French colonial side of the city had broad streets and open parks. Controlling these open spaces by fire was critical, since it allowed the Marines to compartmentalize the battlefield. Carl Fleischmann observed, "It was pretty neat. Hue City, the streets were like spokes of a wheel." A tank would be positioned at one of the major intersections. The commander's cupola would be turned to fire the heavy machine gun down one street, the turret with its coaxial machine gun down another to prevent the enemy from moving between blocks of buildings.

"In the streets we were advancing down, they used us like an artillery piece or for a gun platform for the big machine guns. I remember many times having people run across the street and we're trying to shoot down the street at these people. They were carrying boxes that we found out later were mortar rounds and stuff like that they were carrying from one side of the street to the other."

Reminiscent of the battle for Seoul in 1950, the tanks were also used as battering rams. "We would come up to stone walls. They couldn't get through, so they would have our tank go through the walls.

"Many times we got through the walls, and Gee! That's where the enemy was. They didn't have to worry about the tank being hurt by small arms fire, and they always thought well, an RPG is not going to hurt the infantry or anybody else. The tank will take it."

In the narrow streets the tanks were sometimes critical to extracting infantry caught in an ambush. Casey recounted one incident in which his platoon leader won the Silver Star. "The grunts were really pinned down." The platoon leader stood up out of the tank commander's cupola, exposed to the intense fire to use the heavy machine gun. "He grabbed that fifty gun and just started walking. Laid down some suppressive fire and broke them loose."

Tanks were far more likely to be called upon to provide direct fire support, eliminating snipers or enemy positions in the sturdy masonry buildings that were impervious to the fire of infantry weapons. Casey: "I remember one morning where they had a whole infantry platoon pinned down by some NVA that were in a Catholic church, up in the bell tower. They called for tanks to come in there so we sent a pair in.

"They walked mortars right down on top of the tanks, but never did get a direct hit on them. We sat there and pumped round after round after round into that church. Literally destroyed that church. But finally we silenced that sniper up there, which allowed the infantry to start to move."

The tanks were used not only to suppress enemy positions. One of the basic principles taught Marines was that entry through doors or windows exposes the infantry to concentrated fire. Tank fire was also used to "mousehole" the heavy walls to allow entry. "Depending on what the building was made out of, but usually you could almost knock a hole in there big enough to drive a jeep through.... Sometimes it would go right through the masonry and then explode in the interior of the building."

The vast majority of the ammunition expended was HE, with a few anti-personnel flechette rounds.[15]

Eventually the *crachin* cleared, and the A-4 Skyhawk fighter bombers could fly. Casey: "The first thing they did was drop CS [tear gas] on the north bank. Of course the doggone wind was blowing out of the north, back toward the south. We were in the MACV compound, that's where we had our headquarters and we were all wearing gas masks, because the doggone CS was all over us. They were firing eight-inch artillery from Phu Bai … and we were getting huge chunks of shrapnel from that stuff…."

The tankers quickly rediscovered an old lesson: basic bodily functions could be deadly. Carl Fleischmann: "When you got to go to the bathroom, you just go. We used our drinking cup … if it overflowed, so? The smell didn't get to you. It was a normal thing." Of course the stench of the city, with no sanitation or running water, and bodies decaying in the rubble was itself intense. "When it was time to clean up, boy-oh-boy was that horrible." Fleischmann was even sleeping in the driver's seat. After seeing the fate of Hicks, Hall, and others, "You don't take a chance. You stay inside the tank."

Casey recalled that Lt. Colonel Ernie Cheatham, the CO of 2/5 later said that the RPGs were so numerous they "….'sounded like gravel on a tin roof.' Every one of those eleven tanks had at least one penetration into the turret, and numerous hits all up and down the tank, from both sides."

The RPGs could not usually destroy the tanks, but were deadly to the crewmen. "They had to hit it just right to penetrate. Initially they had the old RPG-2s, and then they went to that RPG-7, which was a hell of a lot more potent than the earlier RPG. But both of them could penetrate. When the thing penetrated, it was a chemical energy type penetrator. It goes in about the size of a silver dollar, and then when it hits on the inside, the metal from inside the turret just spalls off."

An RPG penetration made a small round hole through the armor, but the spalling typically did little mechanical damage to the vehicle. As Karl Fontenot explained, "Just weld them up. Nothing spectacular. Replace whatever damage they did inside."

None of Casey's tanks were disabled during the fighting, but the shards of hot metal inflicted brutal wounds on the tank crews. Of the fifty-five original Alpha Company tank crewmen who entered the city, only eleven remained after six weeks of fighting.[16] "I think I had four

KIAs, and the rest were WIAs they had to medevac out.... The ones that took it the hardest when that RPG would penetrate of course were the gunner and the loader. The TC would get some in the legs every now and then, but the driver was safe down there, because he's down below that turret. That shrapnel, as it spalls off in there, wouldn't hit him. They always aimed at the turret. They always tried to hit that thing on the side, because that's the thinnest part."

Replacement crewmen continued to be flown into Phu Bai by fixed wing cargo planes, then into the landing zone near the boat ramp.[17]

As the Marines established control of the south side, the ARVN were struggling on the north side of the river. Within forty-eight hours of the initial onslaught, fifteen South Vietnamese battalions had fought their way into the city, including elite airborne, Ranger, and South Vietnamese Marine Corps units. Despite numerical superiority, leadership was lacking and the NVA still controlled most of the north side. At midnight on 10 February, 1/5 was abruptly ordered to break contact with an enemy unit and march nine kilometers back to board helicopters. By 1045 the next morning helicopters had landed the first elements of Marines inside the Citadel.

The same day two companies came up the Perfume River aboard U-boats, accompanied by five more of Casey's gun tanks. The tank units that were brought in were using whatever vehicles were available, as photographic evidence places Casey's command tank, A51, with the group on the north side.

The effort to clear the Citadel was at first stymied by the ARVN. Just after dawn on 13 February the NVA attacked A/1/5 inflicting heavy losses. An ARVN airborne unit had simply pulled out, leaving the Marines rear exposed.

The Marines' task was to clear the northeast wall of the Citadel. Casey's tanks advanced parallel to the wall, as the infantry attacked along the crest of the high, broad wall, actually two thick walls of brick with earthen fill between. The toughest objective was the massive Dong Ba Tower that dominated the Dong Ba Gate. The tanks could not elevate their guns enough to engage the enemy in the tower, and fought their way through streets so narrow that they could not traverse their main guns. The Marines captured the tower on the afternoon of 15 February, lost it to an NVA counterattack that night, and regained it the next morning.

For days the depleted battalion and tanks fought their way along the wall, suffering brutal losses. Reinforced by L/3/5 on 21 February the fresh company and the tanks turned the corner and began the attack to clear the southeast wall—parallel to the river—on 22 February against collapsing resistance.

On the other side of the river the Marines had swung about and started advancing to the east, clearing the edge of the city near the soccer stadium. John Wear said that "right before we left … they brought up a compressor, and a mo-gas, and the napalm powder, and we filled up the bottle."

When the south side was declared secure, the remnants of the wandering 3rd Tank Provisional Platoon were at last sent on their way to Quang Tri. John Wear had spent three weeks in Hue. He said, "There were only two other guys who didn't get Purple Hearts out of those four tank crews. And two or three were killed." Carl Fleischmann: "I was the only one left. Out of all the guys that originally went up to Hue, I was [the only] one of the original ones there who made it through the whole thing."

Though the attention of the American public was riveted on Khe Sanh and Hue, positions allover the country came under attack. Previously unthinkable risks were taken to relieve isolated bases. Air resupply of an isolated Special Forces base failed when aircraft were shot down or driven of by heavy fire. What Wokaty described as "a bastard group" was organized from available infantry from several battalions, mounted in trucks, supply trucks, all escorted by a platoon of tanks. Along much of the route, "the road looked like there had been nobody down through there since the French had been down through there, because the vehicles were left there, old French vehicles and stuff like that. There were big holes in the road, I guess where mines had been put in that area.

"We got to Hill 10 and spent the night, and we pushed off from there the next day going out to the Special Forces camp. You could see it out in the valley out there." Everyone in the camp was expecting an attack. Years later, back in the US, Wokaty ran into a Special Forces soldier who told him, "You looked so damn good that day I wanted to kiss you, because I knew we were dead meat out there."

The encircling enemy forces were content to fire at aircraft and harass the camp, and declined to directly attack the powerful column. "They mortared us. You could hear them all night out there, the mortars tubing."

The *Montagnard* tribesmen in the camp amazed Wokaty. "Every time a mortar would hit, if it didn't go off, the chief of those *Montagnards* would tell them to go get it. They had a big old pit over there that they were putting them mortars [dud rounds] in." Despite the risk of explosion, "They'd go grab it and throw it in there."

The 3rd Tank platoon in Hue loaded out on boats and went down the Perfume River to the sea. Wear said, "It was kind of funny, because we wanted to recon by fire, off the sides of the boat. We had two tanks on this one boat, so we just started shooting, didn't get permission or anything, just started shooting. The [boat] captain just about had a fit." He did not want to attract attention from any enemy still about.

Carl Fleischmann said, "We landed just going out of the river toward the ocean. We went down so far and we pulled over to a thing on the lefthand side, and offloaded. We built a camp there." This was a logistical base to support efforts to clear the coastal strip. "We laid barbed wire down, put LPs—listening posts—out, and built everything up right from there.

"That's where I picked up my second Purple Heart. We were laying barbed wire." The tankers had met up with additional crews sent from Phu Bai, and were unloading the wire from a truck. "We noticed a couple of kids in the field, carrying something, but we didn't think anything of it.

"Then before we knew it, the kids were running, and we looked over and we saw the ground that was fresh-dug. Before we could yell to the truck driver, he ran over something and the truck blew up.

"His name was Pepper, Sergeant Pepper, just like Sergeant Pepper's Lonely Hearts ... That's exactly what his name is—Benjamin A. Pepper. He got severely wounded, and I was wounded. People came down and said leave him out there, it's a minefield. Ben was a friend, like I said, a tanker. I ran out there, picked him up and got him out. We put him on the chopper with the other wounded people. Again I wasn't bad enough to be medevaced, and I don't like flying."

At 1700 hours on 25 February the Citadel was declared secure. A few days later the 5th Marines returned to their operational area south of Phu Bai. The 1st Marines were moved north toward the DMZ, to participate in Operation PEGASUS, the attack to open the road to Khe Sanh.

After the city was secured and the coastal position established, the Marines worked out into the coastal strip between the city and the sea.

Tear-off calendars in many of the abandoned homes, all dated 29 January, were a poignant reminder of the Tet Offensive.[18]

Casey sent a heavy section into the strip with the ARVN, and "They got into some hellacious mess out there. In fact I lost one of the best Staff Sergeants I ever had.

"That doggone machine gun, that fifty cal, that heavy machine gun in the TC's cupola, was mounted on its side. It fed at a ninety-degree angle, and it would do nothing but jam. So … we pulled that thing out, mounted it on a tripod, sky-mounted the thing, where the TC had to pop up to fire it. And that was dangerous."

Casey continued, "They got the message early on that as soon as that cupola on that tank opened, they knew a head was coming up. They would put those snipers just zeroed in on that cupola.

"I lost a couple of TCs, and of course this platoon sergeant that way."

Dan Wokaty: "Novak was the one got killed up there. It's hard for Colonel Casey to talk about that…."

The tanks had been sent out to help sweep the area between the beach and the river, the only supply route into the city, since the road from Phu Bai was still closed by enemy activity and mines. The tanks were moving along a road when they were ambushed. Casey: "The ARVN left those tanks." The tanks had to extricate themselves by backing along the narrow road under close attack.

Jim Carroll eventually got command of a line platoon after two of Casey's tank commanders had been killed or wounded, and arrived in Alpha Company near the end of the Tet fighting. One of his first assignments was a sweep out of Phu Bai. It was very poorly planned. "The infantry wanted to do a sweep up into the highlands just south of Phu Bai. There was a paved road that the French had built … and it was overgrown with stuff, and there were some villages up in there. It was really no-man's land….

"We conducted a convoy where the grunts were on trucks, and my platoon was interspersed with their trucks. It was a scary experience, because the damn elephant grass had grown up over this road." The vegetation was actually brushing the sides of the tanks, and "If anybody had been in there to ambush us, we would have been in a world of trouble. We went up a little pass, and we got up to this so-called village area by a stream, and the houses had been blown away…. There was nobody in the village."

Carroll was convinced they were in a trap at the end of the single road, and "I told the grunt commander we need to get our butts out of here." One of Carroll's tank commanders said, "'Gunner, I'm going to recon by fire.' I said, 'Go ahead, Tal.'

"He'd be firing bursts of fifty off to the left and right, so if there was anybody in the grass, why they were keeping their heads down or they didn't make their presence known. We got back down there without taking any fire ... but it was really a bad, bad situation. A dumb enterprise that luckily didn't turn out to be a bad one."

The rest of Karl Fontenot's scattered 3rd Tank Battalion had also suffered heavily, between Quang Tri and Dong Ha, far from the spotlight of the press coverage focused on Hue and Khe Sanh. "We had half our officers in the battalion killed or wounded in one week. It got pretty hectic there at times. A third of the battalion was at some time a casualty over a period of three months.... Of course part of that too, we dismounted the headquarters and used it as infantry in the Tet Offensive, and that didn't help much." The Marine Corps had long had a three strikes policy; a third wound meant an automatic trip out of the combat zone. "When I had an officer wounded twice, I generally tried to find him a place on the battalion staff. Of course then you put that infantry company out, with nothing but officers in it who'd been wounded twice. It was kind of funny. I thought to myself, 'Hey, that wasn't too bright a move' when I had to put them out as an infantry company."

Lt. Luli's platoon from B Company, 3rd Tank was isolated at The Rockpile. Wally Young: "The supply route by road was shut down. So there for a good long while all we were getting was one C-ration meal a day." The Rockpile was a base for the Army's 175mm long-range guns firing in support of Khe Sanh, and Young recalled one memorable episode. The gun crew swabbed the chamber as usual before loading a new round, but somehow the swab got caught up in the tube by the hydraulic rammer that seated the projectile.

"The whole barrel blew up. Wounded some Marines on the perimeter there.

"When they got the new barrel in, they came up there and asked me did I think my tank could move that barrel. I said 'There ain't no doubt in my mind it'll move it.'"

The tank was used to drag the crated gun tube to the gun position.

Despite his primary MOS as a maintenance man, JJ Carroll was made a tank commander in Alpha Company of 3rd Tank because of his long experience and the shortage of combat veterans. Just before Tet the platoon, reinforced with a flame tank, was sent to support an infantry company at The Washout. They listened in amazement to the intelligence assessment of enemy strength, and plans for a last ditch defense of the position. "Me and the other tank commanders are looking at each other, going like 'Well, if you guys know all this shit, why ain't you smoking these gooks up with some air strikes?'"

A few nights later an infantry officer climbed up onto the tank to advise JJ Carroll that seismic intrusion sensors had detected motion outside the perimeter. Through an infrared vision device, Carroll could see an NVA recon team atop a small knoll, a feature marked on his night range card. "We had these new flechette rounds, dart rounds. I said 'Hmm, this is great.' I show this lieutenant, I said 'I can smoke these dudes up for you. I know the exact range to that spot.' Here you didn't have to worry about getting too much permission. It was just 'kill them.' I centered that ninety on these guys and fired one of the dart rounds.

"Next morning the grunts sent out a patrol. They came back and I said 'Hey, you guys find anything?'

"They said 'Yeah, man! Teeth, eyeballs, knuckles.' Said 'You nailed them fuckers to the tree out there.'"

Two nights later sensors indicated heavy movement in the tree line. Two of the tanks opened fire. "I fire four or five HE rounds with a five-second delay, so they'd ricochet into the jungle. I swing back to the center, and I fire one of the dart rounds. I backed it off enough to where it would fan out to the whole tree line." The report was "'Yeah, we got movement now! The shit's moving the other way!'"

Like most of the tankers, Carroll and his crewmates named their tank, though "I had so many tanks, so many names" that he could recall only a few. "My tank I named the best, I named it, was 'The Angel of Death.' That was really cool, being an Irish Catholic boy. And I had it painted in red, of course."

Throughout the Tet Offensive the logistical lifelines still had to be protected by scattered units like Luli's platoon at The Rockpile. On the roads, vehicles were supposed to keep a 'dust interval' of fifty meters between vehicles, both for security and to avoid rear-end collisions in the poor visibility.

One day near the end of the Tet fighting Wally Young's tank was the last vehicle in a convoy coming along Highway 9 from Camp Carroll.

At the Rockpile they converged with another convoy bound in the opposite direction, and "Naturally when that happened, we got hit with rockets. Big time." The tank crew could see the flashes from two enemy firing positions far out to the northwest, inside North Vietnam and beyond normal artillery range. The whole road was blocked under the rain of rockets. "Everybody was just sitting still. Nobody was returning fire." Even the long-range artillery was out of the action. "They hit the ammo dump, and the ammo was going off. The illumination ammo dump. It was all different colors, smoke, and stuff like that. They hit the fuel dump, and they hit the mess hall."

The tank commander tried to get Platoon Leader Lt. Roger Luli on the radio, but he was trapped in a bunker and out of communication. The tank could not fire its flat trajectory gun from inside the perimeter. The tank commander took over as gunner. Young drove slowly around tents and structures inside the perimeter wire, working their way toward a bridge to exit the perimeter as the rockets began to fall around the bridge.

As the tank approached the bridge from the side of the road, "A large artillery rocket landed right there and blew a big hole in the ground, just this side of the bridge. It was right in my face, because I was up out of the hatch driving. The concussion of it, once I realized that it didn't kill me, I just stood up."

The tank commander told Young he did not think he could make it over the bridge. "I had stood up, and I barreled it. I figured I could make it. So I went on. He said that we had at least two or three road wheels and the sprocket on the left side was hanging off that bridge."

The tank moved out about two miles and chose a good firing position. "We pumped about fifteen rounds into those two positions. They stopped the rocket attack, stopped shooting.

"The Lieutenant he came over the air and he asked me, 'What do you need?' I said 'I need some Hotel Echo,' HE.

"He said 'We're loading it now, and it's on the way to you.' They ran up there with a six-by with more rounds, and we reloaded."

THE AFTERMATH OF TET

The enemy had been soundly defeated in the aftermath of his Tet Offensive, but the political cost to America would eventually prove decisive. Media coverage placed the carnage of the war firmly in the face of the people, and questions about the cost and purpose of the war grew more strident. Lyndon Johnson stepped down as a contender for a second term as President, a divided Democratic Party self-destructed in an orgy of recrimination, and Richard Nixon stepped into the Presidency with promises of a "secret plan to end the war." It would be a costly secret, for the peoples of both South Vietnam and the United States.

Jim Carroll's platoon joined Casey and the rest of the company near Hue. The tanks were helping run patrols to help extricate Ernie Cheatham's depleted command in continuous ambushes as they ran patrols around the perimeter of the city.

The region consisted of scrub brush, paddies, little villages surrounded by windbreaks of trees and bushes, and areas of barren sand. "It wasn't bad tank country, as far as operating, and visibility—it wasn't jungle at all. We were able to see what we were doing."

Like many tankers, in later years Carroll would be told in no uncertain terms that there were no tanks in Vietnam, to which he replied, "'Well, I'll tell you what buddy, we ain't going to argue over it, but I was in tanks, and I was in Vietnam.'"

Jim Carroll's platoon was sent out into the dunes in support of the Army, and that's when he "had the million dollar wound. I got hit in the arm and the hand, and my butt." Such a wound always made the victim the target of typical Marine dark humor, but the fact was that "I was asleep on the back of my tank outside of Hue about two o'clock one morning in May, just before Memorial Day....

"The NVA, we'd been playing cops and robbers with them. By day we'd be looking for them. I was working with the 101st Airborne, Screaming Eagles, because they didn't have any tanks up there. They had just moved up to Hue-Phu Bai. Colonel Casey was my company commander, Captain Casey then, and he would rent us out, rent-a-tank to the Army."

The cops and robbers routine consisted of the Army troopers searching for the NVA by day, and the NVA turning to harass the encampments at night. One night the tanks were drawn up inside an Army company perimeter, when the NVA attacked with rifles, machine guns, and RPGs.

"One of their RPGs, probably, hit short of my tank, and a piece of it flew up and hit me.... That's a wakeup call you don't want to get too often. Myself and my driver were the only ones that were wounded."

The driver was asleep under the tank. The wounded Carroll and the platoon sergeant started to try and determine who had been hit without showing a light. The driver "wasn't moving. We thought he was dead. Then he started twitching a bit.... Couldn't find any blood. Finally we eased him out from under the tank, and he had a very small pencil-eraser size type hole in his temple....

"They put him and me and a couple of other guys on the chopper." They went to triage and on to the hospital ship. "He recovered okay. Just one of those things. He had a piece in his head, and I suppose he's still got it."

Casey's assessment of the night's action was that, "When they opened up from the wire, Jim opened those tanks up with flechette. I mean they had them hung in the wire out there, locker boxes full of them. That was one where you could really see what the tank could do ... although it was in a defensive situation, which is the worst thing for a tank."

On 1 April Operation PEGASUS began. Far from the glorious advance Westmoreland had planned, it was anticlimactic. The 1st Marines moved west out of Cam Lo, with tanks and infantry protecting the engineers who would rebuild the road. The Army's air cavalrymen assaulted mostly undefended landing zones.

After months of exposure to torrential rains and NVA demolition the road required considerable repair and reconstruction. Wally Young said, "We had two pontoon bridges to build. I crossed them, but I'm sitting there looking at the tank in front of me cross that thing, and the tracks get wet in that river" as the bridges sagged under the weight. "I didn't like that too much."

On 8 April the "rescuers" met a patrol out of Khe Sanh. On 11 April in Washington, Westmoreland announced to the press that the siege had been lifted. The Marines continued to agitate for closing the base, but Westmoreland refused; the personal symbolic value was too great.

Some of the tanks at Khe Sanh had been hit by mortar and artillery fire. The repair crews repaired the damage on site, so the tanks could be driven out.[19]

Also, on April Fool's Day, JJ Carroll made sergeant. "I said 'Yeah, alright, April Fool's, I get it. I didn't believe it, but sure as shit this warrant shows up, signed by Colonel Fontenot, or whatever his name was." Like so many, he had never met his battalion CO, despite Karl Fontenot's travels about the vast operational area.

Boats picked up the 3rd Battalion's wayward tanks that had been in Hue for transport north along the coast. At sea they were caught in a typhoon, and according to Fleischmann, "That's when I found out I get seasick real easy. We couldn't come into shore. We stayed out there. I remember a Chief [Petty Officer] coming up to me. I laid in that tank sick as a dog. I remember the Chief coming up to me and giving me saltine crackers.... I was like, 'Get them out of my face!' But it got me through."

At Con Thien, Carl Fleischmann was assigned to C Company. Still craving revenge, he started sleeping with a knife. His experiences in Hue were far more traumatic than his brother's wounding. "I was also pretty pissed at people at that time. Robert Hall died in my arms. I was mad as a hornet about that. All my friends were wounded. I hated it.

"That's when I said I didn't want to have tanks any more. I wanted to become a tunnel rat. I wanted to become a grunt, and they said, 'Well, you'll be a tunnel rat,' so I said fine." Tunnel rats were men chosen for their slight or thin build to explore the numerous underground tunnel complexes that were the specialty of the VC. It required a high tolerance for tight spaces, snakes, and other animals that infested the dark tunnels, and of course the risk of encountering the enemy or his booby traps deep underground.

"When the third Purple Heart came, I said 'Okay, this is it.' I got shot in the leg, and then I guess reality set in. It was like 'Okay, you're running out of body parts here. Let's just get you back to tanks,' which I did. Then my orders showed up to come Stateside. That's when I found out I made E-4 (Corporal). I was an E-1 (Private) when I got there." Fleischmann still does not know whether it was the accumulated effects of his wounds, or the Corps' 'three strikes and out of country' policy, which seems to have been somewhat erratically enforced.

John Wear's flame tank came up the Cua Viet River to Dong Ha. They spent only a few days there, only long enough "to get a shower and a hot meal" before being sent out to relieve another flame tank. "They needed their quarterly maintenance, so we spent about a week up at The Washout."

In early April John Wear got a new assignment. "The CO of H&S Company called me back in and said, 'You either can be flame tank commander, or I can send you to any gun tank company you want to go to.'" Wear chose command of a brand new flame tank.

Unlike the gun tanks, the flame tanks served primarily on call for special operations. "If we went through a bunker complex, and they couldn't get the guys out of the bunkers, we'd burn it out. Or if they had a huge stash of [captured] stuff they wanted to get rid of, destroy, they'd call us up and we'd take care of the munitions or whatever it was. The rest of the time we were used for making a lot of noise."

The entire Leatherneck Square region, bounded by Gio Linh and Dong Ha on the east and Con Thien and Cam Lo on the west, was by now a free fire zone. All civilians had been evacuated. In April, "Two flame tanks went with the Seventh Cav, Army. They came up to show us how it was done. There was a huge sweep where we were the blocking force, south of Cam Lo. That wasn't part of the free fire zone, and there were farmers out there, kids begging for food, and all that kind of stuff. We really didn't interact with them, but it was just amazing to see. Three clicks away you're in a free fire zone, and anything that walks around you can shoot it with impunity. Then we go south just a little ways, and we had to watch our Ps and Qs."

THE NEW WAR IN NORTHERN I CORPS

While most attention was on Khe San and Hue, the 3rd Marine Division had launched its own offensive on 30 January, Operation SALINE, to clear the important water supply routes along the Cua Viet and Bo Dieu rivers near the DMZ. Resistance and intelligence indicated that the NVA *320th Division* was moving south to threaten the Dong Ha area. The division continued to conduct sweeps in the Leatherneck Square region, continuing Operation KENTUCKY.

Operation PEGASUS had opened Route 9 as far as Khe Sanh, but securing the narrow, twisting road required constant patrols. On the night of 25 April a tank from C Company, 3rd Tank conducted a road patrol with grunts from G/2/3 mounted on the tank. Garry L. Hall was the tank commander of the vehicle moving down the pitch-dark road, the crew all riding exposed for better visibility in the darkness.[20]

At about 2130 hours numerous explosions lit up the night as the patrol was ambushed. The gunner got off one round of canister, obliterating an RPG team, but other attackers fired RPGs and hurled satchel charges. The tanked jerked to a stop, and Hall dropped down into the turret to radio the command position. Just then the tank lurched forward. Apparently the driver, Jim Jaynes, was dead. The tank veered off the road and careened about four hundred feet down the jungle-covered mountainside. Battalion commander Karl Fontenot: "The driver was killed instantly, they hit it right on the front slope with an RPG, penetrated and killed the driver. The tank went do the slope to the bottom of the hill, hit the bottom of the hill tracks still turning, and the driver wedged in place." Hall also believes that a satchel charge was thrown into the driver's compartment.

At the bottom of the ravine Hall found the tank so firmly wedged that he could not traverse the turret, and the still-churning tracks were beginning to smoke from grinding on the rocks and debris. Hall had the crew don gas masks in an attempt to stay with the tank as long as possible. By the time flames coming into the crew space forced them out, machine gun ammunition stored in the gypsy rack above the engine was cooking off. The loader, a PFC Rodriguez, dismounted the coaxial machine gun, and he and the gunner, Charles W. Tucker, followed Hall out, loaded with the tank's grease gun and some grenades. The three survivors went to ground in a shell crater about thirty feet away. All night long the 90mm ammunition in the tank cooked off.

In the pre-dawn hours a flashlight flickered through the darkness, and Hall told his men to hold their fire to avoid revealing their position. They all felt that the grunts would wait until daybreak to search for them. At last the light moved away and up the ravine.

At first light a face appeared through the broken vegetation in their path, and the crew hunkered down for a fight. Then a black face appeared, and they knew that the grunts had come for them. There was little of Jaynes's body left to recover, and the burned-out tank was left at the bottom of the ravine.

In the early days of 1968 the 3rd Marine Division was already experimenting with flexible organizational structures that would allow it to fight a more mobile and more conventional war with limited resources. Karl Fontenot recalled a division reserve of which he was the XO, consisting of a tank company, Army self-propelled twin 40mm and quad .50 caliber AA guns, Amtracs, and a company of Ontos. "It was set up to take any number of infantry attachments for particular operations. Run completely off notebooks and things, with no typewriters or anything of that type. It was in the center of the area sitting between Dong Ha and Camp Carroll."

The mobile reserve was the forerunner to the only armored task force the Marines formed during the course of the war. In response to the perceived threat of an NVA armored attack, the 3rd Tank Battalion formed Task Force Robbie, based at Cam Lo. It consisted of a truck-mounted infantry company, a tank company, plus supporting units. John Wear was assigned to TF Robbie. He explained, "There were representative tanks from all three Marine tank companies, some Ontos, quad fifties from the Army, mounted on trucks. I know there were some one-five-five self-propelleds [M109 armored howitzers], but they just kind of stuck around. They didn't go out on road marches with us or anything. They were there at Cam Lo Hill when we were there. There were also some Dusters, the twin-fortys." The main force was whatever infantry company was available, typically drawn from 1/9.

Task Force Robbie was used more as a reaction force and division reserve. When asked if Robbie ran into trouble "a couple" of times, Wear laughed. "A couple?" Official histories state that on 29 April the Task Force headed to the assistance of an ARVN unit that was under heavy attack.[21] "Mai Loc was the name of the town they were in. They hit some trouble and we went out hell bent for leather, just the tanks. The CO, Robichard, said, 'Don't stay on the road, go across country.' My tank and five others hit mines, within ten minutes of going out on the sweep to see if we could go rescue the grunts.[22]

"The guys that did make it to where the grunts were getting their asses handed to them, they did shoot up a bunch of the North Vietnamese. It was a company, maybe part of a regiment of the NVA."

Wear's tank was heavily damaged, and "We think ours [the mine] was probably an unexploded one-oh-five [round]," either a dud that simply exploded, or an improvised mine rigged by the NVA. "It blew off one set of road wheels, I'm going to say maybe a hundred yards away.... Tore up the suspension, enough to where we had to short-track the tank, and we were able to limp back to Cam Lo." The ubiquitous retriever hauled the tank back to Dong Ha, where "It took about four days of really bustin' heavy to really get the tank back together. A lot of that stuff was wrecked, so you had to go out and get new, either steal it off another tank or go to the Army and beg for it, or whatever."

This battle was the opening round in a series that revealed the NVA was now operating far to the south of his previously known positions, and planned to interdict critical river traffic. This triggered a series of savage infantry fights in the swampy terrain along the river east of Dong Ha.

By spring 1968 the tempo of operations had settled back down enough to pass for 'normal.' Jim Coan was a tank platoon leader for 1st

Platoon, Alpha Company, 3rd Tank at Con Thien. One morning he was summoned back to headquarters at Dong Ha, which usually meant hot food and a shower. His tank was speeding along when they came upon a lone grunt trudging down the road between C-2 and Cam Lo, alone in hostile country. He said that his CO had sent him off for R&R, so the tankers offered him a ride, telling him to hold on to the gypsy rack.

When Coan looked back, the man was gone, lying in the road. The tankers turned around and were looking him over for wounds when a jeep with two senior officers sped up and asked what happened. Thinking fast, Coan explained that they had found the unconscious man, who had likely fallen off the back of a truck. A few minutes later a medevac helicopter landed nearby. The corpsman roused the grunt and explained to him that he had fallen off a truck and would be okay.

The officers congratulated Coan, who took the opportunity to depart at speed.[23]

Dan McQueary was returned to duty and was on the I&I staff of a Reserve unit in Ohio, then went through the Warrant Officer program and Officer Candidate School at Quantico. He returned to Vietnam in the late summer of 1968 as a Captain.

The Battalion Headquarters was at Quang Tri. McQueary was assigned to Dong Ha. "We had a company of tanks at Dong Ha, and H&S (Forward) Company, which included the Maintenance and Headquarters and Service department." McQueary began with A Company, and then took over as the forward commander of the two elements. Later an officer was assigned to lead A Company, and McQueary assumed the position of area commander. "I was what they called A Company/H&S Company Forward.

"In the H&S Forward I had the battalion maintenance, ordnance, the recovery, and coordinating. They put another Captain up there in A Company, and I coordinated the operation of H&S with A Company, and provided him with Headquarters tanks if I needed to fill in on some of his operations."

As maintenance officer, McQueary thought that the fire control system was the most difficult maintenance burden for the M48A3s. "They really had to be calibrated quite regularly, and really checked because of the humidity, getting moisture in the optics and things of that nature.

"Then of course the other thing, I'll be up front with you, was the spare parts situation. It was unbelievable. The other thing was the mine damage."

The mine damage kits, as described by Joe Sleger, were "Kind of like a mount-out type thing that you do when you mount out to go somewhere. We made up a kit of what we felt from experience of [parts] where we received the most damage. In the suspension." The kits were mostly spare parts put aside, since "You come up and all of a sudden parts are not available to put a unit back in service. That was really our reserve. We kept that right up to snuff all the time. That got us out of the woods quite a few times, as far as keeping things operational."

The slap-hammer was a heavy inertia hammer used to knock out damaged torsion bars, and was the 'official' tool for the job. When asked if it was much used, McQueary answered, "Well, yes," without much enthusiasm. The hammer was slow, laborious, and unpleasant.

Explosive was as always the tool of choice for removing the heavy torsion bars, even for the maintenance crews. McQueary explained that "only about a thumbnail of C4" was used to pop the torsion bars. "Funny thing happened one time, we had a Lieutenant up in Bravo Company. He had heard about how this was done. Anyway, he performed the operation, but he stuck enough C4 in there, about the size of a baseball. It did a nice job.

"We had ammunition inside the tank at the time. It detonated that, too.

"It was damaged. Really bad. Basically, the total price for that vehicle, I think he's probably still paying for it, maybe. I was a little hostile over it when I went up there and took a look at what he'd done."

On 5 July the Marines launched Operation THOR, an incursion into the DMZ to destroy enemy artillery positions. The 3rd Marines attacked north from near Dong Ha. Between 17 and 31 July the 3rd and 9th Marines and the 2nd ARVN Regiment swept the area south of the DMZ as far west as Camp Carroll. John Wear recalled that virtually "every single tank that could run ... was involved in that."

Often in combat, survival is simply a matter of pure chance. Wear's tank had been detached to carry a load of wounded back to the LZ and was returning just as the Marines struck a bunker complex. "I got out my binoculars and was looking out from the TC's cupola... I felt something warm. That next evening one of the grunts said, 'Did you see that RPG almost hit you?' and I said no. What had happened was my tank pulled forward, and as we were pulling forward the RPG went over and missed me. If I had stayed where I was, I would probably have gotten hit in the face with an RPG."

The bunker complex fight was the only incident where John Wear could recall the NVA heavy artillery firing upon tankers who were trying to recover a disabled tank. "We were attacking a bunker complex, and one of the tanks—the driver was buttoned up—didn't see where he was going. The tank fell into a B-52 bomb crater." Tanks that fell into the huge craters were usually invisible from ground level.

When Wear dismounted to help, the rest of the crew were already out of the hole, but the tank commander, Jesus 'Chewy' Bonilla, was missing, "... and I said 'Where's Chewy?'

"They said 'He's inside the tank,' and I said 'Why?'

"A huge piece of shrapnel, about ten inches by about four inches, pranged off a tree and smacked him. He still had his helmet on. Smacked him in the forehead, and knocked him on his ass. Hit him flat, so it didn't hurt him at all, but bruised his pride. He was inside the tank saying his Hail Marys.

"It slid sideways down, and threw one track inside (under the hull) and one track out.... We hauled the tank up and took off the track and put it back on and locked the tank up. The whole time we were getting those shells....

"Some place close by there was a spotter, an FO, and they were throwing shells in on us."

Like most combat veterans, Wear recalled being subjected to artillery fire as the most frightening experience of the war. "That was absolutely terrifying.... Just because you're all by yourself. It could land on you, or it couldn't. And there'd be thousands and thousands of these things, and they just wouldn't stop. Scare the living dogmeat out of you.

"Loud, and it's huge, it's like a freight train. You're absolutely helpless."

Third Tank inherited responsibility for the Civic Action Program in a local village. Karl Fontenot: "I got real lucky one time, I drew a former Viet Cong village. Everybody in it was mostly relocated Viet Cong, which was interesting. Always got an itching in the middle of the back when I went down there.[24]

"All the battalions that stayed in one area for any length of time were assigned these various villages to try and secure their rice. The tax collectors for the Viet Cong used to come around and people kept their rice in their houses. The [VC] would come around frequently and take the rice, assess 'taxes' against them to support the Viet Cong activities. You'd try to get them to help centralize the location and guard their rice and stuff like that, along with helping try to improve the health of the village.

"My corpsman found one kid with a cleft palate. We flew him out to the local Navy hospital ship ... and they repaired the cleft palate. What I thought was amazing was his mother. His mother of course could speak no English, but she came and got on the plane and left with him. She wanted her child taken care of enough to go with him to a strange ship and eventually get back on a plane. We just attached a tag to her, telling where they were going. She got there, got the child repaired, and brought him back.

"Of course you don't hear much about those things, either."

For some reason known only to the military bureaucracy, the battalion was also assigned a dentist, so "We used to put him on a tank. We'd take him out to local villages and he'd work on their teeth."

Other incidents were less happy. "One night there was a misguided air strike...." Fontenot explained that the villagers constructed elevated houses, "So when a bomb hits, they're right in the area to take the blast coming up. By far it's the worst area you could be in."

Third Tank was the closest unit and the corpsman and dentist were the only medical help available. "The corpsman had to perform some amputations there before we could get helicopters in and airlift all these casualties out to the hospital ship. I think we had eighteen or twenty that night."

Life was far different for the gun companies. In general the line company tankers did not associate with the villagers, probably because, as Fontenot noticed, the tankers could not develop a settled lifestyle. In the closing days of Korea the tankers had lived in one area for lengthy periods, and accumulated masses of things like stoves and furniture to make life more comfortable. In Vietnam the tanks were constantly in the field, and "they learned how to live in their tank, basically. They had small containers welded on the back of the tank, five-gallon ammo cans, and all their belongings were in a can. They learned how to live with that tank, move from one unit to another wherever they had to go, and that basically was their home."

Also unlike Korea, the tankers were better trained before arriving in country, but it was still prudent to provide additional training at battalion level as the companies in the field did not have sufficient time available.[25] Even so, there were harsh lessons. "We had one officer killed. Stuck his head up to look. The gunner reached over and tried to pull him back down, saying 'Don't stick your head up there, lieutenant.' Somebody shot him right through the head."

Major General Raymond Davis assumed command of the 3rd Marine Division in May, and quickly implemented plans for airmobile operations that would allow the overtaxed division to respond more effectively to the constant NVA incursions across the DMZ. Most of these operations were conducted in the rugged terrain west of Con Thien. The infantry was largely helicopter borne, and supported by local Fire Support Bases hewn out of the hilltops.

The rising level of NVA activity caused MACV to reinforce III MAF with additional Army units, and at the end of July an Army mechanized unit, the 1st Brigade, 5th Infantry Division was assigned to the DMZ area. The first indication for the Marine tankers were when men like John Wear who "were guarding the Cam Lo Bridge outside Dong Ha, when all of a sudden a whole gaggle of Army tanks came trundling up the road, and they were gasoline-powered tanks at that. They had just offloaded from the ships. They came and relieved us and were attached to Third Marine Division."

III MAF concluded that the mechanized unit was better suited by organization and training to secure the open terrain around Gio Linh and Dong Ha, while the Marines shifted westward. Years later, as a General, Army Colonel Donn Starry would write in reference to the short-lived mechanized operations by the 1st Brigade, that the NVA were:

> .... unaccustomed to fighting U.S. armored forces. The U.S. Marines operated in this region, but used their armor in small groups whose primary role was support of dismounted infantry. Thus, the 1st Brigade enjoyed some immediate success against enemy troops who tried to stand and fight, believing themselves to be facing tank-supported infantry as before. These encounters were usually one-sided, with the North Vietnamese losing significantly in men and equipment. However, the enemy quickly learned the futility of a stand-up fight against the consolidated mechanized force of the brigade, and changed his tactics to avoid the mounted formations.[26]

The remembrances of the Marine tankers are somewhat less rosy. JJ Carroll was at the Dong Ha tank park when the new Army unit rolled in. "Brand new extra road wheels strapped to their searchlight mounts.... We're lickin' our chops" said Carroll, probably thinking of the potential for theft of much needed spares. "I'm on the back of my tank cleaning the old M1919 Browning [pistol]. These doggies came over and said 'What is that?' They said, 'We saw them in the movies.'"

The Marines marveled at the excess of equipment, like APCs loaded with extra ammunition, spare parts, and most of all the cockiness of the new soldiers.

Carroll: "They go off toward Gio Linh, and there's a big sand flat there. No grunts. Going out, they're General Patton, right?" The NVA quickly "whacked their ass big time."

Without faulting the courage or professionalism of the Army tankers, doctrines developed for fighting against opposing mechanized forces were inherently not the best suited to fighting the NVA. The NVA was not intimidated by the tanks, but simply adapted to a new situation. Changing tactics to "avoid the mounted formations" was a primary NVA survival mechanism, and one at which he was very good. Despite Starry's optimistic assessment, the brigade was quickly withdrawn from the DMZ area proper, and used primarily in sweep and cordon operations farther south in Quang Tri Province.

During the Army's stay, Dan McQueary marveled at their practice of abandoning equipment for later recovery by the ordnance repair units. "They had an abandoned retriever up there, an [M88] and we had our retriever up there. They had hit a mine with it. The only thing it did was it broke the track off it." There was also minor damage to the road wheels.

"The crew just evacuated, got up and left. They left the whole retriever there, the weapons on it, communications equipment, everything on it.

"We got all the communications equipment out of it when we were up there. We stopped and got that, and all the weapons off it. We didn't have the capability to recover it and bring it back to Dong Ha at the time.

"They didn't want it after we got through with it. They blew it in place."

In addition, "They did that up at Con Thien. The First of the Forty-Fourth went in country up there, and they relieved, I think it was Third Platoon up at Con Thien for a period of time. They brought tanks in there, and boy they took a beating up there. They walked off that hill up at Con Thien and left everything just sitting there."

McQueary preferred not to refer to removing parts from abandoned Army tanks as scavenging, but rather as "selective interchange. It's kind of a nice thing. Not stealing."

John Wear later became friends with an officer in the Brigade, then Captain Stovall of the 1st Battalion, 69th Armor, who was the company commander in the only action in which the NVA used tanks against American tanks, at Ben Het in March 1969.[27] The Army tanks inflicted a one-sided defeat on the enemy and the NVA never again attempted to pit their own tanks against American armor. The battles along the DMZ area would continue to be fought largely by Marine infantry, accompanied by Marine tanks.

When the tanks were not out on sweeps they occupied positions protecting the perimeters of the bases. "My tank was on the line" at Con Thien, explained Wear, "and we had this tiny little hooch. There were three of us living inside this fairly small hooch. There were racks [wooden beds], and we just put—we called them rubber whores, rubber ladies, air mattresses—in there, and slept in those." The little bunkers were an architectural mishmash of ammo boxes filled with dirt, steel engineering stakes, tarps, and sandbags.[28] The usual procedure was for one person to stay on watch inside the tank, and "When there was more than one person on the tank on watch ... one guy would sleep on the back of the tank.

"The platoon commander, and a lot of the people, had these huge Dye Marker bunkers, built with twelve-by-twelve (inch) timbers. They were nice."

The improvised homes were not suited to the climate. "When it rained a lot, then you got wet....We went up to Con Thien right at the very end of the rainy season, so it started getting not so bad.

"Rats and mice! The rats, they were huge. The rats could pick up a whole bag of M&M's™ in their mouth, the quarter pounders, pick them up and walk off with them." The rats usually came out at night.

"We had wild pigs, pythons, once in a great while you'd see a tiger...."

The pythons were more common in the bush. "The grunts would be on both sides of the tank, walking, and all of a sudden 'Oh, God, look out! Look out!' and there'd be a python lying across the path. They'd just slither off. Almost always you'd just let them go. Once in a while a guy would shoot them. They might take them back and eat them, make a stew out of them or something" to relieve the horrendous tedium of C-ration meals.

C-rations came in nine menus, and the variety was further reduced since some were considered highly undesirable. Ham and lima beans, usually referred to as 'ham and mothers,' induced flatulence. Ham and scrambled eggs were simply a soggy, unseasoned goo. Ham and mothers also were unpopular because the sweet included was canned apricots, considered bad luck by the Marines, and by tankers and Amtrac crews in particular. John Wear thinks the tradition originated with 1/9 as a bad luck or 'dead man's meal,' but the tradition seems to be even older. The aversion was so strong that Wear said "I didn't eat apricots until about five or six years ago," three decades after leaving Vietnam.

Even at bases with mess halls the food was uninspired, featuring overcooked canned vegetables, potatoes, lots of bread, stews, and less than choice cuts of meat that the troops referred to as "scabs."[29]

Because of the limited diet, food was often a major obsession. Units in the field subsisted for months on the C-ration menus, with an occasional hot cooked meal of A- or B-rations brought out in large insulated cans. Anything else was a windfall.

"We went to The Washout once," said Wear, "and the grunts had all left. We were snoopin' and poopin' around there, and I found two big number-ten cans of dehydrated steaks. We went back to Con Thien and we had a steak fry. We soaked them in water, and broke up some pallets [for wood], and had a steak fry. That was like a month's highlight."

On the sweep operations the tanks were occasionally able to surprise the normally vigilant NVA. On 15 August ten tanks escorted troops of the ARVN 2nd Regiment and the 11th Armored Cavalry into the area northeast of Gio Linh. Dan McQueary: "We had a very good operation one time called Lam Song 260 [250?]. That was up right on the border, on the Ben Hai River. We had an operation with an ARVN group up there. We took a platoon plus of tanks up there" from A and B Companies, 3rd Tank.

"We caught an NVA battalion on the south side of the river. We had an excellent Army advisor, a great guy, a Major. He brought us in during the middle of the night up there, and we ran into them just pop! Caught them still cooking their rice.

"They made their evacuation toward the river at the time, so we got a good kill rate on them, just excellent. It was interesting, because when we got to the Ben Hai River, we did some scooping and everything, we noticed they had a sapper base, kind of like a UDT [Underwater Demolition Team] base, right across the river. They were over there training in rubber boats and things, and we spotted them. We put some ninety millimeter on them, and we had some pretty good results." Tank fire was credited with inflicting 198 of the estimated 421 enemy dead from the *1st Battalion, 138th NVA Regiment*.[30]

Field operations were of course interspersed with road sweeps, protecting the engineers in the never-ending effort to keep the roads open. Mostly the sweeps were slow, boring crawls in the intense heat, with occasional disasters. Wear said that though mines seemed less common up north, on one such sweep, Clem Matye's tank hit what was probably a command detonated mine. "He was sitting up … on the TC's clamshell. They think it probably was three one-five-five rounds linked together blew up, and blew his leg off. It blew the entire side of the tank off. There was nothing left on the one side of the tank, other than the turret and the body. Fenders, every bit of suspension was gone."

The situation was not much better elsewhere. "We'd go to Dong Ha for quarterly maintenance or if we hit a mine." Aboard the sprawling base, "We'd walk from our tank park across this kind of little gully, and up a hill to a chow hall, the 9th Motor T chow hall. It was way up on top of the hill. They knew that we'd break for lunch. Every day at lunchtime, they'd fire off a major salvo and sometimes it would hit in the Motor T, sometimes it would hit the mess hall, sometimes it would hit our tanks."

Fortunately, "You can hear stuff, and you know it's incoming. Even it it's not incoming, you get in a hole."

One day at Dong Ha random chance again intervened. "It was really hot one day, and we both happened to be back at Dong Ha. I said 'Come on, Peavey, I gotta leave tomorrow, so come on and have lunch with me.' He said 'Nah, I'm going to go to my tent and take a nap.'

"I convinced him to go, and we went to chow. Two rounds landed in the middle of the tent, and would've killed him. You're always on edge, and you always think something's going to happen, and … eighty-five percent of the time nothing happens."

Under the constant threat, the men grew blasé. "As you're there longer, things don't bother you nearly as much." Some things even became a fixture of life. "The B-52 ARC LIGHTs … just outside of Con Thien, they would make your teeth rattle, they were so loud." The bombs were exploding "At least a half mile, maybe longer" away from the base, "but it seemed like they were right there in the wire."

Over the final months of the year the tempo of the war slowed in northern Quang Tri. Wear's flame tank was assigned to Alpha Company, and then to Charlie Company, shifting all around the region. Wear and Bob Peavey's tanks were both sent to Ocean View, a Marine outpost where the DMZ met the seashore. Wear said that from Ocean View "You could look through the binoculars, the periscope, and see the North Vietnamese on the other side. They'd be taking baths out in the water, and we'd shoot at them every once in a while."

One of Wear's last assignments was to Quang Tri, the location of the tank battalion and division headquarters. "We spent most of the time—a gun tank and my flame tank—from eight o'clock at night until eight o'clock the next morning doing staggered Rat Patrols going between Quang Tri and Dong Ha to keep the road open." The tanks were also a rapid response group to come to the aid of Combined Action Platoons in the local villages if they were attacked.

It was both boring and terrifying duty.

Their strength spent, both sides staggered to a near halt in operations along the DMZ as the year drew to a close. Wally Young left Vietnam early, diagnosed with a "fever of unknown origin." His last indignity was being issued a new uniform and being mistaken for a man fresh "in-country."

THE NEW WAR IN SOUTHERN I CORPS

The enemy had built up considerable strength in the region south of the Hai Van Pass, but the Tet Offensive was largely thwarted. Marine reconnaissance teams identified the *2nd NVA Division* as it moved toward Danang, and air strikes and infantry drove the division back. Danang suffered rocket attacks and minor ground assaults.

After Tet, southwest of Danang in Quang Nam Province, the *2nd NVA Division* controlled the old *1st VC Regiment*, and the *21st, 36th, 38th,* and *141st NVA Regiments*, with heavy firepower provided by the artillery rocket regiments *68B* and *368B* of the NVA. In Quang Tin and Quang Ngai Provinces the *3rd NVA Division* controlled the *2nd VC Regiment*, the *3rd, 22nd,* and *31st NVA Regiments,* and the *401VC (Sapper) Regiment*. They were reinforced by the *Q81* and *Q83 VC Local Force Battalions*, and the *220 Transport Regiment*. To counter this force the Americans had deployed not only the 1st Marine Division, but the Army's Americal Division. The requirement to protect the Danang Vital Area and the conduct of the pacification and village security programs inherently meant that the initiative would remain with the enemy, but the Marines were intent on disrupting the enemy's plans.

Westmoreland trumpeted the victories against the Tet Offensive, but warned that the enemy was not spent. He requested another 206,000 additional troops. This was yet another blow to an American public increasingly disenchanted with the war. On 23 March the President announced that Westmoreland would be "kicked upstairs."

As part of the buildup, the 27th Marines were alerted to move to Vietnam, arriving between 17 and 28 February. After recuperating from his wounds, Ken Pozder went to Charlie Company, 5th Tank at Camp Pendleton. "When that Tet Offensive hit, they came in the barracks one night, and every tanker that was in the barracks got transferred to the infantry. They put them on planes, and then they brought amphibious tractor people and stuff like that in to be tank crewmen.

"We were left with one company, Bravo Company 5th Tank, and we trained all those people. There were Motor Transport people—pretty much a hodge-podge of people that got transferred in, and we had to train them. Luckily we had a month to do it...."

The reconstructed company was shipped to Vietnam after Tet, but "As soon as we hit Danang, they kind of broke up the tank company. I went to Bravo Company, 1st Tanks. I don't even know what they did with the people from the rest of the company." The separate bits of the company took their tanks with them, to be functionally absorbed into the other battalions.

In late February of 1968 Pozder was assigned to a unit primarily because he could get along with T.J. Siva, who was notoriously hot headed. The First Sergeant threatened to send him out with Siva's platoon, and "I said 'Oh, yeah! Put me in with Siva.'

The First Sergeant was incredulous. "'You wanta go with Siva?' I said 'You're damn right. I'll take him any day.'" Pozder was sent out with Siva's 3rd Platoon, Bravo Company, 3rd Tank.

One of the first things Pozder noticed was that the opposing side's weapons had changed, and with them the nature of the war. "They had recoilless rifles, RPG-7s, good machine guns.... Of course it was almost all NVA by that time."

The NVA "...were good soldiers. They were well disciplined. They didn't turn and run. They did their strategic retreats or whatever. If they were overwhelmed, they'd just boogie. But it was orderly. That's the way you stay alive."

Bob Embesi was also with the 5th Tank Battalion, in support of 2/27. The 27th Marines assumed responsibility for the 5th Marines' old area, and the 5th Marines began a prolonged sweep, Operation HOUSTON, between the Hai Van Pass and Phu Bai. On 12 March the 7th Marines began Operation WORTH southwest of Danang, but this operation was suspended when it became apparent that at least an enemy division was entrenched around Go Noi Island, another traditional stronghold.

Siva was one of the characters who would figure prominently in 1st Tank's actions over the coming months. Dan Wokaty: "I never did have problems with old Siva. We always got along good. I went on liberty with him, but whenever he started drinking, I cut out. I had better sense than to stick around, because I knew what was going to take place next."

In one memorable episode Siva had been wounded and medevaced to a hospital ship offshore. The Navy lost track of him, and the 1st Tank Battalion was carrying Siva as missing, believing he had fallen overboard from the hospital ship. In reality, he had gotten aboard a medevac helicopter on its return trip. "He was coming across the area ... and he had a body cast on with one arm out. He was wanting me to cut that body cast off of him. He said, 'You know I can't stay on them damn ships because they make me sick.'"

Wokaty got some tools and cut away the cast. Siva boarded a helicopter and flew back out to Hill 55. "I'm glad he was on our side, not their side."

The war was steadily heating up, and the tank units in southern I Corps were also tasked with support of ARVN units. In April, Dan Wokaty's 1st Platoon, A Company, 1st Tank was assigned to bridge security between at the Tuy Long Bridge on Route 5 between the infantry battalion positions on Hill 10 and Hill 37, west of Danang.[31]

One day about 1400 a group of ARVN came up to the platoon position to report VC in a village to the south. After receiving permission from the battalion, the platoon sent A12 and A13 to assist. Dan Wokaty: "One of them [A13] got hit with an RPG. It came back. I took the next one [A15] down there. They were really shooting down there.

"When they got down there, they found it was a little more than what they thought it was.

"This corpsman was telling me 'We got a lot of dead and wounded we got to get out of there.' so I pulled my tank around there and I told him 'Only load up the wounded ones on the tank, and I'll take them out of here.' One of them was Captain McPherson.... Warrant Officer Carroll was telling me 'There was some good kids killed out there that day, and some good kids that got shot up.'

"When we were pulling out, they were shooting B-40s and RPGs at us, and goldang, it was hot. We got them out so they could get medevaced, but there were about eight bodies there, and it got dark on us. They couldn't carry them out of there."

The infantry had thrown both dead and wounded onto the engine deck, and the wounded were shouting that the enemy were firing at the tank. "I remember looking over my shoulder, and I could see them things [RPGs]. Have you ever seen one of them coming toward you? They're moving about as slow as bringing you finger toward your face. It's a bad feeling."

The dead infantry, even though they could not be carried out, needed to be identified. "I told this lieutenant I had there, 'This is your job.' He said 'I can't do that' because some of them, part of their head was missing, and part of the torso was missing. I said, 'You got to go over there and identify those guys for them.'

"I went over there and identified all of them, and called it in to Captain Casey, and he turned it in to battalion.... The next morning some of them you couldn't even load them up...." The bodies were already frozen into the awkward postures of death.

Wokaty later found out that he had been recommended for a Silver Star for the action, but the battalion commander did not like him, so "if I was written up for one, he probably put it in that A to Z file."

Months later Wokaty encountered McPherson in California, and the officer thanked him for saving him that day.

Wokaty went back to battalion for a couple of days, and when he came back, "the lieutenant told me, 'There's two ChiCom grenades out there that you got to get rid of.' I said, 'What do you mean there's two ChiCom grenades?'

"He said 'Yeah, a kid brought them up here and I gave him two cases of C-rations.'" The child had found two grenades that had been armed, but failed to explode. "It took a lot of thinking on my part in deciding whether I wanted to touch those things or not. I finally made a decision and was going to get rid of them. When I threw them over in the river, the first one didn't go off, but the second one did."

Go Noi Island is lowland bounded by the wandering channels of the Ky Lam River. Highway 1 and a long-abandoned railway traversed the east end of the island. Otherwise it was overgrown, roadless, and generally inaccessible, ideal terrain for the VC and NVA. The region also lay athwart the boundary between the ARVN and South Korean TAORs, and neither would aggressively enter the area.[32]

Operation ALLEN BROOK, the effort to clear the island, would be another example of the war of attrition that the Marines—and America in general—found so frustrating. The basic plan was to march back and forth through one of the enemy's strongholds looking for a fight. On 4 May, 2/7 was airlifted to the western margin of the island and began to sweep east, meeting the first heavy resistance on 8 May, with heavy fighting near the old rail berm at Xuan Dai on 9 May. On 13 May, 3/7 replaced the worn battalion when it reached the eastern end of the island, and swept back to the west.

Embesi's heavy section joined up with four tanks from the unit supporting the 7th Marines near Liberty Bridge, and he provides an account of the fatigue, confusion, and brutality of a prolonged operation. The officer from the other platoon, a Lieutenant Scott, would be the Platoon Leader, with Embesi as the Platoon Sergeant. As on most such operations the tanks served as assault guns for the infantry; direct-fire cannons at the infantry's beck and call. The enemy was adept at avoiding the Marines, and even after it was "cleared," an area remained infested with enemy.

"When we first went in there ... we got all the way up to the railroad tracks, that's in there ... ten miles, maybe more. We had gotten in there with no resistance. A firefight, maybe a little bit. I was reconning by fire all the time. We turn around and come back, and swept around, trying to make contact.

"We found that these NVA were coming through the lines ... dressed like women. We found a few of them, they got in a firefight and killed them, found they had wigs and shit on them, and female clothes and such."

The NVA roamed freely about the areas the Marines had already swept. The enemy polluted the village wells, and even such vital supplies as water and food were scarce. One day, "We pulled up there and they said 'Okay, everybody take a detail down to get water…' We get a bunch of grunts going to go fill canteens, and we took a couple of water cans.

"The river's full of dead bodies. NVA dead bodies laying everywhere. We get that water in the tank, and after two or three days, hot as it is, that old [water can] starts spewing and stinking. God, it smelled. You had to put Halazone in there to drink it. You had to change it every other day … it was just nasty."

Embesi watched the hungry infantry kill livestock they found in the villages. "One guy had a pig, and a couple of guys had chickens…. They're going to cook it, eat it raw … however they could do it. They were hungry."

Resupply was perilous duty. "As we came through we had a lot of wounded and dead infantry from the ambushes. We were up there at the railroad tracks, and the colonel says we need to get resupply. Every time resupply would come in they couldn't get in there with anything, because they put up such a fire in the air. They'd shoot the helicopters down. So helicopters didn't want to come in there." On the ground, no area was considered safe, so the tanks were used to escort the convoys through "cleared" areas behind the fighting.

"We went out for a resupply. We had Amtracs carrying the dead. We had a company of grunts with us and we were going to take them out and get resupplied. We didn't even have good drinking water, and hardly anything to eat. We got about halfway out" when the column plowed head-on into resistance in an area that had—in theory—been swept twice. The enemy, entrenched in a hedgerow, opened fire from near point blank range.

"Reinforced bunkers in there. They started shooting RPGs, and they were flying all over…. We were stopped, and the arty guy, the FO, came over and called in a fire mission right on top of us. Near right on top of us, they were probably [impacting] thirty, forty yards, not even that, in front of us. The grunts were of course pinned down, laying down" in the face of intense machine gun and mortar fire.

Even after the artillery impacted, "Then they come at us again with RPGs, and more mortars. Hell, we ran out of ammunition in the tank. I got up, and I had a lot of dead grunt's rifles hanging off the top of the tank. Had them set on automatic. I just got up and started shooting the bastards…."

He told Bob Peavey to fire off the last round from the main gun—an armor piercing solid shot.

"We broke the ambush. We decided to move. Once the artillery came in a couple of times ... we busted through and just took off, got everybody in line in column and just left....

"We got resupplied and we turned around and went back in there the same day.... On the way back in, we got ambushed again. We broke that one, pushed through it."

The tanks were regularly used to escort such convoys between the fighting and the resupply point at Liberty Bridge. On another occasion four tanks were called upon to escort another resupply convoy, with Embesi's tank in the lead. The small convoy, with its awkward Amtracs, had to pass through a tunnel in the railway berm, rather than climb over it. Normally the more heavily armored tanks would lead the way, but Embesi refused to believe that the tunnel was not mined. After multiple searches by the engineers he still refused to move through the tunnel. Finally another tank led the way. "They swept it five times. Kimbrew gets up there.... He starts into that tunnel and 'WHAM!', there it goes. Hit a mine....

"Then they're under fire. The NVA had come up on the west side of us." Embesi moved over the berm. "I get in front of Kimbrew, and I hook onto him, and I said, 'Okay, I'll pull him out. I'll lead the column pulling one.' So I'm pulling him, we got him on the other side."

The other vehicles passed through and drew up about eight to nine hundred yards past the tunnel to form a column. The explosion of the mine had initiated another of the usual ambushes, but now the action started to resemble something out of an old Western movie. "We started moving a little at a time. All the time we were moving forward, I was shooting NVA off to the left side. The tanks were taking these guys under fire. They were running ahead of us. As we started the column we were still taking them under fire. We probably killed two or three hundred with machine gun fire.

"We're moving the column forward at a steady pace, and we got up so far and they made a stand up there and ambushed us." The NVA had set up a classic L-shaped ambush, firing at the entire column from the front and one flank. "We ran out of ammunition on the tank, the big ninety was out. We were shooting machine guns. I was up shooting rifles. At one point they climbed on the tank, and I shot a couple with my pistol." Another tank fired a canister round at Embesi's tank to sweep NVA infantry off the engine deck.

There was intense fighting on 15 May around bunkers in Phu Dong, an area already swept by 2/7. This was probably the action where Bruce Van Appledorn Sr. accidentally drove C22 into a bomb crater concealed in the tall grass, a constant hazard for tanks. By the time the other tanks helped extricate the tank the sweep line had moved on.[33]

The tanks rejoined the infantry just in time to be thrown into a frontal assault against a bunker complex hidden in a tree line. The gunner, LCpl Lenny Mendes, was pouring fire into the tree line while the tank commander hammered away with a sky-mounted M60 machine gun. The intense fire wrecked some of Van Appledorn's vision blocks, nearly blinding him to the outside world. Suddenly the gunner came over the intercom to tell him to back up the tank; the tank commander, Lieutenant Williams, the C Company XO, was lying on top of him and the loader was down.

Van Appledorn carefully backed the tank, fearful of running over grunts that might be in the enormous blind spot behind him. When they were able to assess the situation they found that a single round that entered the gap in his flak jacket under the right arm had killed the young officer. The badly wounded loader was medevaced, two grunts were shoved into the tank and told to drive and load, and the tank was sent back into battle.

Bob Embesi: "We got back to where the CP was at the railroad tracks, and we sat in there." All together Embesi and his men were in the field for sixteen days, and he lost track of time. "We're back there behind the Amtracs, and the general is calling the colonel and saying 'You gotta find that NVA headquarters.' We thought they were further in there."

The next morning the tanks stumbled into another of the bogs that made the coastal plain so treacherous, and two of the tanks sank in positions where the tankers could not get their tow cables out to them. "We had to call out to get cables from the ships. We ended up pulling them back out ... on the hardpack up by the railroad track." Meanwhile, "The generals are still screaming at the colonel to make contact."

That night the tank was set up on the railway berm, which commanded the surrounding countryside. Seven or so grunts were sent out on a listening post without advising the tanks. Equipped with an infrared night viewer, Embesi could see the NVA moving about to his front when the grunts started crawling back toward the berm. "I called the tank and said 'I'm going to shoot a burst. Wherever that burst hits, put some rounds on that sucker.'

"Consequently, a friendly fire [incident]. We had seven injured Marines. We got them back in. They popped a green flare and there was a cease fire." The rest of the night was a madhouse. The medevac helicopter was fired on, and "we put out a base of fire to pin everybody down so the choppers could come in. The choppers, they didn't want that happening, because then they didn't know who to fire on. So they called Puff in.[34] He came in ... and dusted them down on the outside of the perimeter."

Embesi was worried about the angry grunts. "Everybody was hot under the collar, and I had everybody go on one hundred percent alert, because the grunts were pissed off at us.... Fifty watching back and fifty watching the front. Next morning everything kind of cooled down," but Embesi had to write a report of the incident on a C-ration box.

A few days later Embesi loaded a platoon of grunts aboard two tanks. "We were going to make a high-speed recon, so we took off." The patrol went in a large loop. "We got ambushed in there. I told them 'Don't get off. Just fire off the sides of the tank. We're going to break through it.'"

Embesi admits that after a while many of the numerous ambushes and actions ran together in his mind, but tried to sort out the story. On one day a medevac helicopter was shot down and the crew killed. Tanks and infantry were assigned to guard the site until a recovery crew arrived the next day. "Everybody's nearly out of ammunition, so the Platoon Commander [Lt. Scott] says 'Call up the reserves' and that's the people left at the railroad track. So we call up ... two tanks, bring all the ammunition, all the grunts, everybody moves forward. They got ambushed twice coming up to us, and broke through, got to where we were.

"We redistribute the ammo. I think everybody had three rounds of ninety left. It's getting dark, and we got hold of the Lieutenant and said check everybody. We're set up in a big semicircle. Let's check all fields of fire, do what we're supposed to do. We went around to all the tanks, talked to everybody."

When Embesi returned to his tank "Some young grunt walked up and said 'Hey, Sarge. Them NVA is right out in front, and they all got them damn tubes.' By that time they started shooting them. I was off the tank, and they're coming all over the place. Lit up like the Fourth of July.

"They look like they're coming at you in slow motion.... One over the head, one down to the right, one here, one over there, they're coming over the tank ...

"One lands right between my goddamn legs. Knocked me on my ass." Embesi and Scott scurried for cover trying to get under Embesi's tank. "There's no way in hell a man can crawl between the road wheels and the bottom of that tank. It's impossible.... The lieutenant's a little bitty man, and he couldn't do it." But they did.

They quickly decided the position under the tank offered no protection. "I told the Lieutenant, 'Make a run for your tank. Soon as I get in mine I'll tell them open the hatch for you.'

"I don't know how the hell I got up on the tank ... I got on the radio and said, whatever the Lieutenant's tank was, 'Open the hatch.' He came back on the radio and said 'I'm already in.' He actually beat me."

The shaped charge blast had expended itself into the ground, but had burned Embesi and broken his hip, though he did not discover it until much later.

"We're sitting there the rest of the night. There's an NVA in a house, probably not thirty feet away from me. You could see him in there smoking cigarettes, and a candle burning.... We didn't have any ammunition left. It was like a Mexican standoff. I don't think they realized we were out of ammo, and they were scared to make that move."

At daybreak the Marine officers decided that they would destroy the downed helicopter in place. The Marines pulled back, with Embesi's tank towing another disabled tank. The column fell into yet another ambush, with heavy fire directed from a flanking tree line.

"We couldn't get started, and Lieutenant Scott and [Johnny Cash] did a flanking movement and turned toward the hedgerow that the ambush was coming from on the west side. The [machine] gun jammed on one of the tanks. There was a brand new crew in there, that had just taken over that position that morning." Three men had been wounded by mortar fire, and none of the replacements could drive the tank. Cash, the usual tank commander, was driving, and a green Sergeant was in the cupola. "He raised the gun tube up to clear the jam, didn't know how to do it. Nobody was shooting out of that tank. An NVA jumped up with an RPG and shot right through the bow and killed Cash." With Cash dead in the seat the tank was immobilized. The three replacements "jumped out of that tank and ran off. They ran all the way up to the head of the column, and I never seen them again."

Scott's tank drew back from the melee and "backs into an Arc Light hole. A big B-52 bomb hole. You could put five tanks in there and not see them.... He went down in there, he couldn't get out. We got dead and wounded grunts laying everywhere. That battalion don't have twenty walking men, thirty maybe."

A relief force with more tanks arrived, including one commanded by Siva. A new infantry Captain started making elaborate plans to attack the enemy. Embesi: "That Lieutenant Colonel's on the ground, and he says 'We gotta go get my men!'" The tankers were not about to leave the casualties, the abandoned tank with Cash's body, or the stuck tank. "I told that Captain, 'Get the hell off my tank.' He was all slick-headed, shaven, come out of the rear. He was right there, full of everything in the book. That Colonel told him to stand down.

"We lined up with what we had left. We went in there and his grunts were picking up dead and wounded, throwing them on the tank." The platoon got four tanks on line, and headed toward a hedgerow that was the source of most of the fire. "They're at us like no tomorrow.... All we have left is machine gun ammunition. Fifty and thirty. Lots of it."

The tanks laid down fire on the hedgerow, but someone would have to dismount to attach a tow cable to the stuck tank. "I opened the hatch up to get out. I looked out and Siva's right next to me. He opened his hatch up to get out." Machine gun fire raked the tanks, driving both men back inside, but then Siva climbed back out and took shelter behind his turret. "I knew it was his game."

Siva ran out into the fire, dove into the crater to hook up the tow cables, and then attached them to his own tank. The tank pulled the officer's tank free; it backed away and the other tanks moved forward to rescue Cash's tank.

"Siva was still on the ground. Ran in and got into Cash's tank, swung the turret around, and got him [Cash's body] back into the turret. Got in the driver's seat, backed that tank around, and drove it out of there."

The other tanks continued to place heavy fire on the tree line, and the NVA were either dead or had gone to ground. The infantry Colonel "was pretty well beat." Embesi was most impressed with the infantry battalion's Sergeant Major. "Every man that ever got wounded or killed, he was right there. The wounded ones he would give water to."

The column eventually got moving again and had almost reached Liberty Bridge, the resupply point. The engineers had just swept the road, but Embesi's tank, still towing another, hit a deeply buried mine as it passed them by. It broke the track and "sandblasted them kids. We got them picked up, put them on the tank and fixed the track. It egg-shaped my road wheel, so by the time we got to the end, the wheel was smoking." By the time the column limped into Danang the wheel was on fire.

After four days of nearly continuous fighting the depleted 3/7 was replaced by 3/27. That battalion would slog westward again toward An Hoa, against savage resistance. After being berated for the appearance of the tanks and crews, a master sergeant gave Embesi a fifth of whiskey, and Embesi said he got drunk. The tanks were badly in need of repairs and maintenance, so "That was the end of *our* ALLEN BROOK. Then ALLEN BROOK started."

The operation would drag on until 24 August. Special heavy engineer units with Rome plows[35] arrived to put an end to the Go Noi sanctuary. "They went in and bulldozed it from A to Z. They found underground reinforced bunkers, everything under ground. We were on top of them all the time. That's why they was all around us when they wanted to be."

Meanwhile, on 18 May the 7th Marines opened Operation MAMELUKE THRUST in what the Marines sardonically called Happy Valley, southwest of Danang. For the rest of the summer months the Marines in the two operational areas would march to and fro through the baking, dusty countryside, fighting infrequent but exceedingly vicious battles. In July the 5th Marines shifted MAMELUKE THRUST south toward An Hoa, and in August pushed an enemy force against blocking positions set up by 2/7. MAMELUKE THRUST would drag on until 23 October.

On 11 June Westmoreland departed and General Creighton Abrams replaced him as head of MACV. There was one significant point upon which Westmoreland had absolutely insisted: the Marines could not abandon the Khe Sanh base until after he had departed. A week later the Marines began to destroy the base that they had never wanted but held so valiantly.

In July, Lieutenant Luli's B Company platoon, with Wally Young, were with the force that helped dismantle the Khe Sanh Combat Base. Traffic going into Khe Sanh was not molested, but when convoys lined up to leave, "They hit us with everything they had."

Young was standing on the fender next to the loader's hatch, "Just milling around." When the shelling began Young dove through the loader's hatch. "That little spring-loaded seat in there, my foot hit that seat" and the seat collapsed into its folded position. Young looked up and realized "I slammed the hatch on my bird finger, on my right hand. I'm just hanging there, and can't find the seat. And I can't touch the floor."

With no purchase for his left hand, "I had to pick myself up with my right arm, and find that seat with my feet. Then come up with my head and push that hatch up and get my finger out."

Crush wounds are among the most dangerous and difficult to treat, so the Platoon Sergeant ordered Young to get onto one of the numerous medevac helicopters.

Staff Sergeant Baldwin was helping organize the wounded for evacuation. Baldwin was quite large, and "More than once I saw him come back with a man under each arm." Young started helping load wounded, and "He'd holler at me and cuss me. Once he found out I had that crushed finger, he took my pistol. He told me, 'Get your ass on a chopper and get out of here, Young!'"

Young ran back to the retriever to find out if the convoy was about to move out, and asked for a ride. Baldwin hunted him down as the last helicopter came in. "He cussed me again" and again ordered him onto a helicopter. The Sea Knight helicopter was already off the ground, hovering, when Young ran under it and signaled it back down. The pilot looked out the side. "He stuck both his hands out, like 'What for?'

"I just stuck my right hand up there and shot him the bird. My finger then was about as big as a banana. He saw it and came back down there and got me."

At Danang the doctor at first wanted to amputate the end of Young's finger, but tried a new technique. "He saved my finger. It's about twice as big as the other one, but it worked." Young was sent to Camp Carroll on light duty.

Creighton Abrams did not concur with Westmoreland's strategy of attrition. Although the best opportunity for winning the war through pacification was long past, III MAF was at last given an opportunity to fight a more mobile war, pursuing the enemy into his sanctuaries, and to renew their pacification efforts.[36]

After the return from Go Noi Island, Embesi's platoon was given extra equipment and personnel—a cook and stoves, medical corpsman, and wheeled vehicles—to make them semi-independent, and sent to support the Korean Marines. His predecessor was gone, but told him over the phone that relations with the Koreans had been really bad. Apparently some trading deals among the troops had aroused hard feelings. The Koreans had booby-trapped a building and blew his cook's legs off. "His platoon was really pissed off ... and tried to kill some of those Koreans."

Embesi was hearing reports of considerable Korean activity against the enemy. One morning Embesi heard a radio report of a tremendous firefight the night before, and walked over to see if the Koreans needed ammunition resupply. "My troops are telling me that the Koreans never leave the compound, and they set the [nightly] ambush up there inside the wire. There was absolutely no contact." The reports coming back from higher headquarters were fabricated.

As for trading, the tankers told the Koreans to stay away. A few days later Embesi's driver left the hut to walk down to an abandoned fishing village inside the compound that was being used as a recreational area. "Right on the trail, they booby-trapped him. Blew his leg off. I was the first one there, and I probed in there and didn't find any more booby-traps or mines." Digging revealed an ammo can that had been used to hold a grenade; it had all been issued to the Korean Marines. The tankers forbade the Koreans entry into their compound, and kept watch at night to defend against their allies.

On the periodic sweeps the Korean infantry would hang back two hundred yards behind the rear tanks, too far back to protect them. When the tanks would back up, the infantry backed up. The tanks were ambushed and a driver temporarily blinded by an RPG, and the Marines had seen enough.

"I got pissed off, and I went over and woke the [Korean] general up, in his French quarters," an old mansion he had commandeered. "I had a good Lieutenant, name Perkins, from Louisiana, and he let me do what I wanted to. I got that General up, dragged his ass out of bed and showed him what close infantry support was on his blackboard."

The Korean NCOs were soon driving their men harder, but "The next day some Army attaché comes over in civilian clothes, finds me, and chews my ass out for causing an international incident. I said, 'Wait 'til the next one. They don't support me next time, you'll see a bigger one.'"

When it came time to leave, the Koreans demanded that the platoon leave its tanks and equipment behind. It required the unofficial assistance of Marine infantry to escort the tanks out, moving along the beach.[37]

In September the 1st Marines were returned to operational control of 1st Marine Division and the 27th Marines were freed to leave Vietnam. The supporting tank units left with the 27th Marines. Embesi said they went to Okinawa, then "to San Diego, had a big parade, and then went on liberty." Ken Pozder spent about ten months on his second tour, and came back with RLT 26. He said the welcoming parade at San Diego was "about the only one I ever heard of."

October saw one of the few truly innovative operations, MAUI PEAK. The NVA attempted to overrun, then laid siege to the isolated Special Forces camp at Thuong Duc. Anticipating the usual NVA ambush of a relief column, 2/5 pushed down Highway 4, and on 6 October ran into an ambush. This time 2/7 and two battalions of ARVN swooped in by helicopter behind the ambushers while 2/5 fought through. The operation was closed on 19 October.

In November, 1st Division began a series of sweep and clear operations designed to reassert control over the local villages and eradicate the VC infrastructure built in the aftermath of the Tet Offensive. MEADE RIVER was designed to clear Dodge City, another stretch of swampy lowland dotted by villages south of Danang, It was home to the *36th, 38th*, and *368B NVA Regiments,* as well as local VC.

Near the end of his second tour, mortar fire eventually caught up with Dan Wokaty while the tanks, again without infantry, were providing security for engineers rebuilding a bridge south of Hoi An. "I got caught outside of the tank. I was trying to get inside the tank when a mortar round went off on the other side of the tank." Wokaty was climbing onto the tank by putting his right foot into the sprocket when the shrapnel came under the tank and tore into his left shinbone.

He tried to ignore the wound for several weeks, until "The corpsman said 'They prob'ly gonna want to cut your foot off, cut your leg off.' I said 'They ain't cutting my leg off.' I was running around with one boot on and one boot off, and my durn foot was turning black. I guess it was cutting off the blood circulation through the bone to my foot."

Wokaty was evacuated to the large hospital at Cam Ranh Bay, where they were "shooting him in the rear end" with massive doses of penicillin and streptomycin four times daily. The leg was draining fluid.

"You know how you see sap coming out of a peach tree, or some kind of a fruit tree? That's the way it was coming out" and the doctors were indeed debating amputation.

While in the secure island hospital—one to which not many Marines were sent—Wokaty was amazed at the lavish lifestyle. "They had big old four-way intersections with signal lights." The soldiers in the hospital told him they got at least one hot meal a day in the field. "They'd fly out and drop their meal, and I guess a helicopter would bring their stuff [vacuum cans] after they'd had their hot meal."

Wokaty eventually recovered and was ordered to report back his battalion. The problem was transportation, since Cam Ranh Bay was outside the I Corps area. "They said, 'Well, there's a transport station office over there [at the airstrip]. Just go over there and they'll find you a plane.'

"I asked this guy, 'You got anything going north that I can get on it and fly back to Danang?' There was one of them old Goony-birds (ancient C-47s). He said 'There's a plane out there getting ready to take off, and its going to Danang. Go out there and see if you can get on it.' I looked in there and there's a bunch of Vietnamese with pigs and chickens, and all that mess. I guess it was one of the Air America planes the CIA had over there.

"I asked the guy, I said 'You got any parachutes on there?'

"He said 'Naw, what you see is what you got.'"

Wokaty decided against the first flight, and later in the day hopped a flight on a C-130.

With little time left in country, Wokaty was assigned the cushy duty of running the Staff NCO Club for 1st Tank. "That wasn't too shabby there."

By the time Wokaty left, the war was starting to wind down, and the KEYSTONE redeployments were beginning. He noted that some wanted to get into a unit that was departing, while others wanted to stay.

Beginning on 7 December, TAYLOR COMMON was intended to disrupt and deny the enemy the use of a major base; unlike most similar operations, the Marines and their allies intended to establish a long-term presence deep in enemy territory. The plan was to proceed in three phases. The Marines and ARVN would clear the Liberty Bridge—An Hoa—Arizona Territory region, destroy the *2nd NVA Division,* and establish self-sufficient fire support bases. Then four battalions of Marines would invade Base Area 112, primarily by helicopter assaults.

In the final phase, reconnaissance and surveillance operations, resulting in air and artillery strikes west of the Song Cai, would prevent enemy movement from Laos.

Between 7 and 10 December the 1st Tank Battalion helped sweep the road between Danang and An Hoa in preparation for the operation. A week later 2/7 moved into Go Noi against little resistance, beginning an operation that would drag on into mid-February of 1969, when troops were withdrawn to secure base areas against another anticipated Tet offensive.

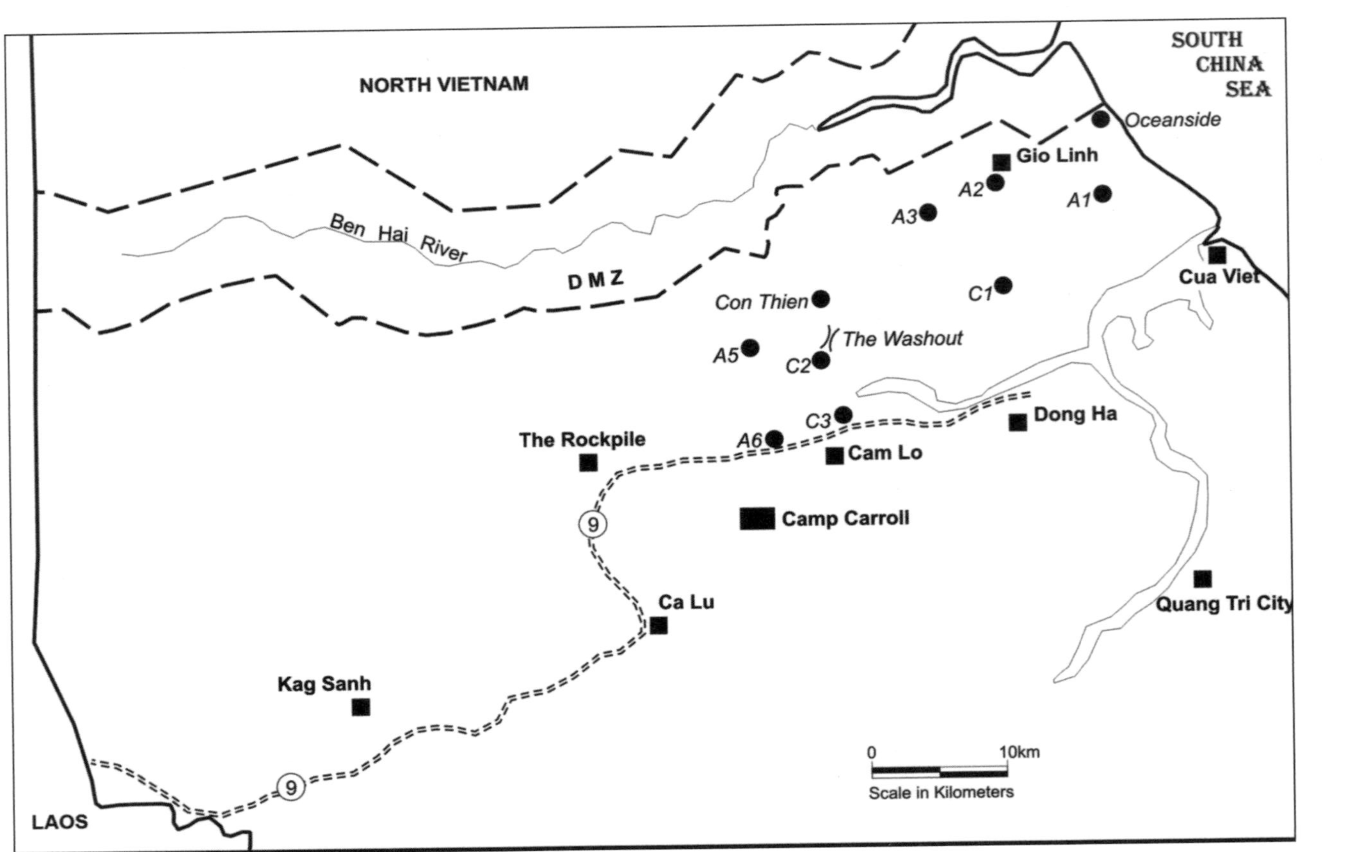
NORTH VIETNAM
SOUTH CHINA SEA
Oceanside
Gio Linh
A2
A1
A3
Ben Hai River
D M Z
Cua Viet
C1
Con Thien
The Washout
A5
C2
C3
Dong Ha
A6
The Rockpile
Cam Lo
9
Camp Carroll
Quang Tri City
Ca Lu
Kag Sanh
0
10km
Scale in Kilometers
9
LAOS

CHAPTER 6

1969: ON THE ROPES

"You will kill ten of our men and we will kill one of yours, and in the end it will be you who tire of it."

Ho Chi Minh, speaking to the French, 1948

After the horrific bloodlettings of 1968 both sides were exhausted, and backed off from major operations as if by mutual consent. The VC infrastructure had been all but destroyed in the failed Tet uprisings, when secret cadres had emerged from hiding and their units had been ripped apart in open battles that exposed them to Allied firepower. NVA units were similarly decimated, and it would take time to rebuild its ranks with troops and equipment moved laboriously south from North Vietnam. Only units along the DMZ, in immediate proximity to sanctuaries in the North, could hope to engage the Marines in conventional fighting. The Communists were forced to shift to a strategy that attempted to gradually exhaust American forces and to disrupt the threatening pacification effort.

The Americans and South Vietnamese had decisively defeated the Communists in every battle of Tet and the following months, but the cost to the morale of the American people was felt politically and on the battlefield. General Creighton Abrams would attempt better integration of the "big war" against the NVA field forces and the "little war" of the pacification program, but henceforth his resources would be limited. Abrams had better ideas than his predecessor of how to defeat the enemy: disrupt his base areas, protect the population, and extend the pacification programs that Westmoreland had derided. Unfortunately Westmoreland's imperious demands and perceived failure to anticipate the Tet Offensive had poisoned the well. No longer would political leaders write blank checks for ever-larger allocations of money and manpower. The newly elected president, Richard Nixon, who had promised a "secret plan to end the war," was about to implement a simple process: US forces would be progressively withdrawn. "Vietnamization," a focus on turning the prosecution of the war over to the ARVN, was the new order.

Ironically the Marine operations from 1969 until the withdrawal would achieve new levels of tactical sophistication, with large airmobile offensives, better reconnaissance, and fewer blind sweep operations. The Combined Action Program (CAP) would reach its peak with 114 platoons in the villages and hamlets.[1] The Communists were on the run, but it was too late. The American public no longer supported the war.

Of course all this made little difference to the Marine at the dirty end. His life centered about the same spirit-numbing series of brutal battles, large and small, one after another. The tanks were called upon to support sweeps by Marine, Army, and ARVN infantry units. In an effort to keep critical supply routes open, the tanks ran night patrols along main roads, and were occasionally diverted to assist CAP units and local militias under attack by the VC or NVA. There was never enough infantry, and personnel from the tank units were called upon for local security, running foot patrols that searched out bunkers and tried to forestall enemy attacks.

The roles that the two Marine divisions would play were growing more polarized. North of the Hai Van Pass, where the mountains reached down to the sea, the 3rd Division would fight an increasingly conventional struggle against the NVA, the two sides pounding at each other with artillery in savage battles fought amid rugged and generally sparsely populated terrain. To the south, the 1st Division would fight for control of most of the ICTZ's civilian population and rich agricultural land. No less important, that was one battle the Americans were winning, with about 70 percent of the population living in what were considered secure areas.

When Ken Zitz and Mike Wunsch returned to Vietnam in 1968, neither was assigned to a tank unit. "They made us language officers, they called it 0250, language officer. They gave us Interpreter Teams. Mike had Interpreter Team Fifteen, I had the Fifth. We went to Danang and we had enlisted Marines working for us, interrogating prisoners."

Unable to speak Vietnamese, "We didn't have a lot to do there. Mike said to me, ''What are you going to do?'" Despite the cushy life in Danang, both wanted a tank company. Zitz volunteered to run the night watch at the III MAF Combat Operations Center. When Zitz requested a split tour and transfer to a tank company, the Colonel in charge recommended against the reassignment. "But they were really hurting for company commanders. All of the combat arms."

Wunsch had gotten Alpha Company in 3rd Tank, but when Zitz reported to 1st Tank in January 1969 he faced one more hurdle. First Tank was not short of company-grade officers, and a friend in III MAF personnel advised him not to join the company—turn over his record book—until he got the promise of a company command. Sure enough, the CO tried to assign Zitz to an administrative billet, in charge of the battalion Civic Action Program, just outside Danang. Zitz told him he was going back to Division for reassignment, "Because Captain Lutke has fourteen rifle company commander slots, and he said I could have any one I wanted."

Zitz started to walk out and the Colonel called him back. Zitz was given B Company. "The next day I was on the road with a jeep driver, going down to take over my company." The headquarters was located at Hill 55, the "gateway to the west." The company supported both 5th and 7th Marines, and their area of operations would include Ah Hoa, Go Noi, the Arizona Territory, and the Que Son Mountains.

THE DMZ WAR

Along the DMZ most of the month of January was marked by a lull in the fighting, though intelligence identified at least five NVA regiments, plus the specialized *126 Naval Sapper Regiment*, active in the area. Most were in base areas in the remote interior where the NVA was clearly building up strength for renewed offensives against the population centers. There were also sporadic artillery bombardments and probes of the Marine bases. Search operations like DAWSON RIVER, SCOTLAND II, and KENTUCKY were intended to seek out and disrupt the enemy plans.

KENTUCKY, with 2/3 supported by elements of the 3rd Tank and 1st Amphibian Tractor Battalions, was to support pacification efforts around Cam Lo and Con Thien. Third Tank also conducted road sweeps along the vital road artery between Quang Tri and Dong Ha, and around Con Thien. Along the central DMZ sector, Task Force Hotel, built around the 4th Marines, hunted the *246th NVA Regiment*.

The shift toward the rugged interior was a reflection of the strategic planners on both sides. The badly mauled NVA could best offset the superior mobility—and to some extent the firepower—of the Americans by taking advantage of the terrain. For their part, MACV was still obsessed with a potential "right hook" by the NVA through the A Shau Valley, a conventional offensive to carve away Quang Tri Province.

The shift toward the rugged mountains to the west, and the consequent change to an emphasis on airmobile operations, meant that the tanks played a smaller role in the big, well-publicized operations. The most aggressive American operation was DEWEY CANYON (19 January through 1 March), the major incursion by the 9th Marines into the NVA's Base Area 611 in the Da Krong Valley along the Laotian border. The rugged, trackless mountains decreed that DEWEY CANYON be a strictly airmobile operation, supported by airlifted artillery.

JanWendling had three older brothers who were Marines, and his father had been an Army artilleryman attached to the Marines on Guadalcanal and Bougainville. "He always talked about the Marines in a high light."

The two older brothers both received orders for Vietnam, so "My mother wrote a letter to the Commandant of the Marine Corps asking why he was sending two of her sons into combat. He nixed their orders so they didn't have to go, either one of them. My oldest brother John, thinking that Joe would end up there anyway, volunteered to go. So Joe saw what John did, so he volunteered to go. They both went anyway. They spent a tour there in sixty-six and sixty-seven." The next brother, Jim, was then sent.

"I graduated in sixty-eight, and I wanted to get him out of there because I was afraid something bad was going to happen with him. I was afraid the law of averages with our family was going bad." Jan was assigned a tank MOS, which came as a surprise; he did not know the Marines had tanks. At Infantry Training Regiment he acquired the nickname Turtle, because his helmet always looked too big. The nickname would follow him through the rest of his service. At tank school Wendling signed a waiver to go to Vietnam, calculating that it would allow his brother to leave the combat zone, and in January 1969 he left for Vietnam.

The 19 January flight on Continental Airlines from Okinawa was "Scary. The stories I heard from my brothers, I figured they'd be running under the plane shooting at me. We landed and that door opened, and I can still smell the smell that hit me when I got off that plane.

"We had to go for registration. We went into this little building and we were assigned our units. We had to stand by on the flight line for a C-130 to come in to take us up to Dong Ha. I was sitting next to this kid who looked about thirteen years old, and his camos were rotting off of him and his eyes were way sunk back in his head. He had a shotgun slung over his shoulder, with a bandoleer with shotgun shells.

"I looked at him and I said 'Doggone, man, how long you been here?'

"He said 'I been here three months.'

"I said 'Oh, God! It's going to be a long tour.'

"We got on the C-130 and the pilot came on and told us that he was Major So-and-so, and that there was a good possibility that we might get shot out of the air today. If that occurred we were going to land in the ocean and a helicopter was going to come. I just started shaking all over. That scared me to death."

The cargo planes had no seats so passengers sat on the metal deck. "This pilot said, 'If you hear a bell go off, just tuck forward and grab the guy in front of you.'

"By the time we got up to Dong Ha this guy in front of me probably thought I was a little funny. All I heard was bells going off in there. The guy kept slapping my hands down. He goes 'What are you doing?'

"I said 'I hear bells!' He goes 'Well, those are [cargo] shackles banging together.'

"I go 'Oh, Jeez.'"

The plane landed safely and Wendling began his search for the 1st Platoon, Alpha Company, 3rd Tank Battalion. He did not think that it would be too bad, staying in wooden structures with screens to keep out insects. Unfortunately, "I got sent out to the bush on February first. I got sent to a place called Charlie-2. It was a little fire support base just south of Con Thien. It was just a little dirt hill, and there wasn't anything out there. You could see Con Thien up to the north, about three miles away. There was nothing out there, no villages or anything. It was a free fire zone."

Wendling met up with his crew on tank A14, commanded by a Texan named Ed Meirs. He stuck Wendling in the gunner's seat for a ride down to Cam Lo village. "Doggone, that tank was going down this dirt road at what seemed like a million miles an hour. I was afraid we were going to crash. That just scared me to death too."

Joe Sleger had returned to Vietnam in June 1968, serving the first half of his tour as the G-4 Operations Officer for the 3rd Marine Division headquarters at Dong Ha. Sleger thought it was beneficial since by mid-tour he was "on a first name basis with a lot of the battalion members and their staff." He assumed command of 3rd Tank on 1 February.

When Sleger assumed command of the battalion, "We had our tanks at eleven different locations in the Division area. I just personally considered that that was too much of a spread. I didn't like the fact that we had just a few tanks at some of the locations."

On 26 February, Wendling was on a road security position when the resupply truck came up the road. His brother was on the truck, and "I just went nuts. I ran off the tank and out in the road to hug him and everything. We're hugging and everybody's yelling 'No, no no!' and I thought they're yelling 'Go, go, go!'

"Here I ran right through the edge of a minefield to get to him.

"He was with us for five days. He was a sergeant and I was a PFC at the time. I was trying to show him how to work the machine guns on my tank, because we didn't have a gunner at that time. There were three of us on the tank. We received word that the North Vietnamese were massed on the other side of the DMZ and they were going to come down south with two and a half regiments. We had forty-four guys on our whole base."

His brother quickly made Jan aware of the desire to get below ground level that dominates almost all infantrymen's lives. "He said, 'If the shit hits the fan, I'm outta this thing. I'm just going to jump out of here, because I'm going to go on the ground where I belong.'

"We had night defensive fires shooting all around the base all night long to hamper them from coming in. Nothing happened. We didn't get hit." The artillery dropped rounds at random all around the base.

Jan Wendling quickly adopted the free-wheeling attitudes of the tankers, who often operated with only limited command oversight on their lonely outposts. One morning he was driving the tank, escorting a truck on the resupply run to Con Thien. His brother Jim was riding in the loader's hatch. The older brother was unaware that tanks could not cross the frail bridges, but had to divert through bypasses and ford the streams. Wendling recalled that "I cut and went down, and I could hear him screaming up there" as the tank suddenly veered off the road at high speed.

At the bases within artillery range of the DMZ, the tankers lived in subterranean Dye Marker bunkers. The interiors of the bunkers were about ten by twenty feet, with two exits. Cots with rubber mattresses (which soon went flat) and a poncho liner were the sleeping arrangements.

Jan Wendling: "We had rats all the time. I remember I had three rats on my back one night. I rolled over and knocked them off, and three more jumped on me.

"The living conditions were horrible. There were centipedes, scorpions, and of course snakes. There were snakes everywhere over there. We got rocketed one day, and one of the rockets hit our outhouse. When we went out the outhouse was blown away, and there was half a cobra sitting in there. Apparently he lived in there. That really scared us. No one wanted to go to the bathroom at night any more."

When a typhoon came through the men were confined to the leaky Dye Marker bunkers. "We were soaking wet for days. You get that wrinkled skin, you just can't get rid of it. That was terrible. Rats were running everywhere, so what I did was I took a clicker [electrical detonator] for the Claymore mines, rubbed it in peanut butter and let it lay over in the corner. At night you could hear those rats over there fighting over that peanut butter. You charged that thing and blow them up.

"We put a board up to a fifty-gallon drum with that caraway-flavored [C-ration] cheese that nobody ate down in there. In the morning they were crawling over each other. You'd just walk over with a forty-five and pop them."

On 1 March the 4th Marines initiated PURPLE MARTIN, another largely airmobile operation designed to block NVA incursion in a huge area extending from the vicinity of the Elliott Combat Base, formerly known as The Rockpile, to the Laotian border, and south almost to the abandoned base at Khe Sanh. The fighting continued into early May.

MAINE CRAG was conducted south of Khe Sanh and west of the DEWEY CANYON area, and would see the only use of an airlifted mechanized unit. The NVA were using the region as an alternative logistics route after the destruction in Base Area 611, and unlike the Americans, had the advantage of a dense network of trails and roads that entered the region from the Laotian side. This raised the concern that the NVA might be able to employ tanks.

The Marines began the preliminary establishment of air-supplied logistics and artillery bases on 10 March. Dan McQueary: "We had some intelligence that we thought there was going to be some infiltration through a certain area up there. We had a platoon of Ontos attached to us up at Headquarters and Service Company also, at Dong Ha. Somebody came up with the idea that they wanted to helicopter some Ontos in up there as a blocking force. We went into a training cycle. We took the one-oh-sixes off the Ontos.' We trained on that—taking them off, helicoptering up to a certain area, set them down, and mount the one-oh-sixes on them right away."

"They stuck the plywood on them so they'd look like dozers, the dozers they used to clear fire-support bases." The disguise was simply a large plywood panel across the front of the Ontos.

On 30 March the Ontos were lifted by helicopter into the remote mountainous area, and the guns remounted. The Ontos section operated with the 3rd Marines through 30 March.[2] The operation discovered large caches of food and ammunition, but failed to meet expectations and was suspended in late April.

The last of the great campaigns in the interior was APACHE SNOW, a coordinated effort by the 9th Marines in the Da Krong Valley and the 101st Airborne in the A Shau Valley. The 9th Marines sought the enemy in vain. The paratroopers found them in abundance, and were severely mauled in the "Hamburger Hill" battle. The 9th Marines would continue operations in the Da Krong for several months.

As the officer in charge of forward maintenance support at Dong Ha, Dan McQueary also spent a surprising part of his time in the field. "My battalion commander felt that he wanted control in the field. If they had a section of tanks go out, or a platoon go out, I usually went out. If we had a platoon of tanks that was in an operation, regardless of what it was, he always wanted a recovery vehicle there with them." McQueary said of Joe Sleger, "He was constantly in the bush."

McQueary's task was to provide or coordinate second and third echelon maintenance. First echelon maintenance at the crew level consisted of daily tasks like track tension and battery checks, and "Repairing the track, replacing road wheels, fire control systems." Second echelon was company maintenance of slightly more complex tasks. Third echelon was battalion. Force Logistics Command, "They got the fourth echelon—complete overhaul. They had one up at Dong Ha, FLSU-B (Force Logistics Support Unit Bravo), they called it Floozy Bravo. They did mostly the major overhaul on tank engines, transmissions, fire control systems."

As Sleger noted, the tanks were spread over northern Quang Tri

Province, and moreover were constantly being shuffled about. The activities of this battalion are a useful illustration of the confusion inherent in tank operations in Vietnam, even to the participants.

In March, the first full month of Sleger's command, Company A, including Wendling's platoon, spent its time marching across the full width of Quang Tri Province. A part of the company first moved to the Vandegrift Combat Base far to the southwest on 3–4 March to help secure that area after DEWEY CANYON.

The 1st Platoon remained at C-2 to support Army units that had moved into the area. Working with the Army's 5th Mechanized Brigade was always a logistical boon. The Marine tank units were chronically short of parts like tracks that were routinely damaged by mines, and the Marine tankers liked working with and near Army tank units because of the excellent scavenging opportunities. Army tankers were not trained or tasked with recovery of their own wrecked vehicles, which were left sitting to wait recovery by specialized ordnance repair units. Wendling, like other Marine tankers, was also amazed that each crew position in an Army tank was a separate MOS.

"They'd always go out and get their tanks blown up and then they'd leave them. We could get anything off of them we wanted. We'd steal the tracks, we'd cannibalize them."

As usual, mines were the big problem. On one brief operation west of Charlie-2 the force consisted of two platoons of tanks—one Marine, one Army—plus supporting vehicles. "It was starting to get dark and one of our guys was leading one of the tanks, he was on foot, showing them where to go across this rice paddy. They hit a mine and the guy got wounded, so we set up on the other side of this rice paddy that night.

"The next day when we came back, we started off with five tanks in our platoon. They had a platoon of tanks, and five APCs and three tank retrievers. When we got back we had four tanks, and they had two, and I think two retrievers and two APCs.

"We told them not to go up this hill. They just went up this hill and all you could hear was boom, boom, boom. They kept hitting those mines."

Wendling's wandering platoon joined the rest of the company at Vandegrift on 5 March. The company supported 3rd Marines by conducting road sweeps around Vandegrift, and one section was detached under operational control of Company C.

On 19 March the company briefly moved back to Cam Lo to support I/3/3. A land that had been fought over for decades contained historical dangers. Two platoons of tanks were assigned to escort a platoon of infantry to reoccupy a base in the hills west of Charlie-2. It was to be a quick trip, in and out the same day. Wendling: "I was the lead tank and everybody was following in my tracks. We got right in the middle of their compound and the ninth tank detonated a mine. They were old French mines from the fifties. I'd go over them and loosen that dirt a little bit, and the next one would go over and loosen it a little more, and the ninth tank back detonated that mine and blew that tank up.

"The second one was the tank right behind me. That was the first time I saw an American get wounded real bad. That poor kid that was on that fender. They medevaced nine people from that one mine. They were all grunts that were riding on the tank."

The temperature was over 100 degrees F, and the crews were trying to keep the tanks closed up because of the mine danger. Wendling's crew found a can of beer that some prior crewman had forgotten in the bottom of an empty water can, and opened it with an old-fashioned can opener. "We popped that thing and that stuff shot fifty feet in the air. Everybody was trying to get their mouth over it to get some in their mouth.

"We passed that beer around, and I'll never forget taking my slug. It actually burned. I could feel it burning going down. It reminded me of sticking my hand in my mom's dishwater, because it was always too hot for me to put my hands in. I swore then I'd never drink another hot beer. But I did."

Every tank but Wendling's hit a mine, and his threw a track in a bomb crater. Helicopters shuttled water in to help offset the intense heat.

The only contact with the enemy occurred while tanks were engaged in one of the repair operations. "Somebody says 'I got movement.'" In the distance the tankers could see an oblivious NVA mortar team making its way through a valley. "One of them had a base plate over his shoulder, the other one had the tube, and the next guy had ammo strapped over him." The group disappeared behind a small hill.

Captain Mike Wunsch must have seen this as a morale-building opportunity. The captain brought his tanks on line and had them train their main guns on the spot where the NVA would likely emerge from behind the hill. "The captain says, 'Okay, on my say-so, we're going to fire.' Everybody loaded up with a beehive round.

"Those three guys walked out, and I mean you could see them. You didn't need binoculars. They had no idea we were up there. There must have been fifteen tanks fired a round at those three guys. There's a tracer that goes out with those [rounds] and then there's a puff of yellow smoke that lets you know they've opened up. They airburst, and then they go out about seventy-five feet wide, seventy-five feet high, and there's eight thousand of those little steel darts in the shell. They go out at you like a pincushion.

"I'd love to have seen those guys after they got shot with those things. I bet you could have used them for a peppershaker. That was really neat to see that happen, because you never see those guys."

The following day the tanks moved northeast of Cam Lo, where "The next morning Gunny Dodge hit a mine coming down into a creek. It was a command detonated mine that blew a couple of road wheels off. I think it broke the driver's leg, and I think Gunny Dodge was wounded with that too." A search also located a five hundred-pound dud bomb that a tank track had missed by a few inches.

As part of operations in the western area, the 1st Platoon of Alpha Company, 3rd Tank was moved from Charlie-2 to the Vandegrift Combat Base on the far western edge of the 3rd Division's zone, "And that's when the monsoon hit," said Wendling. Before conditions deteriorated too badly, in late March the platoon left the base to support an infantry sweep into what the tankers called the 'tank graveyard.'

"March 22nd we moved into this valley. The valley was shaped like a horseshoe. The lead tank saw a North Vietnamese running. We went into the valley a ways and then we went up on one of the hills, the highest hill we could find, and set up on there like a wagon train around the hill."

Captain Wunsch sent a heavy section into the trackless, brush-filled valley. "My tank was the last tank, and my lieutenant's tank was right in front of me. His name was Paul Tank.

"It was a real nice day, and I thought if anything happens I've got an M79 grenade launcher in my driver's compartment, and I'll just shoot it out of the front of the tank." The tanks and infantry found and destroyed bunkers and a hospital complex, but one of the tanks threw a track in a bomb crater, delaying the withdrawal.

"The only road we had was what we knocked down in the bushes." The column moved back along its trace, approaching a spot where the path made a right angle turn to climb toward the top of the hill. "As we're approaching that turn, I look up and I see Paul Tank spin around in his cupola with the fifty, and start firing. I looked off to the right and I saw an RPG team running. My tank commander says 'Turn right, turn right, Turtle, turn right.' He says 'Go in about fifty feet and back up,' so I did."

The tank commander was trying to find a location where he had an open field of fire in front of the tank. "About that time an RPG team ran right out in front of us, and we shot them with a beehive round. They didn't get one shot off. We had three tanks, and there were three RPG teams coming to get us. The grunts all jumped off the tanks of course, and engaged them."

The infantry remounted the tanks and the column started up the hill again, but the captain radioed down from the hill that he could see yet another RPG team lurking near the bend in the trace, where the column would slow down as it made the turn to start up the slope. The RPG team had set up below a large, isolated tree that formed a landmark and a perfect aiming point. "We got on line and fired high-explosive rounds at it, and he said, 'Okay, you got him.'"

The column returned to the top of the hill and A-6 Intruder aircraft began to work over the valley. "They came down that valley, and they were eye-to-eye with us when they pickled their bombs. One guy even gave us a thumbs-up." The Intruders had to climb steeply away from the target in the enclosed valley.

"The bombs were those high-drag bombs [Snake Eyes], that thing pops out of the back and it looks like they're in slow motion. Doggone those things started going off and all the shrapnel was hitting our tanks, they're hitting real close. Then we got out of there and went back to Vandegrift."

During the monsoon, maintenance was a particular nightmare as mud clogged tracks and the moisture required extra lubrication. Guns had to be cleaned and oiled daily, and ammunition kept wiped free of moisture in a tank that leaked through old rubber seals and gaskets. Jan Wendling: "There wasn't really much you could do with the inside, climbing in and out of the things you were muddy all the time. You had to wait 'til the weather broke to really clean them up. Then you really had to clean them."

There were always too few infantry maneuver battalions to hold ground once the NVA had been driven out. Like most small tank units, the 1st Platoon of Alpha was shuttled from place to place, backfilling for units involved in the big operations. On 25 March two platoons were moved back to the Con Thien/C-2 area, and a separate section replaced Company C tanks in the Mai Loc area.

There the Marines occupied an old ARVN position, a triangular earthen fort. Jan Wendling: "Every morning we'd go down to a water point to fill our water cans, and we always got sniped at when we got down there. This guy was such a bad shot you could see the rooster tail [the trail of bullet impacts] sitting way out in a rice paddy, so we didn't shoot back. We were afraid we'd hit him, and they'd get somebody in there who could shoot."

At Mai Loc, Wendling found out how permeable the American and South Vietnamese operational security truly was, from an eight year-old child. "There was a little girl up there, her name was Mai, and she came down to the water point every day. I'd give her cigarettes and C-rations to take back to her family. All the little kids smoked over there.

"Her brother had jungle rot all over his hands, and I put iodine on his hands, and after a while his hands were fine. He'd come down and take all the five-gallon cans off my tank and take them down and fill them up and bring them back every day.

"One day the girl says 'Toto, you go to Vandegrift Combat Base tomorrow.'

"I said 'No, no, we're not going anywhere.' She says 'Yeah, you leave. You go Vandegrift Combat Base.'

"We left there and went back to base, and they told us 'Pack your stuff. We're going to Vandegrift.'"

At the beginning of the month Company B was in direct support of 3rd Marines, but on 5 March was pulled out and sent to Gio Linh to support the 2nd ARVN Regiment. It remained in support of the ARVN through the remainder of the month, except for one section that replaced a section from Company C in support of 1st Amtrac Battalion at Ocean View, the outpost on the extreme eastern end of the DMZ near the coast.

Company C began March with one platoon at Ocean View, and another at Vandegrift, in the diagonally opposite corners of the Division's operating area. The bulk of the company provided night sweeps of Highway 1 between Dong Ha and Quang Tri, and supported the 3rd Reconnaissance Battalion by providing road drops. On 5 March one platoon was sent to Mai Loc. At the end of the month the company was relieved by Company A, and moved back to Quang Tri Combat Base.[3]

Bravo Company's support of the 2nd ARVN Regiment resulted in the award of a Navy Cross to one of the company's maintenance crewmen. Late in the day on 24 March the company was supporting a sweep between Con Thien and Gio Linh when one of the gun tanks struck a mine. The company's M51 VTR was called out to assist, and en route it too struck a mine. As the retriever crew tried to repair their own vehicle, they were attacked by an NVA platoon concealed in dense vegetation. In the initial onslaught two of the VTR crewmen were killed and two others critically wounded, leaving Staff Sergeant Harold Riensche, the vehicle commander, as the only man capable of resistance. The lightly armed and thinly armored VTR had large side hatches, and the box-like superstructure produced blind spots on both sides that masked the fire of what few weapons the vehicle possessed. It was even more vulnerable than a tank in close quarter fighting.

As the NVA closed in, Riensche fired the .50 caliber machine gun mounted atop the vehicle until an enemy round disabled the weapon. Riensche scrambled across the roof of the vehicle and dismounted an M60 machine gun. Standing in full view, he fired the M60 from atop the vehicle until it overheated and vibration caused the barrel to fall off. Riensche grabbed the red-hot barrel as it fell, and ignoring the pain of the burns on his hand, screwed the barrel back in and resumed firing.

The overheated M60 again malfunctioned. While Riensche was attempting to clear the jam, he noticed an NVA soldier rushing the vehicle. Riensche killed him with his pistol. As night fell the encircling enemy had closed within point bank range, so Riensche grabbed the box of grenades carried inside the retriever. He began to hurl grenades in a protective circle around the vehicle until the NVA was forced to break contact. Riensche grabbed an M79 grenade launcher, and lobbed shells into the darkness at the retreating enemy.[4]

He continued to pursue the retreating NVA with fire until one of the company gun tanks, alerted by the firing, arrived.

Sleger said, "The original citation came in to my hooch back there at Dong Ha, and I said 'No way! Send this thing back' because it was for a Silver Star. I said we're going to write him up and we're going to get him a Navy Cross, and lo and behold, we did. I was very proud to be able to get him that."

Sleger: "We sort of consolidated some of the positions and we were able to reduce the locations, but we were also able to have the company CP located at a real vantage point, where they could respond quickly in the Division area of operations."

Corporal John Wear's flame tank section was at Quang Tri, but a new sergeant had arrived to take over the section. "I was short, and my First Sergeant liked me," so Wear's tank was able to avoid the routine convoy escort and road sweep duties, with the other NCO going in his place.

Sleger found it necessary to be continually on the move, with the main CP at Quang Tri and his maintenance CP ("quite large") at Dong Ha. "When I would go out to make contact with the unit that was on the coast, I would go by Navy fast boat up the Cua Viet [river] to the coast. A tank, would meet me, or a jeep, and take me up to where the tanks were."

Sleger had started his combat career in Korea under the leadership of officers like G.G. Sweet and Harry Milne who led from the front. "I was a tank riding battalion commander. Having been in Division headquarters I was familiar with obtaining things, so I put in a request to division headquarters for three APCs for the battalion, on loan from the Army."

These M113s, the only ones used by the Marines, were marked as Marine Corps vehicles. "I had been to a couple of schools at Fort Knox. I saw how the Army had operated, and I thought their mobile CP was quite good, and it would be unique for the Marine Corps. I used those three APCs as a mobile CP, along with the command tank."

Dan McQueary was not quite so impressed with the M113s. "They were a maintenance nightmare. The other thing was a lot of mines up in that country." The M113s were vulnerable, and "It wasn't so much the crew as troops in them, when they were carrying troops."

The M113s were also used as logistical vehicles in convoys with the Division motor transport units, at times serving in direct support of infantry units.[5]

The mobile CP was known as the Alpha Command Group and was first used in March, operating with a section from Alpha Company.[6]

Sleger: "My routine, I would spend a day back in the CP at Quang Tri, and then a day in the field. I maintained that rotation unless we were on an operation, and then I decided to stay for ... maybe a couple of days." Sleger was able to maintain this practice because of the support of an unusually able staff.[7]

The battalion had numerous other responsibilities. It provided security for part of the Quang Tri perimeter, logistical support for the Chieu Hoi Village, and provided MEDCAP medical care for hundreds of civilians in the local villages. The tanks also emplaced recon teams by the simple method of having them drop off the tanks along the roadside, coming back to retrieve the team days later.[8]

Tank combat in Vietnam was totally unlike what Sleger had experienced in Korea, but the main threat was still the same—mines. During his term as battalion commander there were over fifty mine strikes.[9] The design of the M48A3's hull provided far more crew survivability. "Any casualties that we had were just bruises.... The damage to the tanks as the result of those particular types of mines was quite predictable."

A report dated early May reported some forty mine strikes, involving gun and flame tanks, retrievers, and the battalion's M113 personnel carriers. The 3rd Tank Battalion Staff Journal recorded sixteen mine strikes in March alone, involving fourteen tanks (one was struck twice) and Riensche's retriever.[10]

Engineers managed to recover some unexploded mines, and Sleger said, "They were East German mines. They were like a large disc, circular, and all fiberglass. They were about fifteen to eighteen inches across, and about four or five inches high. The only metal parts on those particular mines were in the detonator. It had a spring that looked like the spring from a ballpoint pen.... Those were the ones that were doing the predictable damage." The NVA seemed to use the mines more as a harassing and delaying agent. Some were simply hidden in tall grass, and there were generally no attempts to attack recovery operations. Sleger also noted that, unlike in Korea, the NVA did not stack multiple mines to create a more powerful explosion.[11] "Since the damage was so predictable, we made up mine damage kits and kept them right on the recovery vehicle. As soon as a tank was hit, if we could get it out of the immediate area we could do some fast repairs in the field and get it back to the maintenance facilities at Dong Ha under its own power."

John Wear left Vietnam in February 1969 with six months and two weeks remaining on his enlistment. At that time Marines who had served in Vietnam and had less than six months left to serve could be discharged to the Reserves, so "I paid a guy a hundred dollars in Okinawa to stamp my orders that I was supposed to get out."

When he got to California, "The guy looked at my orders, he ripped off the top page and said 'Dude, get out!' He put a new cover page on and said 'You're going to Camp Pendleton.'" He was sent on a month's leave, and reported back.

In the first morning formation the Staff Sergeant said, "'Corporal, get rid of that moustache. Sergeants and above get moustaches.' So I went in the barracks and shaved off my moustache that I'd had for twelve months. I went up to the tank park, and somebody yelled at me and said they wanted to see me down at battalion." Wear put on his Class A dress uniform and reported to the battalion CO. "He said, 'You're Corporal Wear. No, Sergeant Wear. Congratulations.'"

Even when the tanks were in the base areas, they were not safe from enemy action. Mortar and rocket attacks were a constant, and infiltrators could reach even into the most secure areas. On 19 March, tank B23 hit a small mine inside the CP at Ocean View, breaking the tracks and damaging a road wheel.[12]

Sam Binion served as a Drill Instructor training officers at Quantico, and returned to B Company, 3rd Tank in Vietnam in 1969. While he was temporarily at the Vandegrift Combat Base in southern Quang Tri Province in June, he happened to monitor a radio communication. One of his officer candidates was the stepson of the actor Jimmy Stewart, Lt. Ronald W. McLean. "He was with Recon. Listened to him talk about being surrounded, and then it just went silent. They had killed him."

Binion thought that it was obvious the Corps' role in the war was winding down. "We went on operations. We'd get mortared—or rocketed—but large scale battles like we had in the early days, it just didn't happen."

He did find the rockets unnerving, mainly because of the sound they made. Such attacks were a regular feature since the sprawling base that housed not only the Marine tanks, but also Navy Seabees and an Army unit, was a huge and lucrative target. The tradeoff was far better living accommodations.

The company First Sergeant traded services with the Seabees, who were renowned for their lifestyle. The company compound was partially paved to allay the dust and mud, with wooden huts. "It was my first experience tasting lobster. We traded the Seabees a week of guard duty for a case of lobster." It was a step down when Binion was transferred to the battalion headquarters at Dong Ha for staff duty.

In June 1969 Jan Wendling was promoted to Lance Corporal. "Captain Wunsch called my name out. I went up to get the papers and everything, and he goes 'I thought your name was Turtle?'"

Wunsch was a highly competent officer who had instituted innovative drills. "We'd run a tank down the road. We had a mortar team set up off the right side of the road, and they'd fire a white phosphorus to the west (left) of us. As soon as that round hit, you had to stop, turn, and fire two high-explosive rounds at that plume of smoke. Whoever shot the best got a case of beer for the crew."

The stand down in preparation for the departure of the 9th Marines left the 3rd Division stretched thin, and the NVA took full advantage of the situation. The 3rd Marines were responsible for the swath of territory from the ridges west of Con Thien, eastward to the Dong Ha area. IDAHO CANYON was the blanket name for daily operations within the 3rd Marines' greatly expanded TAOR. Tanks accompanied operations where conditions and terrain permitted.

In late July 1969, Alpha Company took part in an IDAHO CANYON operation with 3/3. The action was triggered by a massive NVA ambush of infantry, and was supported by Army M42 Duster self-propelled guns near C-2. At the time C-2 was garrisoned only by a platoon of infantry. The reaction to the ambush would be a sweep by Captain Paul Goodwin's K/3/3, supported by Captain Michael Wunsch's Alpha Company, 3rd Tanks. Goodwin suggested Wunsch sit out the sweep since he was scheduled to return to the US to teach at the Naval Academy, but Wunsch had apparently already decided to accompany his men.[13]

Jan Wendling had been recently elevated to tank commander after five months in country. The scattered platoons had to be assembled from several bases. The tanks were suffering from prolonged use, and "one of those tanks couldn't even traverse, but they took it anyway. One of them had a road wheel that was hanging up, and they took that too."

The operation did not start off well when two tanks became mired in a rice paddy. "We actually had to dive underneath the mud to hook these things up because they were so bogged down."

The following day the force headed north toward the river, and turned to sweep west toward the hills. "It was the neatest thing I've ever seen in my life. It was just like in the movies. Everything fell away from us, those fields, and you could look right over into North Vietnam. Then the hills started rolling real slow, and then they started getting bigger and bigger and bigger, and then the mountains shot straight up. I could see Oliver North's group [Goodwin's K/3/3] coming off the finger of a hill to our south, coming out to meet us.

"We all got on line with our tanks, side by side going across. It was just beautiful up there, the colors were green and brown, it was really a beautiful day. There's bomb craters everywhere, and we're going in and out, swerving around those bomb craters.

"Somebody intercepted a North Vietnamese radio frequency that said they saw infantry, and said they were either going to hit us with an ambush, or they're going to hit us at night. About that time our air observer, his call sign was Sky King, called and said he had numerous North Vietnamese moving with bushes, they looked like bushes."

A heavy mortar barrage interrupted the morning calm, wounding several men.

"We went up on this hill and set up for the night, we made that wagon-train thing again. We knew we were going to get hit, but we didn't know when." There is some confusion about the exact chronology of events, but at some point the tanks were hit by mortars. "The first mortar [round] hit right in between all the tanks. It sounded like a machine gun going off way out in the distance, 'poop-poop-poop-poop-poop.'

"I thought, 'What the hell was *that*?' It was mortars. They were dropping those mortars so fast. I saw a friend of mine take off running to his tank, and a mortar went off behind him and peppered his butt and his back with shrapnel. He couldn't get up on his tank, just couldn't bend over, and his crew had him locked out. So he had to lay underneath the tank 'til that barrage was over. We had to medevac him out."

Tank A23 was short a crewman, so the platoon's corpsman, 'Doc' Colton, was serving as gunner. "He got hit right between the eyes with a piece of shrapnel." The wound was not serious, so "He said, 'Nah, I'll wait for my next Purple Heart to get medevaced out.'

"They medevaced Creech out—his name is Bill Franker—they shipped him out. We had a Lieutenant named Ralston that had three little slivers of shrapnel in his back, and you'd swear to God it took half his back off. They just picked them out of there, and said, 'You'll be alright.' He had to stay with us."

Late in the day Goodwin decided to move into a night defensive position, so the tanks left the hill they were on and set up a new position, about a hundred yards in diameter, on Hill 70. "This was going to be the last day of our operation. We had a black staff sergeant who said, 'Man, in sixty-six we set up on this hill and they just annihilated us.'

"I said, 'Oh boy, that's not real good.'"

Wendling had the driver back the tank to the edge of a huge crater to help protect it from any enemy who might try to climb onto the deck from the rear. The blade tank had broken down and Captain Wunsch told Wendling to tow it up the hill. Wendling was concerned that he would lose his carefully chosen spot and have to assume a position on the exposed end of the ridge, silhouetted against the night sky. The driver started the tank, but "The captain came back and said 'Disregard. We'll send Two-Three down there because it's a newer tank.'"

A23 was a Mod B tank with a slightly more powerful engine, so it dragged the blade tank to relative safety and set it up near Wendling. A23 took up the exposed position.

Wendling took water cans to a stream near the base of the hill, and when he came back he noticed that a riot gun, a twelve-gauge militarized pump shotgun, had been removed from the gypsy rack and was lying on the deck behind the turret. When he picked it up the gun went off and the blast narrowly missed the loader's head. "The loader at the time was my ex-tank commander, he was getting ready to rotate, so I became the tank commander." Captain Wunsch gave him a royal chewing out, but it was nothing compared to the guilt Wendling felt at his own carelessness.

That night, 27–28 July, the tanks were on a fifty percent watch, and "About ten o'clock the LP [Listening Post] got hit. They started setting off Claymore mines. This kid came across [on the radio] and he was scared to death. He said, 'We got seven of them, but they're all over.'"

Goodwin recalled that about 0300 Captain Wunsch thought he heard movement to his front, and Goodwin climbed up onto the tank, standing beside the cupola. Artillery illumination revealed nothing. Wunsch fired several rounds from his M79, with no result, and Goodwin returned to his position.[14]

Some time later (Goodwin remembers 0330, Wendling 0300), "Then at three o'clock, man they just hit us with everything they had. They started with mortars and then the shit just hit the fan.

"You hear those RPGs hitting metal, on the other side of that hill up there on the open side." A41, the company command tank, was the first one hit. "The first round out killed the captain. Hit the cupola. Oliver North happened to be standing beside him and he got wounded with the same shell. It was just mayhem after that, all night long."

The RPG killed Wunsch instantly. In his death throes his finger clenched on the transit key, locking the command channel and disrupting communications throughout the position. Wendling: "A second RPG hit the front of the tank and sprayed the driver with fragments. They medevaced him out. I don't know his real name, we all knew him as 'Granny.'"

One tanker was sleeping on the engine deck of a tank. "An RPG hit the tank and blew him right off the tank and peppered him with shrapnel. He got up to get back on the tank and one of their grenades went off in front of him, peppered him with shrapnel and blew him off again. He got back up on the tank and caught two AK rounds in the leg, and blew him off again." He survived.

"I had to send my loader and my gunner to these other tanks, because their crews were so messed up, or dead." Doc Colton and another crewman besides the captain were killed, and many were wounded in the first onslaught. The dismounts had to dash through mortar and small arms fire across the exposed hill.

In the noise and confusion one of Wendling's friends thought that the message was that A14 had been struck. He wore a CVC tank helmet with two distinctive white stripes, and "I saw him coming out of his tank to run over to my tank and I called and said, 'No, no, no, it wasn't One-Four. Four-One, Four-One.'"

When Wunsch's finger was pried off the mike key, Goodwin called for artillery, bringing it ever closer to his positions over the warnings of the artillery Fire Direction Center.

"Then they called in Spooky [a fixed-wing gunship], and they were firing illumination from Charlie-2. You could hear those big canisters open up and hear them come down to ground level, whit-whit-whit, and then you'd think 'Jesus Christ, if those hit us they're going to kill us.' Just the canister."

A machine gun team was set up in the bomb crater, firing over the lip. "I had a mortar go off beside my tank, and it blew my helmet around my head. I thought it killed me because I was blind. My helmet was actually blown in front of my eyes. I couldn't see." The blast had dropped Wendling down into the hatch. "I came back out of the tank, and those guys were just climbing back to the top of the bomb crater. It blew them right down in the bottom of the bomb crater."

The NVA were in among the positions, climbing onto the tanks, but like all men in combat Wendling was zeroed in on his own small part of the battle. "You get tunnel vision, and you see everything out in front of you, and you can hear what's going on around you. I can still smell it. If I close my eyes I can smell it. I can smell the broken branches, and the fresh dirt flying everywhere. That's what I think about when I think of combat. I think of that dirt and that sweet sappy smell of trees getting broken up.

"I've been a firearms instructor for thirty-something years and gun smoke never bothered me. The only thing that's ever set me off was my mom cleaning up her garden one time, pruning the trees and digging the dirt. I walked out back and my legs went out on me." He told his mother it was hard to explain.

"We fought from three o'clock in the morning until about seven o'clock in the morning, non-stop. I fired every round I had on my tank. Every round from my forty-five, and my [M79] blooper, and my M16. Everything I had, I fired them all out. There was just me and my driver, and I told Foxy—my driver's name was Bruce Fox—I said, 'You just stand by, because if we got to get the hell out of here you're going to have to get this thing moving. We're running out of ammunition here.'"

The medevac helicopters came under fire, and Wendling said, "You could hear the rounds going in them, and out of them, in one side and out the other side. Them guys had balls as big as this house. But they loaded those guys up and took them out.

"Then they came across [the radio] with the names. Captain Whiskey, Kilo India Alpha. We heard that and I thought, 'Oh my God, they killed the captain.'

Finally the attack subsided. "Two of the tanks were so badly mangled up that one of the turrets, the barrel just bobbed on one of them because it took a hit through the front that busted the trunnion bar on the front of that turret. We had to pull that one and another one back. It was horrible, it was a bad night."

As usual, the enemy carried off as many of their casualties as humanly possible. "The only guy that I saw the next morning, Vietnamese-wise, was one of the guys that we ran over. He was underneath the track, and they couldn't drag him away. There were a lot of blood trails."

Wendling disputes some of the assertions in Oliver North's book *Under Fire* that gives an account of this action. "Some of the things he said just didn't happen. He said there were two tanks on fire. What he saw was we started a fire there in the bushes with our tracers, and it was burning between my tank and this blade tank they had to pull up there, Alpha Four-Two."

North also said that two tanks were abandoned on the hill, but recovery of tanks was a point of pride, as well as a practical matter, for the tankers. "We never left a tank on that hill. All the time I was over there we never left a tank anywhere."

Despite his young age—twenty-five—Michael Wunsch had been "like a father figure" to many of the tankers in the company. Wendling continued to regret that Wunsch had died so soon after the shotgun incident.

THE WITHDRAWAL OF THE 3rd DIVISION

Everyone knew that the Marine Corps' role was diminishing. The most punishing fighting was in small infantry actions, initiated when the NVA attacked small units at night. The new Division CO, Major General W.K. Jones, placed his troops as much as possible in a force protection mode, limiting small unit patrols, allowing operations near the DMZ only in company strength, and requiring units to move daily to avoid being identified and "pinned" for attacks.

The eager young officer who replaced Wunsch was straight out of Officer Candidate School, and informed Wendling that "I want to get in a firefight" because "that's what I'm here for." Soon enough, in August, "These grunts were in a running gun battle with the North Vietnamese, and they were having a grenade throwing contest. They were throwing grenades back and forth at each other.

"This poor kid on the radio, he's calling and he goes 'Man we got them running up…' Boom! The radio went dead. He goes 'Okay, I'm hit but we're goin' up the ridge…' Boom!

"Seven times he got hit. Seven different times. Then our air observer told us to button our tanks up because he was going to drop white phosphorus right over the hill in front of us because the North Vietnamese were coming up the hill."

The new lieutenant had bumped Wendling down to gunner and taken the TC's position. "He can't get the hatch closed. He's going ballistic. Yelling and screaming 'I can't get the door closed. I can't get the door closed.' He's on the radio breaking into conversations with everybody, that he can't get his door closed, don't drop anything. I had to go up and pull the door closed for him. He just went berserk."

The regular gunner, Christiansen, had moved over to the loader's station. "He pulled the thirty in off its mounts because the extractor-ejector broke. He put a new one in and put the bolt back in the machine gun. He pulled the trigger and we had six rounds go off inside the tank. They were zipping around and one of them hit him in the chest and knocked him down." Then the lieutenant "really went nuts."

The nearly spent round had penetrated the loader's shirt and lodged under the skin, so he just popped it out with his fingers. "I'm telling the lieutenant, 'Just settle down! Just settle down!'

"He never talked like he did when he first got there after that."

That night the tanks and infantry planned to set up a night position on a hill adjacent to where Wunsch was killed, which did not sit well with Wendling. "They started bringing all this gear from these North Vietnamese in there, throwing it up on the tanks, packs and rifles and stuff. They decided, thankfully, to go back to base. I was scared to death we were going to have to sit there again."

The 4th Marines were responsible for the far western reaches of the Division zone, operating northwest of the Vandegrift Combat Base, the ARLINGTON CANYON operations area. Contacts were few in the rugged terrain, and the unit's main task was dismantling any bases that were not wanted by the Army and ARVN units moving in to replace the Marines.

Wendling and the 1st Platoon went back to Charlie-2 and then to Vandegrift, but the Marines were already being pulled out of the combat base as part of the drawdown that would end American participation in the war. The 3rd Tank rear had moved from Dong Ha to Quang Tri, so the platoon was sent to Quang Tri. The long march covered the breadth of the country, all the way down Route 9. "We thought they would really nail us going out of there, because they knew what was going on too. Little Vietnamese kids knew long before we did."

On 22 August the 4th Marines completed dismantling the base at The Rockpile, and concentrated on patrolling the region just north of it and west of Con Thien.

In September, Jan Wendling drew R&R [Rest and Relaxation] leave in Australia, but missed his flight when he ran into a high-school friend at Danang. The friend had connections, and arranged for a flight to Taipei, and—since he did not have the proper uniform—a Staff Sergeant's uniform to wear on leave. "So I went on R&R as a Staff Sergeant. I was a Lance Corporal at the time."

As part of the circus of errors, the flight was diverted to Hong Kong because of a typhoon, and Wendling and his friend finally ended up in

Bangkok. The five-day R&R grew to thirteen days because of transportation shortages. "Of course I got arrested as soon as I got back on the base at Quang Tri. I had to tell Gunny Dodge what happened, and then it was okay."

Jan Wendling's final days in Vietnam were spent packing the tanks for shipment to Okinawa. "They said they wanted all the Vietnamese dirt off of them. They all got painted." The Commandant had decreed that no Marine Corps property would be left in Vietnam. "We packed everything in 3rd Tank Battalion and took it with us. We didn't leave anything behind."

The 3rd Marines had been badly battered, and on 6 October the regiment departed for California. On 1 October, 1/4 closed Vandegrift, and on 22 October boarded ship at Cua Viet. The responsibilities of 2/4 had reached the absurd, and the battalion was now responsible for operations from an east–west line from Dong Ha along Highway 9, north to the DMZ. Soon, though, 2/4 was ordered to Quang Tri and on 6 November departed Vietnam. As the last remaining battalion, 3/4 relinquished the Dong Ha Combat Base, and moved south to Danang.

The 3rd Tank Battalion would depart with the remainder of the division. Jan Wendling reported that in October, "Finally we boarded on little Mike-boats [LCM, or Landing Craft, Medium] in the Cam Lo River. They took us down to Cua Viet, which was an in-country R&R center, and it was real nice down there.

"We had to sit out in the ocean, the Gulf of Tonkin, all night waiting for this big LSD to come in to take us to Okinawa." Jan was with another Marine from Indiana who was badly seasick, and "throwing up all over the place." Wendling rigged a captured NVA hammock between two tanks, which compensated for the rocking of the boat, so "I got a good night's sleep. I woke and everybody was vomiting over the side. I just laughed and laughed and laughed, and then that big LSD came in.

"The *Gunston Hall* was the name of it.[15] It was its last trip. It was getting scrapped when it got back. We went into the *Gunston Hall* and unloaded."

The Marine Corps had no space in the States for all the returning personnel, and the downsizing that inevitably follows a war was already underway. In early 1970 Wendling was given an early discharge from active duty at Camp Lejeune, North Carolina.

On 24 November the last combat unit of the 3rd Division sailed away.

THE WAR IN SOUTHERN I CORPS

The overall mission in southern I Corps was maddeningly complex: provide security for the transportation and logistics infrastructure of the Danang Vital Area and the elongated and vulnerable Highway 1, conduct pacification efforts among the dense civilian population, which was increasingly sympathetic to the enemy, attack the enemy in his base areas, and maintain a reserve force for potential service anywhere in the ICTZ. The terrain stretched from the Hai Van Pass through the rugged Annamite Mountains, to the rugged scrub-covered hills, then southward along the coast to include the cultivated lowland river basins. One area, the Song Thu Bon river basin, included the notorious Go Noi Island that controlled part of a major infiltration route from the Ho Chi Minh Trail to the coast.

The early months were the usual mixture of ongoing operations and new attacks, all against the threat of an enemy Tet attack on the Marine bases. Operation TAYLOR COMMON had begun in 1968, but the final phase, an incursion into the enemy's Base Area 112 in the rugged mountains, dragged on into February. In late February the NVA retaliated by launching a major attack on the An Hoa base, and the end result was another scattering of forces as tanks and infantry were sent to screening positions around Liberty Bridge. Soon they were back in Base Area 112, fighting over the same ground into early March.

The area south of the Hill 55 logistics center, with abandoned hamlets set among scattered rice fields, was another known VC haven. Operation LINN RIVER was another sweep intended to clear this area, lasting from late January into mid-February.

When Ken Zitz assumed command of Bravo Company, 1st Tank in January at Hill 55, the company had seventeen gun tanks and four flame tanks. A company command did not mean an end to administrative duties, but a continuing effort to acquire spare parts and other gear to keep the company in action. One day Zitz and his driver were headed down the road in his radio jeep on this continuing search when they saw five tanks parked by the roadside. "They're all lined up. They look just like a used car lot. I said 'Holy cow, Ski.' Lance Corporal Klimazewski was my driver." The driver turned the jeep around and headed back.

"These tanks were just sitting there, and they were clean, looked just like they hadn't been anywhere except sitting on that ramp. They didn't look like my tanks, all beat up and dirty, road wheels blown off and all kinds of stuff." The officer in charge, a Lieutenant Hughes, explained that they had arrived with the 26th Marines. He had been sent ashore, told that the regiment was being sent north and would not need the tanks.

Zitz raced back to the battalion HQ and told the S-3, Major Turpek, that he had found five tanks. The Major at first thought it was a joke, but Zitz ended up with the additional platoon. Zitz sent them south to reinforce the platoon at An Hoa.

Zitz's company was scattered about the countryside. "I never took my whole company, in seven months, as a company in an armored attack." Even the headquarters section served as a reaction force.

The usual practice was for a platoon to support an infantry battalion. "What happened in the Arizonas, the tanks might not have been in the fray to start with. They'd call them in because the grunts would get pinned down. They'd come into a tree line and work it a little bit, and they couldn't break contact. They'd bring the tanks in to get between the grunts and the NVA with the RPGs and all the other crap, machine guns, so the grunts could break contact. That's how we lost some people in tanks." Zitz lost five KIAs during his tenure.

The greatest threat was a "mini-Tet" launched against Danang in late February. On the first night of Tet, 23 February, rockets hit Danang, destroying ammo and fuel dumps. Ground attacks were bloodily repulsed or disrupted before the enemy assault force was assembled. By 26 February the attacking forces were effectively driven off, though fighting continued into March. Interrogation of the captured CO of the NVA *141st Regiment* led the CO of the 1st Marine Division to launch his own offensive, OKLAHOMA HILLS, into the enemy's assembly areas in the mountains southwest of Danang. Fighting in the river valleys and jungle-covered ridges continued into late May.

The areas known as Dodge City and Go Noi Island were persistent enemy strongholds. A prior operation had cleared the region in 1968, but the enemy quickly flowed back in to reoccupy old and build new positions. PIPESTONE CANYON would be a major effort to eliminate the region as an enemy base.

On 26 May, two battalions inserted into the western margin of the area began to sweep slowly eastward against light resistance, but this phase was a feint. On 30 May, they set up blocking positions near the abandoned north–south railway tracks, elevated on a fill above the flat, low-lying, scrub-covered terrain. The next day, five battalions (1 and 2/1, the 37th ARVN Ranger Battalion, and the 1st and 4th Battalions of the 51st ARVN Regiment), supported by 1st Battalion tanks, crossed the river that formed the northern boundary of the area and swept southward preceded by an intense artillery bombardment and naval gunfire. The enemy fled south, farther into the sanctuary, and resistance was light until 2 June when tanks had to be called forward to eliminate enemy bunkers. By 5 June the sweep had reached the Song Ky Lam River that formed the boundary between Dodge City and Go Noi Island to the south. The allied forces paused to regroup while aircraft showered 375 tons of bombs onto the island, as well as artillery fire.

On 10 June, 2/1 and Korean Marines landed on the southern edge of the island and drove north, and 1/1 supported by tanks moved in from Liberty Bridge. Resistance was light as the enemy slipped away toward the Que Son Mountains to the south, or simply moved out of the way to flow back into areas already searched. The enemy had liberally sown booby traps and mines that inflicted heavy casualties. The infantry developed a habit of riding atop the tanks, which were less vulnerable to the anti-personnel devices.

The big Rome plows moved in to turn another 8,000 acres into a wasteland. The plan was that after the end of the operation ARVN and Korean forces would garrison the eastern end of the island, and roving Marine patrols would secure the western end. The Communists declined to cooperate.

Buddy Reveile (pronounced Re-VEL) arrived in Vietnam in the middle of PIPESTONE CANYON, unaware of what was going on.

Reveile had joined the Marines because "It seemed like the most prudent thing to do with my life at the time." At seventeen he already realized that he was headed for a life on the wrong side of the law, but his brother-in-law was in the Air Force, and Buddy thought the military was an attractive way of life. The Air Force and Army both declined to sign him up, and one night "I was watching the six o'clock news, and I don't know what day it was, but it was during Tet of sixty-eight. Hue City was getting just annihilated, and I had a dream that I was in a firefight that night. Crazy thing. Death wish, I guess. I can't describe what makes the mind work, or what makes the body be controlled by the mind."

The next day he talked to the Navy recruiter. "As I was leaving, the Marine Corps recruiter—his name was [Gunnery Sergeant] Frank

Faulkner—came out and grabbed me by the arm and started talking to me." After talking to his mother, who was against the idea, the Marines enlisted Buddy. "In my opinion they were looking for fresh meat at that time, and I was a good candidate for fresh meat. A guy with not too much between his ears, and that was basically it. And that's how I ended up in the Marine Corps."

Reveile had been a mechanic of sorts, doing complex repairs since he was twelve years of age, and apparently scored high on mechanical aptitude in boot camp. He was made an 1811. "It might even have been that Faulkner tried to look after me, because the guy was a real square-shooter." Reveile had actually wanted to enlist for six years, but Faulkner had talked him down to four.

The Corps provided the male role models that Reveile had been seeking, beginning in boot camp. The most lasting impressions were from the tank school. "There were a couple of people that I really idolized there. One of them was named Sublett, Paul [C.] Sublett." A short tour in 2nd Tank included four months in Cuba. The Corps was constantly combing its ranks for men to send to Vietnam, and at one morning roll call Reveile poked his buddy in the ribs and said, "Let's go. Let's volunteer, man."

Reveile had volunteered to get off thirty days of mess duty. "I didn't realize it was going to take thirty days for the orders to come around. So I had to do my whole—it was more than thirty days on mess duty—before I ever got my orders."

By June of 1969 Reveile was in Vietnam, just in time for PIPESTONE CANYON.

Reveile spent one night in the receiving barracks at Danang and went to C Company, 1st Tank Battalion headquarters. "The first incoming I had ever seen was there. It was a trip, man. I didn't know what to do, to be honest with you. It didn't seem like it was real.

"We manned our tanks, and went out to the berm line."

Reveile was sent out to join the 2nd Platoon on Route 1, where the platoon went on road sweeps, convoy escorts, and a few field operations. One day, "We were on a sweep, in Dodge City, and we ran up on a truck that had hit a mine." One of the combat engineers in the area was Jim Hackett, the guide from Reveile's boot camp platoon. "This has come back to me many times. Hackett got killed two days later."

Reveile's time in Dodge City was spent "blowing away tree lines," without sighting a single enemy.

The cordon and search of Tay Bang An during the closing stages of PIPESTONE CANYON was another of the classic operations of the war. Aerial observation reported at least fifty enemy soldiers visible around the abandoned village, halfway between Route 1 and the old railway line. Intelligence estimated that the village was the base for a sapper company. The village was well sited for defense, sitting on what amounted to an island, bounded on three sides by sluggish streams with a swamp on the east. Only Route 4, a narrow branch of Route 1, provided access to the southern margin, about 2km south of the village. The 1st Marines planned an airmobile cordon and sweep of the area that would in some ways be emblematic of the war: tactical perfection resulting in frustration.

On the morning of 15 July, three companies from 2/1, reinforced with an additional company from 1/1, swooped into four LZs surrounding the village. The helicopters all came under heavy fire. One was badly damaged and had to divert to an emergency-landing site along Route 1, and the intense fire forced the relocation of two LZs, delaying the operation. By 0900 all companies were on the ground and spread out to surround the island on which the village sat. Foxtrot 2/1 met heavy resistance from new bunkers built along the near shore of the Suoi Co Ca, a stream that separated them from the island, but drove the enemy across the stream and into the village. That afternoon a platoon of tanks came down Route 1 and west along Route 4. The tank platoon split up, with the light section on the west bank of the wide Suoi Co Ca and the heavy section on the eastern shore near the village.

All day on 16 July the trapped VC probed at the cordon, and that night launched a desperate attack on the southwest side of the trap, straight into G/2/1 and machine guns of the tanks. The attack penetrated the Marine positions but failed to break through. The next morning, two companies of infantry and the tanks moved into the now empty village and began a series of searches. They found twenty bodies and captured fourteen prisoners. Late in the day the infantry boarded helicopters, and the tanks returned north along the highway.

This little part of PIPESTONE CANYON was executed to perfection, but what had happened to the trapped VC? Somehow they had slipped away or gone to ground, leaving behind a few dead, but denying the Marines any tangible victory.

PIPESTONE CANYON dragged on until 7 November, with infantry companies establishing areas of operation, repeatedly searching the ground as the engineers and their heavy equipment devastated the area. The Marines found new bunkers and killed a few enemy troops, but suffered heavily from mines and booby traps.

Buddy Reveile also recalled the heat casualties among the Marines in Dodge City. With the constant pauses for evacuation of the heat casualties, "You'd spend all day and go half a mile." The country itself was ill suited to tanks. "We got into several situations where the road collapsed underneath us, and the tank would go off into a rice paddy."

Many of the roads were so narrow that "It was a footpath. A guy with an RPG could come right up and take you out." Bogged tanks created yet another problem as troops had to be brought in by helicopter to protect recovery operations.

On one occasion the road collapsed on the outskirts of a village. "We spent the night in that village. It was a pleasant experience, but it still worked on your nerves. The people, they invited us to their house, we ate in their house." The village was host to a Combined Action Platoon unit of Marines who lived, worked, and fought the VC with the villagers. "We were treated just great, very nice."

The family that hosted Reveile and his crew had a one-armed son named Tom, about eleven or twelve years of age. "We ate fish, and something else, and it wasn't bad, it really wasn't bad. I made Tom a slingshot. I got an old tree limb, and found some inner tube, and I built him a slingshot." The father of another boy watched and mimicked Reveile's construction, with one exception. Reveile had Tom help him hold the Y-shaped wooden frame while he tied off the rubber. "This dude held the slingshot with his toes, and tied it off with his two hands."

In later years Reveile would often wonder what happened to Tom.

The 5th Marines were meanwhile trying to establish control over the Arizona Territory plain near An Hoa Combat Base. For two weeks in early June, attacks on and around An Hoa goaded the Marines into undertaking a prolonged operation in the extremely rugged Que Son Mountains base area.

The 7th Marines were charged with defense of the Danang Critical Area, a task they approached with aggressive patrolling and an unenthusiastic repair and maintenance of the Danang Anti-Infiltration System (DAIS). The DAIS was a miniature version of the McNamara Line, which in the densely populated coastal plain was thwarted by local farmers repeatedly breaching it to go to and from their fields.

In late July Ken Zitz was sent on a special five-day R&R in Tokyo. When he returned Klimazewski was waiting for him. The driver advised against running the Red Line, the road toward Hill 55, so near to nightfall. The two went to the III MAF compound, and agreed to meet in the morning for the trip.

"I ran into this big First Sergeant, his name was Jurgensen. He was Mike Wunsch's First Sergeant." He told Zitz that he had been trying to find him, and told him to sit down. The older NCO was visibly distressed. "He said 'Skipper, I just put your best buddy on the airplane today. Captain Wunsch was killed in action two days ago up on the Z.'"

In mid-August, a series of attacks on positions west of Danang resulted in a series of major fights in which the 7th Marines inflicted major casualties on the enemy. Almost immediately the 7th Marines were ordered to move south into the Que Son Valley and take over a region formerly held by the Americal Division. As that division shifted northward, the 7th Marines would assume control of two major facilities, LZ Baldy and Fire Support Base Ross, 16 kilometers to the west.

Reveile's platoon went to LZ Baldy in a convoy with the 7th Marines when they assumed control of the base. The platoon was then sent even farther out to help garrison LZ Ross, the forward operating base. The main amenity was a small stream that ran just outside the wire. "Man, it was an excellent swimming hole. We started getting sniper fire, and those guys couldn't hit the broad side of a barn. They pulled us out and they wouldn't let us go swimming anymore after that."

The enemy's reaction to the change of ownership at Ross was at first subdued, but then, "We got hit eight nights in a row.... Every night, you could forecast it. You knew what time it was going to come, a little after midnight. You'd hear the incoming rockets and then the mortars, rockets and mortars, and they'd wear the whole place out.

"We lost a whole hooch of Seabees one night. The Seabees lived closer to the top of the hill, closer to the headquarters up on top of the hill, and they took a rocket."

The Seabees were unlucky, but others had extraordinary luck. "Right behind our tent, within fifty yards, they had an ammo dump, the ammo bunker. One night we got incoming, and we had a guy named Jimmy Logan.... They had a rocket that hit the ammo dump." Most of the crewmen had made a mad dash for the tanks at the sound of the incoming rounds, and were inside the vehicles.

"We were pulling out on the perimeter, and Logan never got up. He was in the tent. When that rocket hit that ammo dump, scrap metal went all through the tent. And Logan didn't get a scratch. Not one scratch. He slept through the whole thing. He didn't even know anything happened."

By 21 August the 7th Marines were already heavily embroiled in fighting with the *1st VC* and *3rd NVA Regiments*, assisting the Americal's 32nd Infantry to entrap the two enemy units. The fighting in the remote ridges grew in intensity as the trapped enemy sought to escape. The tankers had a tank park at Ross, an open area for maintenance, near their billets. Reveile said that "I've got pictures, and lots and lots of memories of memorial services they had for fallen Marines in our tank park, because it was the only area they could assemble troops."

THE WITHDRAWAL OF THE 1ST DIVISION

Along the operational boundary, the tankers also supported the Americal Division, which had no armor. Reveile thought, "In my opinion they were a dysfunctional group." At this late stage it was quite clear that the United States was disengaging from the war, and the soldiers were reluctant to make the ultimate sacrifice in a cause that was so clearly being abandoned. Reveile thought that lives were lost unnecessarily.

Many officers like company commander Ken Zitz were beginning to suspect that the Marines were leaving Vietnam. "The cat was starting to get out of the bag. It was inevitable that we were starting to draw down on the troop strengths." One clue was escalating demands for lists of gear and supplies for potential redeployments.[16] During planning sessions the tank and infantry officers would plan more carefully. "We tried to keep, I'll be honest with you, as many of our guys alive as we could. We didn't actively and aggressively try to go and smoke out the enemy someplace, because we said, 'Hey, the handwriting's on the wall. We're rolling out of here. I want to take as many troops as we can with us.'"

Buddy Reveile said of the Americal, "They called us in to back them up a few times. On one occasion the officers were basically in mutiny against their commander because of the sacrifice. Sweeping up on a hill when they didn't have to. They didn't call anything [artillery or air support] in on it before they came up on it, and a bunch of them got killed.

They had the Americans stacked out there. That was my first experience to see dead Americans, and it was not a pleasant sight."

The tanks were called in for support only after action was joined, so by the time the tanks arrived the enemy had long since departed. "The NVA and VC definitely had their act together more than we did. Because they chose the time and where they were going to hit, and it was usually in their favor. It was the hit and run deal. They'll take two or three guys, or four or five, or six or seven guys out and then pull back."

Staff Sergeant Sublett, Reveile's mentor in tank school, had joined the platoon in Vietnam as platoon sergeant. On one occasion during the monsoon, "They couldn't resupply us for six days on LZ Ross. So Sublett, he's such an imaginative guy, that he went to the mess hall and he got flour, sugar, and whatever else was involved in it, he got grease, and he made donuts for the platoon."

The bright side of working with the Army was that they were far more lavishly supplied. Buddy Reveile was a scrounger who stashed away things to trade with the Army. "I'd trade for food," things like chocolate milk and even ice cream. "Sublett liked for me to do that because it was good for morale I guess."

On one operation where they were supporting the Americal in the Que Son Valley, "We worked all day and set in for the night on the perimeter.... Here about four o'clock, four fifteen, they broke and here comes helicopters with hot chow. They have hot chow, we're eating C's. The coldest thing I've got is the water in my five-gallon jerrycan that I store down next to my gunner's seat. So that's what we're drinking. Then the next helicopter comes in, and it's got a pallet of iced-down beer on it, a sling of beer, iced-down. They're out there drinking beer, out in the bush! Man, I couldn't believe this."

A friend in the Army told him, "That's the way it was, that's the way they got treated. We never knew that kind of treatment."

Ken Zitz found that his M110 radio jeep was far faster than his command tank for making the rounds through his large operating area. One afternoon in August he was at Hill 37 conferring with a platoon commander. Tank crewman Reggie Thompson was temporarily assigned as his driver while Klimazewski was on R&R. That afternoon Zitz received a landline phone call that the battalion S-4 needed to see him at Hill 55, and he agreed to leave soon. The VC regularly tapped the above-ground phone lines. As a precaution, Zitz arranged a tank, B13 under Lance Corporal Flores, for escort as far as Highway 90.

"Just outside the base there was a little hooch at the foot of the hill. There was this old papa-san with the Ho Chi Minh beard and all, pulled his curtain back, and he looked out. I looked at that guy, and he let the curtain go back. It was an eerie thing, and I said to Reggie Thompson, 'Let's go.'"

As the jeep sped on, both men noticed the absence of people, water buffaloes, and even birds. "When we got to the second culvert, 'Ba-voom!' They blew up a command-detonated box mine. It picked my brand new Mark 110 jeep up in the air. We went down. I didn't know what happened. I was stunned.

"We had about fifty pounds of rock all over our windshield, radios blown off the mounts. I'm sitting there and Thompson's eye was bleeding." The jeep was sitting nose-up in a cloud of dust with the engine racing. Thompson, stunned, told Zitz that the jeep was stuck. "I said, 'Let the clutch out! Let the clutch out!' He pops the clutch and we come flying out of there. As soon as we got out of that hole, they opened up on us with AK-47s. A kill team, about five or six of them."

The jeep raced through the hail of gunfire while Zitz groped for a radio handset among the rocks and dirt in the back, and emptied his pistol's magazine. He still recalls Flores's accented voice on the radio. "'Bravo Seex, Bravo seex. One-three, One-three.' I can hear him, but I can't find the handset."

Zitz at last found the handset and replied. "He said 'Skip are you okay?' I said 'Yeah, we're okay. We're out of the kill zone.'" Behind him Zitz could see a huge column of dust that "looked like a small nuke" had gone off. "I said 'Start putting some fire on that' as Flores began returning fire with the tank's machine guns.

"All of a sudden Staff Sergeant Johnson," a young NCO with a big handlebar moustache who was on his second or third tour in Vietnam, "said 'Six, this is One Alpha. You okay sir? We're going in.'

"'Flores,' he said, 'Cover me, I'm going in,' just like Dodge City." The jeep hit a bump and Zitz's helmet flew off and rolled down the road "like a hubcap." He had Thompson stop the jeep because "I didn't want to leave my helmet for some NVA."

Zitz could hear three machine guns working, "And all of a sudden I hear the main gun go 'Ka-boom, ka-boom.' Thompson made the ninety degree turn. I said 'Slow down, Reggie. We don't want to get killed now. We made it through the ambush, now we're going to flip this jeep over and kill ourselves.'

"To add insult to injury, some NVA sniper started shooting at me." Zitz assumed that the sniper was not going to hit a moving target, and he was out of ammunition. "So I just flipped him off. I didn't want to return fire. I didn't have any bullets left."

Zitz and Thompson headed on up the road to the company HQ and the battalion S-4. "God bless the S-Four. He says 'Where you been Skip? I've been waiting for you.'

"I said, 'Major, all due respect [but] I don't think I have time to talk to you today.'

"He says, 'You mean I've been waiting here all day, and what....'

"I said, 'I've got to get my jeep driver down to the regimental aid station and get him sewn up. We just got ambushed. He got wounded. Do you mind?'"

The S-4 was still agitated. "'Won't somebody tell me next time?'

"I said, 'I didn't have time to call you while I was in that ambush, sir. Sorry.'

"He says, 'Now I'll probably be late for chow back at the battalion.'"

Johnson showed up and reported. "' Skipper, we got no problem. We got six for six.'" He had killed all six of the NVA ambushers. Johnson had fired ahead of the fleeing NVA with his machine gun to force them to ground, and then fired behind them. "He finally says 'Say goodnight,' and killed them with the ninety."

Zitz said that he was fine until later that night when he began to sweat and shake. He had learned his lesson. "After that I never rode that road again in that Mark 110. It was always in the steel monsters. I kind of got religion, you know," and was far more careful until his tour ended in September.

In early 1969 Anthony Rogers and some friends had been students at Texas Tech University for a year and a half when four of them decided to "beat the draft" by enlisting in the Marine Corps. "Went down and checked out the local recruiter there in Lubbock. The fellow said, 'Well, we have a two-year enlistment,' and we said 'Sign us up.' So four of us went in on the buddy system." The Corps did not recruit regional units. Groups of young men could be guaranteed that they would train together, but there was little likelihood that they would serve together.

"We kind of realized we weren't doing what we were supposed to be doing in college. We thought well, if we do this—go serve our country—when it's all said and done we'll have the GI Bill and a different frame of mind when we come back. And we did."

Rogers was assigned to MOS1811, basic tank crewman. "As I recall, the Drill Instructor didn't know what that was. It kind of buffaloed him. It took a while to figure out that was tanks." Following boot camp and Infantry Training Regiment, the tank school at Del Mar "was a blur." The Marines had earlier established Staging Battalion, a field school at Camp Pendleton. Reconstructions of villages and other Marines playing the roles of Vietnamese attempted to prepare young Marines for the conditions they would encounter in Vietnam. The only feature Rogers recalled was "walking a trail with an M16, and having pop-up targets come up, and the live-fire exercises. Shoot the targets as they pop up on either side of the trail." Rogers was then assigned to a three-month Vietnamese language school.

In October Rogers was flown to Okinawa aboard a chartered airliner. "I recall it being a [Continental Airlines Boeing] seven-oh-seven. I don't guess you could find one of those birds in the air today." A second flight took him on to Danang. After one night in the transient quarters he was sent out to 1st Tank Battalion, south of Marble Mountain.

On his second night in Vietnam he drew guard duty. "It was kind of spooky. It was a single-man position, in a sandbag bunker, lights around the perimeter, and all kinds of noises at night. It was kind of strange for a new guy." Within days he was sent out to the Charlie Company position at LZ Baldy, then out to the 1st Platoon at LZ Ross.[17]

At this period of the war Baldy was home to Logistical Support Unit 3 (LSU-3), supporting the 7th Marines. Ross was the artillery base and forward tactical base, the jumping off point for operations for 7th Marines.

The trip to Ross was in an unescorted truck convoy, and particularly memorable. "In the back end of a six-by. I went out with a couple of guys that belonged to First Platoon." One, a sergeant, began to reassure the new guy. He explained to Rogers that "During the stint of time the Army had it, they had lost forty-seven trucks in one month going along this road. I don't know if that was factual or not, but it certainly got my attention. I could see alongside the road that not everything this guy was telling me was BS. There was a lot of debris, like an old tanker truck that had hit a mine. It was off to the side of the road. That eleven-mile trip, or whatever it was, the first time I made it was uneventful, but kind of anxious at the same time." In later months Rogers would come to realize that only the first and last convoys of the day had tank escorts.

"LZ Ross was not a big hill, but it had some elevation to it. From the road you go through the concertina wire and on to the camp there." Rogers recalled that" I drove by a sign that said Mike Company, Three-seven." Mike 3/7 provided the base security, and one of the buddies he had enlisted with was in the battalion. "It was out in the thules. You felt like it was the last stop for mankind, was LZ Ross. That was where the road ended."

Ross consisted of the main position on the low hill with an adjacent open landing zone for helicopters. Wire barriers and a series of bunkers, some isolated around the long perimeter of the landing zone, encircled the entire base.

Individual Marines contracted with the local Vietnamese to do laundry and other maintenance. "They would wash our utilities down there in that river, and dry them out by fires. Kind of fold them up real nice and neat," but the clothing still had river silt in the fabric "and smelled like smoke."

After three months, Anthony Rogers had lost much of his school proficiency in Vietnamese, a difficult language to master. "Most of the time when I would speak to someone there they would look at me with real wide eyes. I didn't know if they were surprised I was speaking Vietnamese, or if I said something real comical."

On one occasion Rogers was sent out to help set up a boresight target about a kilometer outside the wire. This was to be a large white plywood structure with a cross-shaped target, used to correctly align the main gun tube with the optical sight. This was a task usually performed at one of the base areas, and the platoon would soon find out why.

"Across the rice paddies, hump all this lumber and whatnot to erect this boresighting target. Hot, you know, and humping all this stuff, and rifles, and ammo. We get out to this area where we're going to do this deal, and there's a papa-san there. The lieutenant calls me up to interpret. He says, 'Ask him if there's any [VC] in the area.'

"I said what I thought was the question. In Vietnamese you have to end every question with a question word, and that word is *khong*. What I actually said to this old man was that there are VC in the area. Rather than asking him if there were any VC in the area, I told him that there were. He started shaking his head. My reputation as an interpreter went downhill from there. I was never called on again."

The target was eventually completed, a "Nice bright, shiny white with a red X painted on the thing." To boresight the main gun, the crew fitted a reticle with cross-hairs to the gun tube, and aligned it with the optical sight at a known, long distance. This was not a task that had to be done regularly.

"We went back to the base and sighted in all the tanks. We did that all in the same day. The next morning all the lumber was gone. It didn't last overnight."

The platoon at Ross was tasked primarily with the security of the hilltop base, and convoy escort back to the logistical base at Baldy. On occasion the tanks would escort resupply convoys of Amtracs into hostile territory. On one such mission the platoon lost one of the few tanks completely destroyed during the course of the war.

"It was about three clicks out. Two tanks and two Amtracs left bright and early one morning to make a resupply run to the infantry.

"We got out there and offloaded the C-rations out of the Amtracs, and kind of milled around there for thirty minutes or so. The whole doggone thing had a mine sweep [team] in this operation. A mine sweep out and a mine sweep back. The EOD guys were going both ways."

While the vehicles lingered near the infantry, the mine sweep team worked their way back toward Ross, so there was about a half hour gap between the departure of the sweep team and the convoy. "I was on the lead tank. I had been in-country like thirty days and I had been assigned to the loader's position. The lieutenant said, 'Well, I'm going to go.'" The officer bumped Rogers from his position, and he moved to the top of the tank. "The second lieutenant is in the loader's position, and we've got the driver, gunner, and tank commander. The corporal [Tommy Thompson] is in the tank commander's position. I just kind of grabbed an M16 and flak jacket and helmet, and climbed on the top. Back there with the tank boxes, on the gypsy rack. Just kind of riding along.

"When we offloaded the C-rations, a couple of grunts said, 'Hey, can I get up there and ride with you?' I said, 'I don't care. Come on.' Most of them were riding on top of the Amtracs.

"In the course of all this, we ran over this mine. The VC were really skilful at planting this thing. We had kind of bottomed out, kind of hit high center, so there was a belly to ground impact. And that's where the mine was." The rounded cast hull of the M48A3 tank generally allowed the force of a mine blast to vent to the sides, but with the tank bellied out, the ground contained the blast. The bottom of the hull was exposed to the full fury of the mine.

"In the initial report, later on, the EOD guys said they thought we had run over a five hundred-pound bomb. Later on they backtracked and said, well, an eighty pound box mine and we had kind of bellied out on it."

For Rogers and the two grunts, riding on top of the tank had been one of those decisions that by random chance saved their lives. "They survived. There were two dead as the result of this, but I never saw those guys again. I said later that's the last time they'll ever ask for a ride on a tank.

"When the thing went off, I had no clue what happened. It was one of those things where you kind of hear something, and you don't. What I remember was being on the ground. I don't remember hitting the ground, but I was on the ground and I couldn't move very well. I felt something move next to my shoulder, and I could hear the tank engine. And the damn thing—I felt the track move was what I felt. I thought, 'This damned thing is going to run over me.' I kind of blacked out.

"When I came around, there was a guy laying on top of me and we're down in this crater, a crater that was built, carved out, by this mine. It was Tommy Thompson, the tank commander. He had fallen on top of me. He had come out of the TC cupola, and he had gone backwards, back where I was at the ass-end of the tank, and we both slid down in this crater." Rogers and Thompson were the lucky ones, since the mine gutted the tank.

"The tank commander's cupola went to the right. That whole apparatus went to the right, thank the Lord. If that had landed on us, we'd have both been dead.

"When I kind of come around, I pushed him off and kind of got around where I could see him. He's white as a ghost, and I think, 'This guy's dead.' I pulled on him a little bit and he starts groaning. By this time the tank is on fire. I just started yanking on him, pulling him out of this crater and getting him back, and he's screaming bloody murder. I got him away from it, and it was blazing pretty good.

"There's some other people from the infantry, grunts, kind of come around trying to help out. Somebody pulled the fire bottle on the front end of it, and that didn't work." Rogers made his way to the front of the tank where another Marine was standing. He asked about the men inside, and "He said, 'They're dead.' The driver was killed and the gunner was killed."

The officer who had taken Rogers' position survived. Waiting for the medevac helicopters, "I was talking to him before he left. Virtually all of his clothes were blown off. He was a kind of red [complexioned] guy, and he was powder burned from head to toe. But that's it. Nothing broken, nothing bleeding. Just a big flash. Blew his clothes off and burned him."

The mine had blown a gaping hole in the hull bottom of Rogers's tank, and blown the track and suspension apart. The hull bottom escape hatches had been extensively redesigned after so many drivers had been killed by mine explosions in Korea. "It blew the escape hatch in. Terry Rexroat was the driver ... he was killed, I would expect, instantly. The driver's escape hatch apparently came up through this, from the concussion of the whole thing." The heavy steel plate caused mayhem inside the tiny driver's space. "The gunner, we called him Rick but his real name I think is William, last name is Van Cleve, he didn't have any place to go. He had the solid steel above his head. Whoever had checked the inside of it before it started on fire said he was dead.

"The only injuries were in the tank, and luckily there was not an ambush set there in connection with the whole damned thing. It was not command detonated. It was laid where they figured we would come back through. I guess they placed it right after the mine sweep went through."

Rogers had only scratches, which resulted in what he thought was "The cheapest Purple Heart anyone ever got in Vietnam, I'm sure."

The tank was totally destroyed, but the bodies remained inside the burning tank, and the Marines set in for the night. "The grunts we had with us kind of blended into the woodwork there, and got into their fighting holes. I went back to that rear tank, and set up camp on the ass-end of that thing for the night with my M16. Waiting for something to happen. It was a long, long night."

All night long the ammunition cooked off, but "The way I look at it, that stuff cooking off is a little bit different than if you had shot it. It was all inside of that tank. But once that diesel got to burning, that was it. You weren't going to put it out."

The next day the infantry and tank departed, and EOD, graves registration, and the recovery crews came to recover what they could. Two retrievers, nicknamed Bull and Bandit, were required to pull the wrecked tank out of the crater.

Rogers was simply sent back to LZ Ross, and the wrecked vehicle was eventually replaced. "It was business as usual after that. I certainly thought twice about crawling in that tank. But you've got to do what you've got to do."

The tanks in the platoon were named for the four horsemen of the apocalypse, so the replacement for the destroyed Famine was named Famine II.

Even as he entered office, Richard Nixon had decided to withdraw major American combat forces and leave South Vietnam to its fate. Exactly how the drawdown was to be accomplished led to considerable behind the scenes wrangling. Over the objections of Creighton Abrams, MACV was ordered to commence the withdrawal. Nixon publicly announced that after the Tet holiday in February 1970, fifty thousand men were to be withdrawn by the end of April, and 100,000 by the end of June. Naturally MACV preferred that the drawdown be primarily from III MAF. The Marine Corps objected, arguing that a precipitate withdrawal would exceed the capacity of the destination bases on Okinawa and California. Implicit in the argument was the fact that a rapid force reduction would make the Corps vulnerable to the budgetary cuts that were sure to come.

The 9th Marines were chosen to be the first Marine Corps component to be withdrawn, since they were not a garrison for any active combat base. The process of reassigning men between units, so that longer service men were assigned to the departing units, began. Looking forward to commitments after Vietnam, Marine Corps planners wanted to withdraw units as MEBs. The 9th Marines would be accompanied by artillery (2/12), tanks (C/3rd Tank), the rump of 3rd Anti-Tank Battalion, 1st Amphibious Tractor Battalion, 1st Searchlight Battery, and some air assets. By mid-August the 9th Marines had departed for Okinawa, the first major unit to leave Vietnam.

Inexorably, the plan fell into confusion. The plan called for two Marine regiments—the 7th and 26th Marines and their supporting units—to depart in Operation KEYSTONE BLUEJAY. The Army discovered that it did not have the forces required to backfill for the Marines, so the force reduction was reduced to one regiment. But logistical support for the Marines was cut when the Navy proceeded with the original plan, closing the Naval Support Activity at Danang, including the Naval Hospital, and eliminating the hospital ship stationed offshore.

The end was shaping up to be as confusing as the war itself.

CHAPTER 7

1970–1975: WITHDRAWAL AND FINAL SPASMS

"War cannot for a single minute be separated from politics."
Mao Xedong, Lectures

Through December 1969 there was considerable haggling within MACV over how to achieve the politically mandated force reductions. The result was a plan to reduce the Marine contingent to a 10,800-man brigade, with the loss of supporting recon, engineer, and tank units. Though the Marines would be largely left alone to define the terms of their own force structure and withdrawal, their ideas conflicted with those of the Army in small ways.

Colonel Donn A. Starry, an armor officer, in mid-1969 led the task force assigned to plan the withdrawal, and he had the ear of Creighton Abrams, another former armor officer. Both felt that the mobility and firepower of tanks were invaluable in reacting to enemy attacks, and they still feared a conventional invasion from the North. They advocated withdrawing the tanks last. The Marines, charged with the complexities of extensive patrolling in populous areas, airmobile operations to keep the enemy at arms' length, and the defense of the big logistics center at Danang, were willing to sacrifice other assets to keep more infantry and air units in place.

In January, 1st Marine Division accelerated the complex Mixmaster. Personnel with limited terms remaining to their thirteen-month tour were transferred to the 26th Marines and replaced by men who still had months yet to serve. The Army's XXIV Corps would assume control responsibility for the ICTZ, and the rump of III MAF would control only Marine Corps units.

The NVA was known to be massing men and materiel along the DMZ and Laotian border, and reactivating base areas inside South Vietnam. Content to see their most dangerous foe depart, the NVA and VC concentrated their efforts on assaulting the local South Vietnamese units, merely harassing the Marines with mines and ambushes.

The Marines were forced to spread themselves ever thinner on the ground. The Danang Vital Area was expanded and designated the Quang Da Special Zone. III MAF faced the Herculean task of coordinating not only with the US Army and ARVN, but the autonomous Republic of Korea's 2nd Marine Brigade, Civilian Irregular Defense Forces (formerly a Special Forces task), Regional Force companies, Popular Forces platoons (through the CAP programs), and the National Police. All this had to be coordinated through the ARVN commander in the ICTZ and several province chiefs. Added to the load was the responsibility to provide an entire regimental combat team on 36 hours notice to counter any major invasion across the DMZ.

Each of the remaining units (including even the division band) would be responsible for security over a vast and densely populated region. Infantry prowled the Rocket Belt around Danang. Kingfisher (heliborne infantry) and Nighthawk (armed helicopter) patrols responded to sightings of major enemy units. The CO of 1st Tank Battalion, Major Joseph Louder, was appointed Southern Sector Defense Commander, responsible for coordinating defense of the entire area south and southwest of Danang. This region included two critical logistical choke points, the Cobb and Cau Do bridges. The tank battalion and 26th Marines provided a small reaction force.

The 7th Marines and their supporting units fought a tedious, debilitating, and no less deadly war around Baldy and Ross. Anthony Rogers lamented that "Somebody steps on a booby trap over here, and two or three people die. That kind of thing. It was not newsworthy. It was happening all the time."

In general the enemy did not molest LZ Ross itself, but in early January 1970 they launched their only major attack on the base, an assault by an elite sapper unit. The tanks were set up around the perimeter of the hill. Rogers: "These cats infiltrated our wire, and lay there until about one o'clock in the morning. They started a mortar barrage, and that's when they came in. Underneath their own mortars.

"We lost fifteen people on the hill." One tank was struck in the initial stages of the assault. "A good friend of mine was hooking it, trying to get on the tank. He just barely made it inside the turret, and the RPG hit. It hit the fender. A couple of inches higher and it would have hit the turret where he was.

"It hit the fender and blew. Staff Sergeant Doan was scrambling at the same time, getting on the tank, and it blew him off. Blew him down on the ground. He gets up, gets back on the tank, and gets in.

"He could identify with me after that. When an explosion goes off it's kind of like the hand of God, it just picks you up and just throws you like you're nothing."

Rogers and others were awakened by the sound of incoming mortar fire. "When the mortars started hitting, we all jumped up and scrambled on the tank. The tank's wet and you're slipping and sliding." Rogers saw a round impact twenty or so yards away before he ducked into the relative safety of the tank. With the enemy inside the perimeter, there were no clear targets for the tank's big guns.

One bunker isolated at the far end of the position, separated from the main hill position by the broad expanse of the landing zone, was under heavy attack. "This poor guy on the radio… we had called and asked if they wanted us to move, to maneuver where we could give a little fire support to them. They said no." The battalion commander was not aboard the base that night, but the tank crew followed the orders of the officers coordinating the defense. "So we just sat right where we were. Never fired a shot. And they died."

After the attack numerous changes were made to make the base more defensible, but too late for the men who were KIA.

In February Ross was turned over to ARVN control, and the 1st Platoon of Charlie Company 1st Tank went to An Hoa, the base for LSU-1, which supported the 5th Marines. Rogers said that the only bad thing about leaving Ross was that the platoon had to leave its adopted local dog, Private Sam Rowdy.

The tenure at An Hoa was relatively uneventful: hill defense, convoy escort, and a few small operations as the Marine Corps' participation in the war wound down. "You crossed Liberty Bridge en route to An Hoa. We would run convoy escorts along that road."

Sweeps out of An Hoa were small, generally platoon-scale operations. Rogers said, "I do recall going out on one of these things and getting into a whole lot of booby traps, but no VC or NVA." Under the intense sun of the dry season, many of the infantrymen suffered badly from the heat. In an attack on a tree line, a tracer round started a fire.

"The booby traps start cooking off. I counted thirty-five. One of them was a big boy, substantial size, but most of them were anti-personnel kind of stuff."

The Marines were waiting on a medevac helicopter to come for the heat casualties. "Somebody kind of walked out into the bush there. I was sitting there watching him, trying to set up a perimeter, and he comes flying back out. It kind of hit him in the foot and leg, wasn't anything terrible. But any time anybody stepped out of the tank tracks, they were going to step on one of these things. It was really saturated with them.

"We got the last one on the medevac chopper and went home. Didn't fire a shot at anybody. I killed a lizard that day. He was about three feet long."

As part of the Mixmaster, 7th Marines personnel who had limited time in country departed, and were replaced by men from the departing 9th Marines who had six or more months remaining on their tour of duty.

After Sublett rotated back to the States, Buddy Reveile met T.J. Siva, who was back for yet another tour in Vietnam. By this time the platoon had been moved back to Hoi An to support the Korean Marines. "The platoon that was at Hoi An before us, their Gunnery Sergeant, their [truck] driver, and their corpsman had gotten killed. They had gotten killed right out on the beach, I think it's White Beach. Driving down the beach headed for Danang, right outside the compound they'd gotten ambushed. This was right near where the Koreans were, in their backyard."

Despite everything, Reveile thought that morale in the tank units was still good, mainly due to the professionalism of the staff NCOs.

KEYSTONE BLUEJAY had commenced on 28 January, and by 5 March the 5th Marines assumed responsibility for the departing 26th Marines area. Between 11 and 19 March the bulk of 1st Tank Battalion boarded ship, leaving only Charlie Company to support Marine operations. This was in itself the result of more high-level haggling within the government and military.

As part of the troop reductions the word came down that anyone who had less than six or seven months left on their tour would be sent out of country. Anthony Rogers was shipped out in late March, flying to Okinawa on a Marine Corps C-130. His reaction was one that would become familiar to a generation of Vietnam survivors. "Glad to be out of the combat zone in one breath, and in the other it was kind of like 'Boy, what a flake I am, leaving these guys there.'"

As always, others rotated out of Vietnam for more mundane reasons. Buddy Reveile had damaged the cartilage in his knee, the cumulative effects of the everyday small injuries in a tank unit, falls suffered while running for the tanks under incoming artillery, and rowdy games of football. In that era knee surgery still carried high risks, so the Navy doctors put his leg in a cast and sent him back to duty for twelve weeks. When he was eventually called back to the battalion headquarters, "They cut the cast off, and my leg had deteriorated. I had lost three inches [of circumference] in it above the knee. My calf had gotten real small, because it was in a cast, from inactivity. I couldn't put my foot to the ground. The pain would shoot through my leg."

Reveile was sent back to his company to draw his pay and liquidate his non-portable belongings that included luxuries like a refrigerator, an electric fan, and even a hospital bed mattress. All these he had acquired from an old friend from 2nd Tank, Bill Holmes, who had already left Vietnam.

On Buddy's last night Siva organized a card game. "We played poker all night long. By the time I was done I didn't have a nickel in my pocket." Down to his last disposable wealth, "I had a cool pair of shades. As I was leaving, a guy named Kelly gave me five bucks for my shades."

Despite his protests that he did not warrant special treatment, Reveile went out aboard a C-130 medical transport. The plane was loaded with combat casualties, and "The guy in the bunk above me died in transit to Japan."

He was flown to Japan, then to the US for knee surgery.

Five months later, after recuperating from his surgery, Reveile reported back to the tanks in California—and found that Siva was his platoon sergeant. Siva soon retired, with his party at Reveile's house in Oceanside. Buddy never fully recovered from the injury to his leg, and left the Corps.

Anthony Rogers spent additional time with the tanks on Okinawa. Like many others, after the relative freedom and autonomy of Vietnam, he found the duty in a rear area stifling. "You're treated like you're a second-class citizen, for whatever reason."

Rogers took the opportunity to become a brig guard until his tour ended in October 1970. With Vietnam winding down, there were fewer hardcore offenders, and the only notable prisoner Rogers recalled was "A guy that killed his CO. Fragged him, shot him with a forty-five, or something, but killed him. He was bound for Leavenworth but was kind of there for a while. Most of the brig-rats I don't think came out of Vietnam. They were just people going UA [Unauthorized Absence] there on Okinawa and that sort of thing."

Even more political haggling resulted in accelerated reductions, with the Army again favoring reductions in Marine forces, but with XXIV Corps upset over the potential loss of Marine air and intelligence assets.

The incursion into Cambodia in late April succeeded on the whole in throwing the enemy off his strategic balance, but again at enormous political cost. The furor forced Nixon to announce accelerated troop withdrawals. The invasion also raised fears of an enemy offensive in the ICTZ to reduce pressure on his forces further south in Cambodia. The 7th Marines were heavily engaged in preemptive airmobile attacks on bases in the rugged Que Son Mountains to the west, in an attempt to both disrupt enemy plans and to deny him access to the food sources of the Que Son Valley. Individual platoons or sections of Charlie Company tanks supported both the 1st and 5th Marines.

In late April, Joe Sleger seized upon the opportunity to use his 3rd Tank Battalion mobile CP in one of the operations in Leatherneck Square. Sleger and the tank battalion command element were given operational control of two platoons of tanks, with the infantry attached to the tank battalion, a major departure from typical Marine practice.[1]

"We didn't, however, run into any resistance in the sweep." The battalion moved up the road from Cam Lo to Con Thien, then "We swept from west to east, then turned and made a sweep back from east to west, back to Charlie-2."

Another instance when the M113 personnel carriers were used was the formation of an armored task force in anticipation of encountering NVA tanks. This included truck-mounted infantry and a reinforced platoon of tanks. The task force was to travel up the road from Vandegrift toward Khe Sanh, "to see if we could draw out the enemy forces." Sleger set up the mobile CP near Ca Lu, south of Vandegrift, to monitor the column's progress.[2]

On 12 June an enlarged reaction force, Pacifier Force, was set up, including two infantry companies and four tanks.

Tanks participated in many of the small, unnamed operations designed to clear small areas and keep the enemy off balance. In mid-

May, Foxtrot and Hotel Companies 2/5, with Regional Forces and tanks staged a series of raids on hamlets and villages in the Liberty Bridge area that were known VC strongholds. The 2/5 had suffered numerous casualties to mines and booby-traps in the tangle of buildings and hedgerows. Like many units before them, they developed a practice of having the tanks crash through suspect obstacles. This was decidedly unpopular with the tank crews.

On 20 June a task force including companies from the B and C Companies 2/1 and G/2/5, with four tanks, entered the northern Arizona Territory, and in the following week swept northeast along the Thu Bon River toward Liberty Bridge in an attempt to thwart enemy forces reportedly massing for an attack on the Hill 55 logistical facility. Foxtrot and Hotel 2/5, with their supporting tanks and a Regional Forces platoon, took up residence in the Liberty Bridge area as a blocking force, and to search and clear the surrounding hamlets.

The 3rd Tank Battalion was departing the country, and as a member of the battalion staff Sam Binion took part packing the battalion for departure. "We didn't leave nothing behind. You know the Marine Corps. Hell, we didn't have it to spare." The battalion loaded aboard boats at Hue City, moved along the coast and boarded ships at Danang, bound for Okinawa.

As the summer months wore on the Marines continued to pursue the enemy, but their war was clearly winding down. Contacts declined as the enemy bided his time, awaiting the final withdrawal. From early July through late August the 7th Marines continued to sweep the Que Son Valley in Operation PICKENS FOREST. The activities of the other regiments focused on defense of the Danang area, including occasional operations in the An Hoa and Arizona Territory. Charlie tanks were mostly on standby for these operations.

Even in small numbers the tanks could still be decisive in the small operations, though their assigned tasks could at times be unsavory. As part of Operation BARREN GREEN in mid-July, platoons of Marines and Regional Forces moved into the northern Arizona Territory to deny the VC the annual corn harvest "tax." Constant harassment by snipers and booby-traps forced their withdrawal. Between 24 and 27 July, 2/5 and 3/5, with a platoon of tanks, returned to sweep the area in force. The tanks were used to crush the crops still standing in the fields, denying the food to the enemy but also to the farmers.

After leaving Vietnam in May of 1968, JJ Carroll served in a number of billets. Eventually he was assigned to the infantry on Okinawa, and then to the SLF. "We're laying off the coast of Vietnam. Of course all these young studs, One-Nine [were boasting], 'We're the Walking Dead,'" the sardonic nickname the battalion had acquired around Con Thien. Of course none of the young infantrymen were veterans of the hard fighting of 1967–1968. Carroll quickly clued them in that "I was there when you got the name. They were hot to land."

The Communists fought tenaciously to defend the enlarged base areas they were establishing in the South. Through August and September the 7th Marines continued their struggle for control of the Que Son Hills, but everyone knew how that would eventually end. Yet another incursion into the historic A Shau Valley by the 101st Airborne and 1st ARVN Divisions was driven out by fierce attacks on their firebases. The stated reason for the withdrawal was to avoid "a bloody, politically embarrassing, and militarily unproductive battle in the highlands."[3] Clearly the enemy would be granted no chance to achieve a propaganda victory like the one inflicted on the French at Dien Bien Phu near the end of their tenure in Vietnam.

In early August the JCS informed Creighton Abrams that the Army's budget and manpower were such that more Marines would have to remain in place, and more Army units would be withdrawn. The Marine Corps' share of Operation KEYSTONE ROBIN ALPHA was 11,000 men. The defensive responsibilities of the infantry were again realigned, and the Charlie Company tanks were ordered to stand down and pack their gear.

On the way out there was none of the fanfare or political furor that had greeted the arrival of the tanks in Vietnam five years before. In September, Charlie Company, 1st Tank cased its colors and departed Vietnam, virtually unnoticed except by Navy cargo handlers and the friends and families awaiting them at home and at various duty posts back in "the world."

The last major field operation conducted by a Marine ground combat force was SCOTT ORCHARD. The fate of Americans either known to have been captured or missing in action was becoming a major issue as American participation in the war ended. Rumors suggested that prisoners might be held in the rugged Que Son Mountains. III MAF intelligence analysts doubted the information, but from 7 through 11 April 1971, Marine infantry and Recon troops, supported by airlifted artillery, scoured the mountains to no avail.

The Army's Americal Division was replacing the Marines, and the last infantry battalions began withdrawal in Operation KEYSTONE ORIOLE ALPHA. The Combined Action Platoons had long since begun the prolonged process of leaving their villages and hamlets, turning them over to the ARVN. In a televised speech on 7 April 1971 President Nixon told the US public, "Tonight I can announce that Vietnamization has succeeded."

On that same 7 April, Operation IMPERIAL LAKE, the eight-month-long program of aggressive patrolling and ambushes that had involved all the infantry units at various times, ended. The 11th Marines fired their last howitzer rounds. The last combat troops sailed away on 1 June. On 27 June 1971, the 3rd Marine Amphibious Brigade, the rump of III MAF, was formally closed down.

WAR'S END

When the Marines departed Vietnam they transferred masses of equipment and supplies to the ARVN as a final contribution to the "Vietnamization" of the war. Apart from this, however, Commandant Chapman vowed to "not leave five dollars worth of property in Vietnam."[1]

Major Marine combat formations were gone, but the final prolonged consequences of the war, for the Corps and especially for the South Vietnamese, would be years in coming. Marine advisors, or *co vans*, remained with the Vietnamese Marine Corps, though their numbers steadily dwindled. Embassy guards and a handful of ANGLICO teams also continued to serve in the increasingly beleaguered country.

The ARVN occupied Con Thien, Dong Ha, and all the other bases that had been so bitterly contested, but for the time being the NVA were content to let the ARVN stew in the increasingly isolated bases. The northernmost provinces, and particularly Quang Tri, were obviously the part of South Vietnam most threatened by the increasingly powerful NVA. The Vietnamese Marine Corps had long been part of the Joint General Staff Reserve, so two brigades of the VNMC, along with their *co vans*, were transferred north in late 1971. The brigades were soon transferred to the newly formed and grossly inexperienced 3rd ARVN Division that would stand in the path of the veterans of the NVA.

Despite a massive influx of military supplies and equipment, the ARVN was ill equipped to deal with the NVA. The primary problem remained corruption, with the appointment of senior generals based on loyalty to the Saigon regime rather than fighting ability.

Beginning in December there was increased enemy activity in western Quang Tri. The ARVN command in Saigon was convinced that the greatest threat was an attack out of Cambodia, farther to the south. In fact, the NVA had their eye on both.

The 1972 Easter Offensive, a conventional attack involving major artillery and tank formations, was clear evidence that the NVA was increasingly confident of its superiority over the ARVN. The offensive began on 30 March with attacks throughout Quang Tri Province, and by 1 April four veteran NVA regiments supported by PT-76 and T-54 tanks had flooded across the DMZ.

Some *co vans* like Captains John Ripley and Lawrence Livingston played a major role in blunting the 1972 Easter Offensive. Naval gunfire, the 3rd VNMC battalion, and the M48 tanks of the 20th ARVN Tank Battalion, once reinforced by other ARVN units, held on to Dong Ha through a week of desperate fighting against superior forces.

No amount of valor could overcome the fact that other major ARVN units had surrendered without a fight, giving the NVA free reign in western Quang Tri. On 9 April, NVA tanks and infantry overran the 6th VNMC Battalion west of Quang Tri City, and a counterattack by parts of the 1st VNMC Battalion and a scratch force of armor resulted in a major tank battle. The M48 tanks proved more than a match for the NVA tanks, destroying most in a matter of minutes to hold the approaches to Quang Tri City.

Again the best efforts of some units were negated through the failure of others. On 27 April, when the 20th ARVN Tank Battalion was pulled out of Dong Ha to help the VNMC counter another NVA attack from the west of Quang Tri City, the 57th ARVN Regiment fled Dong Ha. It fell to the NVA without a shot fired. The NVA flooded on toward Quang Tri City. The 7th VNMC Battalion watched as the ARVN troops assigned to help them hold the northern approaches to the city simply moved through their positions on their southward flight. On 30 April the defenses west of the city collapsed, and on 1 May the ARVN abandoned Quang Tri City.

Farther south, an ARVN division fled in the face of an NVA attack, and the NVA besieged the city and large base at Kontum. In Binh Dinh, the northernmost province of the IICTZ, the NVA seized several district capitals. Local defense forces fought for their homes, but an inept and vacillating ARVN regional commander abandoned them to their fate. Only close to Saigon did the ARVN fight well, when extra divisions were transferred from other areas and the South Vietnamese "palace guard" was committed. As government forces were moved to resist the NVA onslaught the VC flowed into the vacuum, reasserting control over numerous towns and villages.

The NVA onslaught eventually spent itself, in part because of massive US airpower assistance, but mainly because of inadequate NVA logistics. Negotiations conducted by Henry Kissinger left NVA forces in place within South Vietnam to await another chance.

The North Vietnamese waited patiently until 1975. For the Marine Corps, there remained only one last act to be played out. Operations EAGLE PULL, the evacuation of Pnom Penh, Cambodia, and FREQUENT WIND, the evacuation of Saigon, ended the Marine Corps involvement in America's most protracted and divisive war.

AFTERMATH

The Vietnam War came as close to wrecking the Corps as any event in its long history. The Corps had begun the conflict as a relatively small professional volunteer force. It ended the war racked by social ills, poor morale at all levels, and with its standing in society at low ebb.

Sam Binion was commissioned as an officer, but left the Corps in 1972. "There was too much politics in the officer's ranks.... Especially after that war, you tell somebody to get a haircut, and they'd have you up in front of *the human relations council*! If you could believe that crap."

Drug abuse was rampant. Don Gagnon: "When we were at Camp Hansen ... we had to walk clear to the other side of camp for the mess hall. That's where they had replacements coming in, and people coming out of Vietnam. They had fifty-five gallon barrels outside of the barracks that were trash barrels. The local Okinawans had the contract to pick up the trash on a daily basis. They had yellow barrels ... and those were for contraband." Things like ammunition, weapons, and drugs could be dumped into the drums, no questions asked. "There would be hand grenades, forty millimeter rounds, thirty caliber—all sorts of stuff.

"One day we were walking by the barrels, and Gerry Hodum looks in the barrels and says, 'Oh, for Christ sake. We got a bunch of snow here.'

"I looked at him and said, 'Snow?'

"He says, 'Yeah, heroin.' So we put somebody on the barrel and called the CID, and they came out and picked up the heroin.

"I didn't realize it but when I was in Vietnam we went over to what they called the White Elephant PX, or the Pink Elephant, whichever one. These guys were standing outside the perimeter, selling heroin. I didn't know what heroin was. I was naïve as hell, and I was the Company First Sergeant! I never saw that stuff before. The jeep driver was telling me that's heroin and they were selling it for a dollar a canister. It was one of those medicine bottles, about as big around as a quarter. And it was full."

Drug use in Vietnam seemed related more to boredom than fear, and most rampant in the rear areas. "The people that had access to the PX, who were sent out to buy beer or something, they had the opportunity to get involved in that sort of thing."

When Gagnon returned to the States, "They just took all my gear and shoved it off to one side, and escorted me through the line. But with all the other people they took their talcum powder, all their shaving gear and everything, and literally took it apart. That's when I woke up to what was going on.

"When I went back to Camp Pendleton, back to the tank ramp down at Camp Del Mar ... drugs and gangs were rampant, and it was really a sad situation."

The worst problems were at the junior enlisted level, where all the ills of contemporary society after the late-1960s—drug abuse, racial strife, and a general disgust with authority—were reflected in the ranks. Buddy Reveile served another eighteen months, and saw "People going to jail all the time. People cutting each other, shooting each other. This was Stateside duty. It was very tragic. I was a platoon sergeant, and we were dealing with people's problems continually."

It would require decades for the Corps to recover from the Vietnam experience.

EPILOGUE

"I knew guys who went to Vietnam.
What I notice is that they don't talk about it much."
Tom Wopat (actor)

How do you end any story about Vietnam?

The flame of the war sputtered to an end in 1975, but the coals still smolder in an entire generation, whether you are a veteran of the war, the wife or child of someone who served in the war, or an aging anti-war protestor. No one remained untouched.

The worst served, as always, were the combat veterans. Raised to believe in the national myth of the honored veteran, the young men of an entire generation were denied the recognition they deserved. Veterans of past wars were largely just neglected, but the fate of this new generation was in its own way worse.

Unlike veterans of World War II and Korea, the Vietnam veterans had prevailed in every single battle, but were now called upon to pay yet another price for a war that was eventually lost through simple fatigue and a failure of the national will. The veterans of the long, agonizing war that would not end were at best ignored as an embarrassment. At worst they were scorned and feared as psychological time bombs. They were denied even the private satisfaction of knowing they had served well and honorably, if anonymously, in a war their countrymen regarded as just.

It would require sixteen years, and another war, before America realized that the national embarrassment was not its veterans, but the way they had been treated. Sixteen years later still, and we are involved in another debilitating, frustrating war. This time the veterans are neither an embarrassment nor an object of scorn and fear, whether you are a supporter or an opponent of the conflict in Iraq. Perhaps that is the legacy of those who suffered in and after the Vietnam War—that they made us decisively separate the war from the warrior.

A third of a century later Vietnam is still a word to conjure pain and anger because the old scars still ache. Yet there is love inextricably mixed with the pain.

Wally Young is quite candid in saying, "You don't know for sure. So many things happened, you don't know if it really happened or not. Some of the bad stuff, you just block it out. Some of the good times we had, I've had buddies of mine say, 'Yeah, I remember when you did this or did that,' and I no more remember what they're talking about than the man in the moon."

In 2003, the Marine Corps tankers held a reunion in Seattle. Two weeks earlier the 4th Marines had held their own reunion at the same hotel. JJ Carroll had corresponded by e-mail with one of the now middle-aged grunts, "who was right there when my tank got whacked, was right next to me. When I showed up at the hotel, there was a case of beer stored for me there. It was from the 4th Marines. It said 'Thanks a lot there, tanker, for watching our back. September of sixty-seven, India.' It was kind of a neat Marine thing, you know."

Buddy Reveile tried to seek out the people he had known in Vietnam, or their families. Trying to find the family of Jim Hackett, "I called information and I called him up. But it was his dad, and it was a terrible, terrible experience. I reopened wounds for this man. He was an older gentleman. He got very emotional. He wanted to get me off the phone. I felt terrible about it."

Carl "Flash" Fleischmann recalled that the truck driver, "Ben Pepper, he was blown up pretty bad. They medevaced him out. I was out of the Marine Corps, and one day my wife and I looked out our back window in Danbury, Connecticut, and there was a truck back there. Ben found out where I lived, and came to visit. Now he's the godfather of my son. My son's thirty-something years old now. We're dearest friends. He visits me. I call him. I talk to John Wear, I talk to Ray Stewart, I talk to Dick Carey, I talk to *all* of them. They're all a bunch of great guys."

Harry Christensen wrote that on too many nights, like thousands of others with similar memories, he relives the day that Captain Kent died.[1]

When will the Vietnam War truly end?

Not until the night when Christensen's hopes are finally realized and he pulls Captain Daniel W. Kent to safety.

Dan Wokaty was wounded while close to finishing his second tour.

Carl Fleischman (right, holding the Tommy gun) at Hue in 1968.

Jan (left) and Jim Wendling, shown in 1969, and after the war in 2006.

WHERE ARE THEY NOW?

JOHN BARTUSEVICS was awarded a Silver Star for his actions in Vietnam. He became a Drill Instructor, was appointed a Warrant Officer, and was assigned to 3rd Tank after the tanks were pulled out of Vietnam. He eventually retired as a captain. He now lives in Oceanside, where he rides a motorcycle in the Patriot Guard, which provides escorts at military funerals. He also drives a 1947 Mercury. R.B. English teases him about the color; he calls it cherry, English calls it pink. He taught hand-to-hand combat, and still practices and teaches karate.

SAM BINION worked in real estate in Seattle, returned to Louisiana to work in technical supplies for the oil industry, then moved to Tennessee.

JIM CARROLL returned from Vietnam to the Reserves in the 4th Tank Battalion, and served in various capacities until he retired in 1987.

WILLIAM "JJ" CARROLL left Vietnam in May 1968. He had not originally intended to make a career in the Corps, but just kept re-enlisting and retired as a Sergeant Major just prior to the first Gulf War. Now he says that he and an old buddy from Vietnam, "We looked at each other and said 'Man, this is weird to see these young kids walking around with Purple Hearts on. They are what we were in the sixties." As a businessman, he belongs to the local Marine Corps Council, which provides assistance, family support, and other volunteer services.

CONWILL W. CASEY taught embarkation at the Amphib School at Coronado, California, trained recruits at Parris Island, and after serving in staff positions was CO of 2nd Tank. He retired in 1991.

BOB EMBESI shot rifles and pistols in competition for the Marine Corps, and retired in 1982 as a Chief Warrant Officer Four, or Marine Gunner, one of a handful left in the Corps. He also ran nightclubs ("about broke me and killed me") and shooting ranges, and was a competition shooter. Now he just hunts and fishes.

R.B. ENGLISH spent thirty years in the Corps, then worked at the San Clemente nuclear power plant (along with Bartusevics) for ten years, in a 160-man security detachment. There were so many retired Marines that they called it "Marine Barracks, San Onofre."

CARL FLEISCHMANN still has a bit of shrapnel in his leg from Hue. He tried to return to Vietnam, but was medically discharged. The Army offered him a commission in tanks, but he declined. He worked for Electric Boat as a nuclear machinist while pursuing an engineering degree, then worked for the Navy Department on weapons systems and communications. He is now retired.

KARL FONTENOT retired from the Marine Corps and taught high school briefly, then worked as a hospital administrator. Now he "does nothing constructive except play with my computer, go fishing, things like that."

DON GAGNON retired as a Master Gunnery Sergeant, and is very active in a number of veterans groups. He has been instrumental in the preparation of all three books in this series.

GENE HACKEMACK worked for NASA at the Johnson Space Center for six years, worked as a civilian contractor training Iranian search and rescue personnel before the fall of the Shah, and built and operated "the only German restaurant between Houston and Austin." Eventually his old boss talked him into going back to NASA for another seventeen years until he retired in 2006.

DAN McQUEARY retired from the Marines after twenty-one years. He was the director of support services for a school district until his second retirement. He is an avid fly fisherman.

KURT MOSS worked for General Electric, and then the telephone company. He is now retired.

BARNETT PERSON was eventually evacuated to the Balboa Naval

Hospital in San Diego, and was discharged in March 1968. He became a Drill Instructor at San Diego, along with R.B. English.

KEN POZDER served with 5th Tank, was one of the first Marine instructors at the new joint Army-Marine Corps tank school at Fort Knox, and retired as a Gunnery Sergeant. He worked twenty-four years for a logging company until he retired again. "God, I love it. Do all the fishing you want. Do what you want, period. Every day is Saturday."

BUDDY REVEILE, like many, tried to locate some of the men he had served with in Vietnam, or the families of those who had died there. Today he has a business building and selling custom motorcycles. One day at LZ Baldy he had encountered an acquaintance from his school days. Reveile thought the man was dead until the day in 1986 he walked in and bought a bike.

ANTHONY ROGERS returned to college, attended Officer Candidate School, and became an aviator. As the result of a hydraulic system failure his friends tell him, "You're the only guy I know who's lost a tank and an F-4, both." He eventually became a landman, the specialist who secures exploration leases and assembles deals in the domestic oil industry. It took him twenty-nine years to steel his nerves to talk to Terry Rexroat's mother. They stay in contact by mail.

JOE SLEGER retired as a Colonel after 33 years service. He worked in the nuclear power industry before retiring again in 1990.

RAY STEWART also served with F/2/4 in the early DMZ battles, and did a second tour with the MPs in Vietnam. He attended Arabic languages school and served in a number of billets in the Middle East, and worked for Boeing. He is head of the Vietnam Tankers of America Historical Foundation, which seeks to document the location and activities of Marine Corps tank units during this most confusing of wars. Smith and Schultz still "yank his chain" at every reunion about leaving them parked on a bridge in Vietnam, coming back months later to tell them to "get a haircut and go home."

JOHN WEAR served four more months, and got an early out to go back to college. He became a department store buyer, then sales manager for a cookware manufacturer. He is now an independent sales representative for multiple lines of cookware. His son has done two tours each in Afghanistan and Iraq, and he has three daughters.

JAN WENDLING and all his brothers became police officers in a small one hundred-man department. He now has thirty-seven years service. The brother who was in Vietnam with him was shot on duty, and is now retired. He considers himself fortunate because he and his brothers could "decompress" by talking to each other about Vietnam.

DAN WOKATY became a DI, and retired in 1978 after 26 years service. He worked as a union truck driver for 22 years. Now retired, his part-time job is shuffling rental cars about, including providing government and press pool cars for George W. Bush's ranch near Crawford Texas.

WALLY YOUNG was offered promotion and a position as a Drill Instructor, but elected to leave the Corps. He told the re-enlistment officer that his mind was made up. "He said, 'You sound like you're kind of bitter toward the Marine Corps, Corporal Young.'" Young told him that he loved the Corps and always would, but "I was aviation guaranteed. I been in these pig-iron tanks for four years, and I ain't seen one get off the ground yet."

KEN ZITZ had planned to leave the Corps at the end of his tour, but the night he learned of Mike Wunsch's death, he decided to stay in. He went to graduate school and taught Chinese. Zitz never went back into tanks, but was a CO in the Officer Candidate School. After retirement from the Marines as a Colonel, he built and operated golf courses, and runs a youth golfing program. In 2006 he visited Mike Wunsch's grave near Philadelphia.

CHAPTER NOTES

PREFACE

1. Command Chronology, 3rd Tank Battalion, 1 March to 31 March 1969, page 22.

2. Fisher *The Best 'War Story"–Marine Ontos Style*, Sponson Box, March 2004, p. 15.

CHAPTER 1

1. *Montagnards* (French for mountaineer dwellers) of the Moi, Muong, Man, and Miao tribes were hunters and practiced slash-and-burn agriculture. Brave, loyal, and skilled fighters in their native forests and mountains, they served the French and later the Americans well. The Vietnamese of the lowlands discriminated against them, and they suffered greatly at the hands of their own countrymen.

2. Whitlow, *US Marines in Vietnam: The Advisory and Combat Assistance Era, 1954–1964*, p. 132.

3. The Young Turks were a group of young officers who dominated Turkish politics before and during World War I, and the collapse of the Ottoman Empire.

4. Colonel Zitz distinctly recalled this landing and brief stay ashore, though it is not discussed in the official history (Whitlow, *US Marines in Vietnam: The Advisory and Combat Assistance Era, 1954–1964*). Records kept by the Special Landing Forces did not generally include records for small "supporting" units sent ashore.

5. Marine Corps regiments are numerically designated. Unlike the Army, the function is not specified. For example the 3rd Marines are infantry, and the 12th Marines are artillery, both within the 3rd Marine Division. Abbreviated designations in the format D/1/3 will be used hereafter as

appropriate.
6. Wear interview.
7. An Expeditionary Brigade consisted of two to three infantry battalions, with attached supporting units. Combat support units might include detachments of artillery, tanks, tank destroyers, engineers, and helicopters. Logistics assets were sufficient to make the Brigade self-supporting for brief periods.
8. Starry, *Armored Combat in Vietnam*, p. 52–53.
9. Ibid, p. 55.

CHAPTER 2
1. The LPD (Landing Platform, Dock) was an upgraded version of the Landing Ship, Dock of early World War II vintage. Designed to transport tanks and heavy equipment on long voyages under any sea conditions, the entire stern of the vessel could be opened up and the vessel lowered by flooding ballast tanks, flooding a large open well-deck. This allowed large landing craft carried inside to move in and out for unloading heavy equipment. Addition of a helicopter landing platform over the large open well-deck added an air transport capability. This type was an important component of the amphibious force, though once established in Vietnam the tanks were usually transported along the coastline and up rivers by smaller vessels.
2. Military stores intended to support forward Marine forces in an emergency deployment, they could not be drawn for routine or scheduled operations.
3. A military area; the commander of the area is responsible not only for tactical operations within the area, but for development and maintenance of facilities and traffic control.
4. The "Gunny" was responsible for overseeing logistics, maintenance, and other day-to-day combat requirements of the company. His counterpart was the First Sergeant, who handled administration and personnel.
5. At battalion and regimental level the staff sections were S-1 (admin), S-2 (supply), S-3 (operations), and S-4 (most often civil affairs).
6. A 360 degree compass dial inside the turret, but relative to the tank's axis; zero was straight ahead, 180 straight to the rear, etc.
7. A protractor with a pendulum that sat on top of the main gun breechblock to precisely measure the gun's elevation.
8. A sound-powered EE8 field telephone.
9. Moss, *First Vietnam Tanker Casualty*, Sponson Box, March 2003, p. 10.
10. Moss interview.
11. Shumlinson and Johns, *US Marines In Vietnam: The Landing and*

Buildup, pp. 169–170.
12. Landing Vehicle, Tracked amphibian tractor. In Vietnam the box-like LVTP5A1 was the standard vehicle, though the next generation LVTP-7 saw very limited use late in the war. Hereafter the common USMC terms LVT or Amtrac will be used to denote the LVTP5A1.
13. A village was a political-administrative entity that might encompass many square kilometers. A village might include numerous smaller and isolated clusters of residential and farming structures termed hamlets, spread over the area. In map location terminology, these component hamlets were often distinguished by a numeric suffix, such as An Cuong (2).
14. Excerpt from Official Marine Corps Command Chronologies, Capt. Al Lamb's After Action Report.
15. Stewart, *The History of Marine Tanks in Vietnam 1965–1970*, Sponson Box, September 2004, p. 14.
16. Phase Lines were introduced in World War II. Generally prominent map features, they were sites where rapidly advancing units would pause while units that were encountering more resistance could catch up, to prevent the development of open flanks. They also helped minimize the chance of units calling down artillery fire on friendly units operating in front of them.
17. Recoilless guns were a particularly deadly threat to tank crewmen. The smaller and more numerous Rocket Propelled Grenades (RPGs) would penetrate the tank's armor and kill any crewmen unfortunate enough to be caught in the path of the explosive jet. The bigger recoilless guns packed enough punch to detonate stored ammunition, destroying both tank and crew.
18. This was an extreme example of the difficulties posed by archaic command structures left over from World War II. Embarked troops remained under the control of the naval commander until he declared the naval stage of the operation over. Peatross could not get control of his own troops still afloat. Major General Walter Krulak, Commanding General Fleet Marine Forces Pacific, was visiting the 7th Marines CP ashore; he flew out to the command ship to ask nicely for the use of L/3/7 and the helicopters to move them.
19. McQueary interview. This was apparently Corporal William C. Laidlaw, as listed in Anonymous, *Operation Starlite, 18–20 August 1965*, Sponson Box, April 2004, p. 15.
20. Zitz interview; Anonymous, *Operation Starlite: The First Big Battle (17–24 August 1965)*, Sponson Box, June 2004, p. 15.
21. The LVTE-1 was a specialized mine-clearing Amtrac equipped with a large rake-like plow on the front for scooping out buried mines. On top it carried a launcher for a rocket-propelled explosive line that could be fired

over a suspected minefield to detonate mines by barometric overpressure.
22. This region was the site of the infamous My Lai Massacre, by troops of the Americal Division, in 1968.
23. In the post-Korea era the Corps consisted of three active divisions, with the 4th Division (Reserve) as a strategic reserve. President Johnson also did not want to activate Reserve or National Guard units for political reasons. Thus the need to reactivate a division.
24. Embesi (interview) and Stiegelman (*Dagger Thrust Operations–Vietnam 1965*, Sponson Box, October 2005, p. 11) recall different company designations for this unit. Platoons would often be re-designated, changed from one company to another by the stroke of an administrator's pen, which led to considerable confusion. In this case I have gone with the designation provided by Stiegelman, the platoon commander.
25. Embesi interview. Note that the tank platoon commander, then Lt. Herb Stiegelman, recalls that all three tanks, all but one Amtrac, and Seabee TD-15 and TD-24 bulldozers were bogged down. He also recalls that the TD-24 was blown in place. Stiegelman, *Dagger Thrust Operations–Vietnam 1965*, Sponson Box, October 2005, p. 11.
26. The Landing Craft, Utility or "U-boat" carried three tanks. It was used to land vehicles from the seagoing Landing Ship Dock, and often transported vehicles and cargo along rivers or the coastline.
27. Stiegelman, *Dagger Thrust Operations–Vietnam 1965*, Sponson Box, October 2005, p. 11.
28. Embesi interview.
29. Regional Forces were a standing local government militia.
30. A potential point of confusion, HARVEST MOON was the same name given to some September–October operations to protect the rice harvest and deny the VC the so-called rice tax that fed their troops.
31. Stiegelman, *Dagger Thrust Operations–Vietnam 1965*, Sponson Box, October 2005, p. 11; Howtars were 4.2-inch mortars on a wheeled mount.
32. Shumlinson and Johns, *US Marines In Vietnam: The Landing and Buildup*, p. 170.
33. Embesi interview.

CHAPTER 3
1. The following account is condensed from Rogers, *I Remember*, Sponson Box, April 2001, pp. 3–4, June 2001, pp. 5–6.
2. Bartusevics, personal communication.
3. The following account is adapted from Robinson as told to Randy Conrad, *Operation Eagle Flight 49er—Hill 163*, Sponson Box, September 2004, p. 10.

4. Binion interview.
5. Ibid.
6. Hackemack interview.
7. The Corps' term for being declared unfit for service, or discarded.
8. Shumlinson, *US Marines In Vietnam: An Expanding War, 1966*, pp. 181–182.
9. Stewart, *Marine Tanks in Vietnam: July Through September, 1966*, Sponson Box, June 2006, p. 10.
10. Binion interview.
11. Like many veterans, Gibson cannot recall precisely whether this was Operation HASTINGS or PRAIRIE, but the chronology suggests PRAIRIE. Adapted from Gibson, *Gibson Recalls A Day In Vietnam*, Sponson Box, September 2004, p. 9, and Gibson interview.
12. Stewart, *Marine Corps Tank Operations in Vietnam: 1st and 3rd Tank Battalions, 1 October through 31 December, 1966*, Sponson Box, September 2006, p 15.
13. Condensed from Gibson interview.
14. Stewart, *Marine Tanks in Vietnam: July Through September, 1966*, Sponson Box, June 2006, p. 13.
15. Shumlinson, *US Marines In Vietnam: An Expanding War, 1966*, p. 248; Stewart interview.
16. Stewart, *Marine Corps Tank Operations in Vietnam: 1st and 3rd Tank Battalions, 1 October through 31 December, 1966*, Sponson Box, September 2006, p 16; Anonymous, *Famous Vietnam Tankers—Lt. Col. Wm. R. Corson, USMC/CIA*, Sponson Box, June 2002, p. 7.

CHAPTER 4
1. The general situation assessment is condensed from Telfer, Rogers, and Fleming *US Marines in Vietnam: Fighting the North Vietnamese, 1967*; and Stewart, *Marine Corps Tanks in Vietnam First and Third Tank Battalions 1 January through 31 March, 1967*, Sponson Box, December 2006, pp. 14–17.
2. Millett, *Semper Fidelis*, p. 584–585.
3. Bartusevics interview.
4. Ibid.
5. Artillery gun crewman.
6. Red-line refers to the old system of a painted red line, which marked a deadly-force boundary. A prisoner who crossed the line could be shot. At the time the "red line" was the inner of two fences with a space between.
7. Heavy leather gloves used to remove wounded from entangling wire.
8. Terms used at the time to refer to the enemy's 82mm mortar and the

152mm howitzer, which had longer range than the Marine artillery's 155mm howitzer.

9. The terminology for this site can be confusing. At this time the stream crossing near C-2 was called The Rocky Ford. In September it acquired the name The Washout, but many veterans refer to it retroactively as The Washout.

10. The various legs were about six, four, and six kilometers straight-line distance, longer by the winding road.

11. A light tank chassis, mounting two 40mm automatic anti-aircraft cannon in an open-topped turret.

12. Person interview.

13. The account of the battle is based on Coan, *Con Thien: The Hill of Angels*, p. 63–71; Danner and Thatcher's Navy Cross citations; and Murphy, *Semper Fi Vietnam*, p. 115–116.

14. Reynolds, '*OPERATION HICKORY, May 17, 1967*'; www.ironhorsemarines.com

15. Ibid.

16. Recollections from Lt. Rivero in Coan, *Con Thien: The Hill of Angels*, p. 83–85, differ in some details.

17. Reynolds, '*OPERATION HICKORY, May 17, 1967*'; www.ironhorsemarines.com

18. Ibid.

19. Ibid.

20. Ibid.

21. Ibid.

22. This was Cathy LeRoy. Reynolds's date for her wounding is consistent with other records. It is not clear from records whether LeRoy had returned to the battle (blind tenacity was one of her primary attributes), or whether Carroll or I are confused about the date. I have deliberately chosen to keep the chronology the same as cited by the participants.

23. Low trajectory rockets had to be aimed very precisely at the profile of the hill, and some would miss and impact kilometers to the south. Plunging artillery and mortar fire, which could be adjusted, was far more dangerous.

24. Coan, *Con Thien: The Hill of Angels*, p. 2–5; English interview.

25. The dead were Cpl. David Flaningham, LCpl. Miles Jansen, Pvt. Raymond Ludwig, and Cpl. Manuel Garcia. This account is abstracted from Coan, *Con Thien: The Hill of Angels*, p. 2–5.

26. In the five-tank Marine platoon, One was the Platoon Leader's vehicle, Five the Platoon Sergeant's tank.

27. The following account is from Wear, Carroll, Bores, *My Two Days At Con Thein*, Sponson Box, May 2003, and Carroll interview.

28. Adapted from Reynolds, *Double Ambush on Route 9, September 7, 1967*, Sponson Box, September 2004, p. 15.
29. Adapted from Coan, *How The Washout Got Its Name*, Sponson Box, May 2003, pp. 11–13.
30. Adapted from Reynolds, *A Load of Plywood*, www.ironhorsemarine.
31. Adapted from Reynolds, *Tankers Didn't Do It*, www.ironhorsemarine
32. Adapted from Reynolds, *Tankers Don't Drink (Much)*, www.ironhorsemarine
33. Clark, *M-51 Retriever, The Magnificent Bastard*, Sponson Box, August 2001, p. 5.
34. Estes, *Marines Under Armor*, p. 166; Gilbert, *The US Marine Corps in the Vietnam War*, p. 32.
35. Millett, *Semper Fidelis*, pp. 586–591.
36. Casey interview.

CHAPTER 5
1. Millett, *Semper Fidelis*, p. 591.
2. Estes, *Marines Under Armor*, p. 170.
3. Young interview.
4. Probably a .51calber Soviet made HMG.
5. The following account is condensed from Christensen, *Captain Daniel Wilder Kent, KIA*, Sponson Box, May 2003, pp. 14–15.
6. Karl Fontenot recalls the additional tanks as gun tanks, but Carl Fleischmann and John Wear recall that the two gun tanks were Hotel 51 and Hotel 52, the CO's and XO's vehicles, plus one flame tank.
7. Fontenot interview.
8. Note that Fontenot and Fleischmann disagree in details of the route and transport. The details soon enough became moot.
9. Fontenot interview. The instruction apparently indicates Hue area was considered so safe the tanks could travel with guns trained to the rear and the tubes in travel lock to spare stress on the elevation mechanisms.
10. Casey interview.
11. Fontenot interview; Wear interview.
12. Casey interview; Wear interview.
13. The High Explosive Plastic—Tracer round was a thin shelled projectile that flattened into a "pancake" upon impact, and was detonated by a delayed action fuse after a fraction of a second. It was designed to defeat tank armor by blowing off a part of the tank's internal armor with a shock wave.
14. The M67 flame tank had to be supported by truck-mounted apparatus, including a mixer to prepare the napalm, a transfer unit to pump the mix-

ture into the hull-mounted tanks, and a compressor to provide compressed air to force the mixture out the tube.

15. Casey interview.
16. Ibid.
17. Casey interview; Fontenot interview.
18. Casey interview.
19. McQueary interview.
20. The following account is condensed from Hall, *M48A3 Corgi Die Cast Brochure*, Sponson Box, May 2003, p. 15.
21. It is not clear that the following account by John Wear is of the same action. Wear recalls the unit in distress was from the 4th Marines, but the location and circumstances are the same. Such uncertainties are common, given the "routine" nature of the fighting.
22. Other accounts cite four tanks crippled, if this is the same action.
23. Coan, *The Hitchhiker Incident*, Sponson Box, September 2002, p. 4.
24. A Chieu Hoi Hamlet, or "Open Arms" village for deserters from the VC and NVA.
25. Fontenot interview.
26. Starry, *Armored Combat in Vietnam*, p. 139–140.
27. Wear interview.
28. Ibid.
29. Ibid.
30. Dan McQueary thought this event occurred in 1969, but was not personally present. The account closely conforms to events recounted in Shumlinson, *US Marines In Vietnam: The Defining Year, 1968*, p. 387; and Coan, *Turkey Shoot on the DMZ*, Sponson Box, January 2003, p. 13.
31. The following is from the Wokaty interview, with additional details from a personal letter to the author, July (undated) 2007.
32. Embesi interview.
33. Adapted from Appledorn, *The Tank, The Tankers, The Memories*, Sponson Box, March 2006, pp. 1–2.
34. "Puff The Magic Dragon," an Air Force fixed wing gunship with Gatling machine guns and automatic cannon. The term originally referred to the AC-47, but was generically applied to other types.
35. Huge armored tractors equipped with special plows to tear down all standing vegetation.
36. Millett, *Semper Fidelis*, pp. 594–595.
37. Embesi interview.

CHAPTER 6

1. Millett, *Semper Fidelis*, pp. 600–601.

2. 3rd Tank Battalion Staff Journal, March 1969, p. 10.
3. Sleger interview; 3rd Tank Battalion Staff Journal, March 1969, pp. 7–10.
4. Copy of Navy Cross citation, provided by Colonel Sleger.
5. Sleger interview.
6. 3rd Tank Battalion Staff Journal, March 1969, p. 7.
7. Sleger interview.
8. Ibid.
9. Sleger interview; staff Daily Journals supplied to author.
10. Report to Commanding General, 3rd MarDiv, dated 4 May 1969; 3rd Battalion Staff Journal, March 1969, p. 6.
11. Sleger interview.
12. 3rd Battalion Staff Journal, March 1969, pp. 6, 25.
13. Carey, *Interview with Col. Paul Goodwin USMC (ret),* Sponson Box, July 2003, p.11.
14. This and the following account of Wunsch's death are from Cary, *Interview with Col. Paul Goodwin USMC (ret.),* Sponson Box, July 2003, p.11.
15. The *USS Gunston Hall* was one of the very first LSDs (Landing Ship, Dock) designed specifically to transport and land heavy equipment like tanks, in early Word War II.
16. Zitz interview.
17. Many Marine veterans refer to this installation by its Army designation, Fire Support Base (FSB) Ross.

CHAPTER 7
1. Sleger interview.
2. Ibid.
3. Cosmas and Murray, *US Marines In Vietnam: Vietnamization and Redeployment, 1970–1971*, p. 86.

CHAPTER 8
1. Millett, *Semper Fidelis*, p. 604.

REFERENCES AND BIBLIOGRAPHY

Please note that images of issues of The Sponson Box are available for viewing online at www.usmcvta.org/Sponson Box Archives.htm. New material is constantly added to this site.

Anonymous *Famous Vietnam Tankers—Lt. Col. Wm. R. Corson, USMC/CIA*, The Sponson Box, June 2002, p. 7.

_____ *Operation Starlite 18–20 August 1965*, The Sponson Box, April 2004, p. 15.

_____ *Operation Starlite: The First Big Battle (17–24 August 1965)*, The Sponson Box, June 2004, p. 14–15.

Appledorn, Bruce Van, *The Tank, The Tankers, The Memories*, The Sponson Box, March 2006, pp. 1–2.

Christensen, Harry C. *Captain Daniel Wilder Kent, KIA*, The Sponson Box, May 2003, p. 14.

Clark, Jerry, *M-51 Retriever "The Magnificent Bastard,"* The Sponson Box, August 2001, p. 5.

Coan, Jim, *How The Washout Got Its Name*, The Sponson Box, May 2003, p. 11–12.

_____*The Hitchhiker Incident*, The Sponson Box, September 2002, p. 4.

_____ *Con Thien: The Hill of Angels*, Tuscaloosa AL, The University of Alabama Press, ________

Cosmas, Graham A., and Terrence P. Murray, *US Marines In Vietnam: Vietnamization and Redeployment, 1970–1971*, Washington DC, History and Museums Division US Marine Corps, 1986.

Fisher, Paul *The Best 'War Story"—Marine Ontos Style*, The Sponson Box, March 2004, p. 15.

Gibson, Gary, *Gibson Recalls A Day In Vietnam*, The Sponson Box,

September 2004, p. 9.
Gilbert, Ed, *The U S Marine Corps In The Vietnam War—III Marine Amphibious Force 1965–1975*, Oxford UK, Osprey Publishing (Battle Orders Series), 2006.
Goodwin, Paul and Dick Carey *Capt. Michael Wunsch, KIA*, The Sponson Box, July 2003, p. 11.
Hall, Garry L., *M48A3 Corgi Die Cast Brochure*, The Sponson Box, May 2003, p. 15.
Karnow, Stanley *Vietnam: A History*, New York, Viking, 1983.
Kelley, Michael P. *Where We Were In Vietnam*, Central Point OR, Hellgate Press, 2002.
Millett, Alan R. *Semper Fidelis: The History of the United States Marine Corps*, New York NY, Macmillan Publishing, Free Press Edition, 1982.
Moss, Kurt *First Vietnam Tanker Casualty*, The Sponson Box, March 2003, p. 10.
Murphy, Edward F. *Semper Fi—Vietnam*, Novato CA, Presidio Press, 2000.
Nalty, Bernard, *The Vietnam War*, New York, Salamander, 1998.
Reynolds, Lloyd G. *Double Ambush On Route 9*, The Sponson Box, September 2004, p. 15.
Robinson, Robbie 'Harvey' and Randy Conrad *Operation Eagle Flight 49er—Hill 163*, The Sponson Box, September 2004, p. 10.
Rogers, Pat, *I Remember*, The Sponson Box, April 2001, pp. 3–4, June 2001, pp. 5–6.
Shumlinson, Jack *US Marines In Vietnam: An Expanding War, 1966*, Washington DC, History and Museums Division US Marine Corps, 1982.
_____ *US Marines In Vietnam: The Defining Year, 1968*, Washington DC, History and Museums Division US Marine Corps, 1997.
Shumlinson, Jack and Charles M. Johns *US Marines In Vietnam: The Landing and Buildup, 1965*, Washington DC, History and Museums Division US Marine Corps, 1978.
Smith, Charles R. *US* Marines In Vietnam: High Mobility and Standdown, 1969, Washington DC, History and Museums Division US Marine Corps, 1988.
Starry, Donn A. *Armored Combat in Vietnam*, New York, Arno Press, 1988.
Stewart, Ray *The History of Marine Tanks in Vietnam 1965–1970*, The Sponson Box, September 2004, p. 14.
_____ *United States Marine Corps Tank Operations in Vietnam—1 October Through 31 December 1965*, The Sponson Box, December 2004, p. 12.

______ *Marine Corps Tank Operations in Vietnam: Third Tank Battalion (Rein), Third Marine Division (Rein), FMF 1 January Through 30 March 1966*, The Sponson Box, February 2005, p. 10.

______ *Marine Corps Tank Operations in Vietnam: First and Third Tank Battalions, 1 April through 30 June 1966*, The Sponson Box, July 2005, pp. 3, 5, and 14.

______ *Marine Tanks in Vietnam: July Through September 1966*, The Sponson Box, June 2006, p. 10–14.

______ *Marine Corps Tank Operations in Vietnam: First and Third Tank Battalions 1 October Through 31 December, 1966*, The Sponson Box, September 2006, p. 14–16.

______*Marine Corps Tanks in Vietnam First and Third Tank Battalions 1 January Through 31 March, 1967*, The Sponson Box, December 2006, p. 14–17.

Stiegelman, Herb, *Dagger Thrust Operations—Vietnam 1965*, The Sponson Box, October 2005, p. 11.

Telfer, Gary L., Lane Rogers, and V. Keith Fleming *US Marines in Vietnam: Fighting the North Vietnamese, 1967*, Washington DC, History and Museums Division US Marine Corps, 1984.

United States Government, *Lance Corporal Charles D. Thatcher, United States Marine Corps*, Navy Cross Citation as reprinted in The Sponson Box, September 2002, p. 6.

Wear, John, *My Two Days At Con Thien*, The Sponson Box, May 2003, p. 13.

Whitlow, Robert H. *US Marines in Vietnam: The Advisory and Combat Assistance Era, 1954–1964*, Washington DC, History and Museums Division US Marine Corps, 1977.

ADDITIONAL READINGS AND RESOURCES

The following materials not specifically cited in the text and are included as suggested readings.

Gilbert, Ed, *U S Marine Corps Tanker 1965–1970, Vietnam*, Oxford UK, Osprey Publishing (Warrior Series), 2004. Tracks the experiences of several fictional tankers through actual actions. It provides graphics and photos of the tanker's weapons, uniforms, and specialized "tools of the trade."

Matthews, Frank, *Once A Marine... A Journal ... SSGT Earl Matthews Jr. Age 28 - KIA – 9Sept. '66*, The Sponson Box, July 2005, pp. 6, 9, and 12. This is a poignant series of excerpts from letters to Matthews's wife.

They provide a particularly candid insight into the daily life—and emotions—of a man in combat. Particularly recommended.

Peavey, Robert E., *Praying for Slack*, Osceola WI, Zenith Press, 2004. A view of life in a tank unit (3rd Tank Battalion) from the perspective of a junior NCO.

The *Ironhorse Marines* website (www.ironhorsemarines.com) operated by Lloyd "Pappy" Reynolds is an excellent source of personal accounts and anecdotes, both funny and tragic, as well as unique personal photos. It focuses primarily on the 3rd Tank Battalion along the DMZ. Reynolds is a natural storyteller, and the site is particularly recommended.

MAP PROJECT

Maps of the locations of USMC tank units at different periods of the war are being compiled at www.usmcvta.org/VNMaps/maplocater.htm. At present these maps depict the locations of headquarters and support facilities, which were relatively fixed. The locations of platoons and sections are more difficult to fix, and this is an ongoing project. These maps are a valuable supplement to this text, though would be impractical to include within the volume.

INDEX